HISTORY COMICS

THE STONEWALL RIOTS
MAKING A STAND FOR LGBTQ RIGHTS

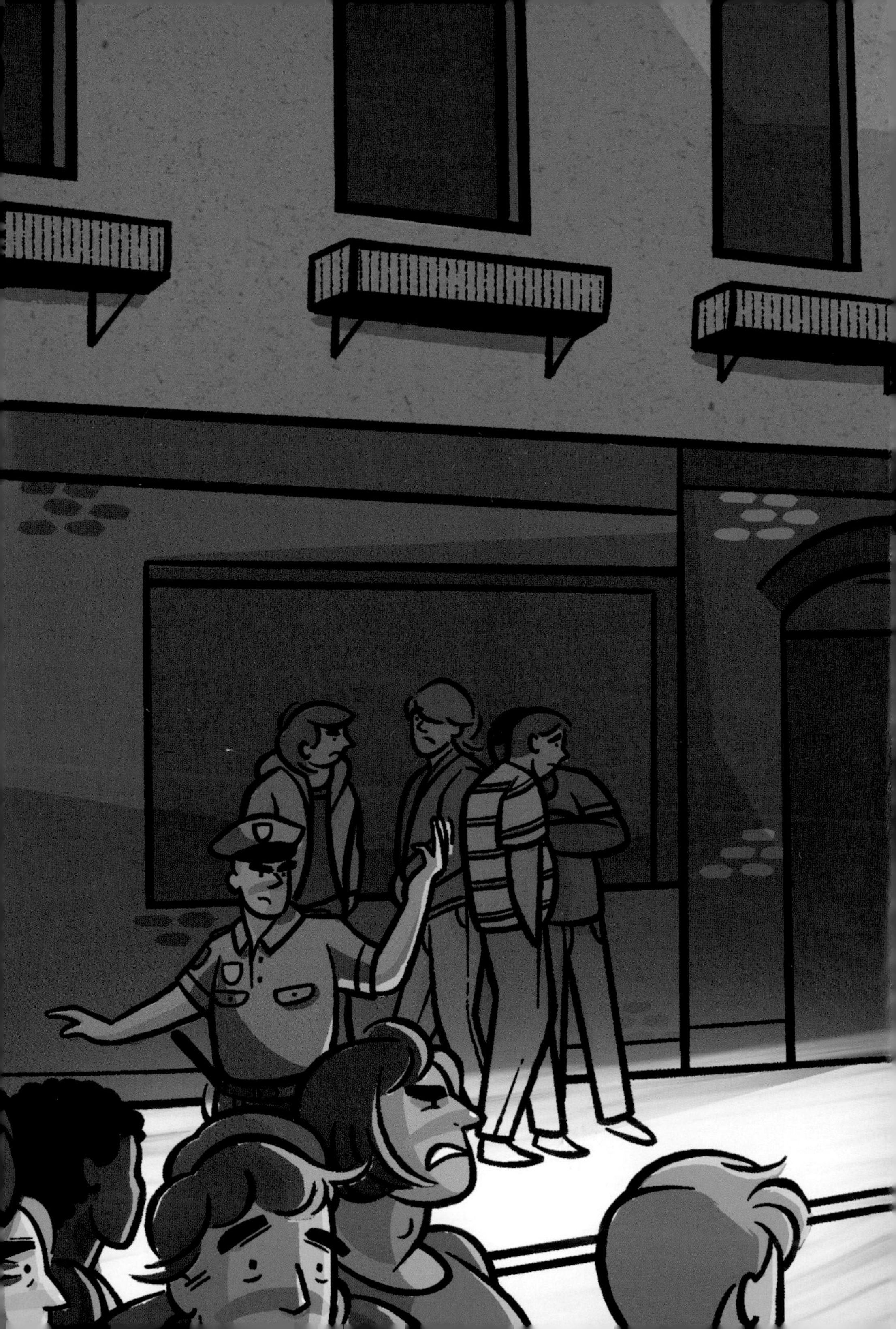

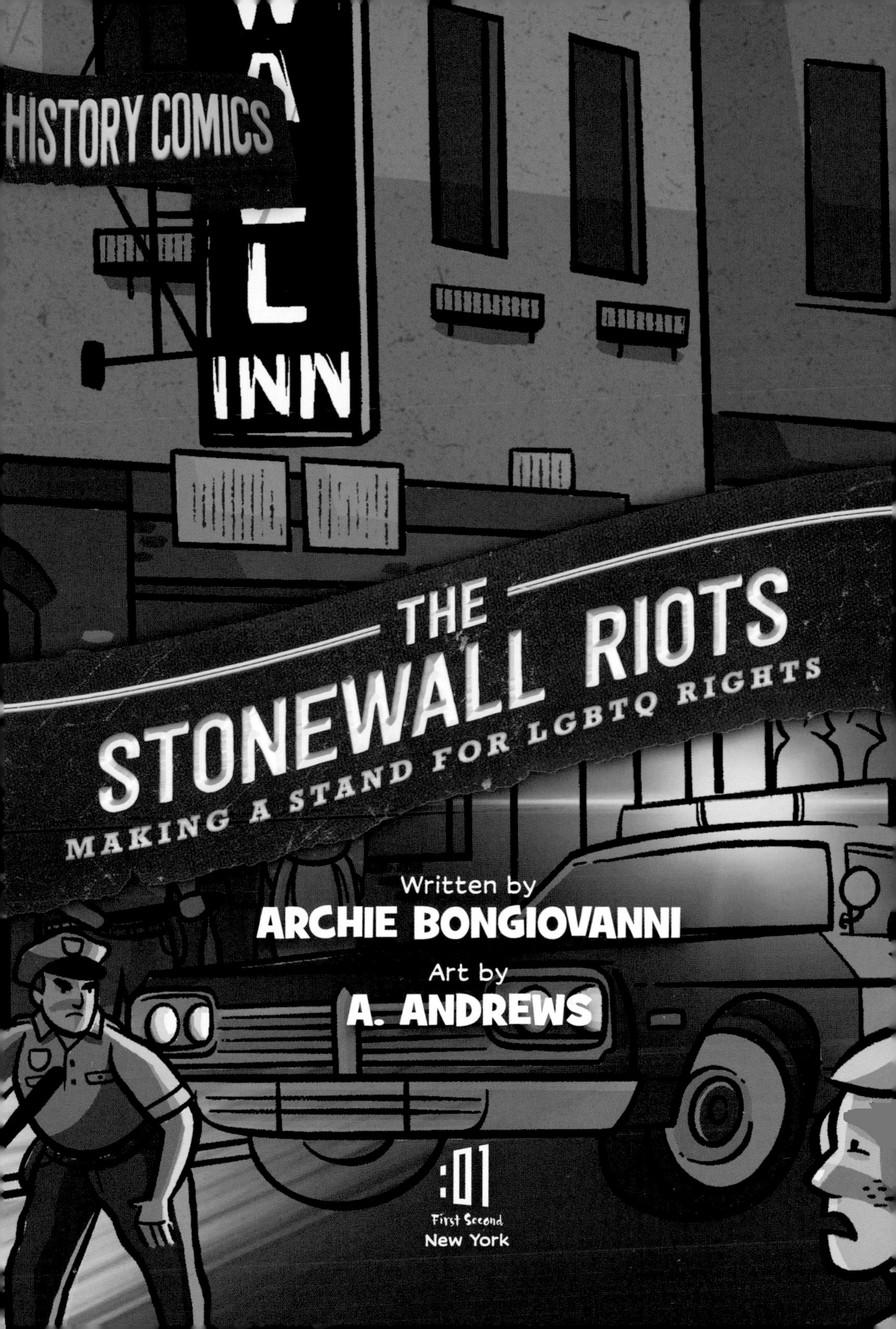
INN

HISTORY COMICS

THE STONEWALL RIOTS

MAKING A STAND FOR LGBTQ RIGHTS

Written by
ARCHIE BONGIOVANNI

Art by
A. ANDREWS

:01 First Second
New York

First Second

Published by First Second
First Second is an imprint of Roaring Brook Press,
a division of Holtzbrinck Publishing Holdings Limited Partnership
120 Broadway, New York, NY 10271
firstsecondbooks.com
mackids.com

Library of Congress Control Number: 2021921632

Our books may be purchased in bulk for promotional, educational, or business use. Please contact your local bookseller or the Macmillan Corporate and Premium Sales Department at (800) 221-7945 ext. 5442 or by email at MacmillanSpecialMarkets@macmillan.com.

First edition, 2022
Edited by Dave Roman and Alison Wilgus
Cover design and interior book design by Molly Johanson
Series design by Andrew Arnold
Authenticity readers: Tessera Editorial and Francesca Lyn

Penciled and inked in Procreate for iPad Pro with ProInker round pixel.
Colored digitally in Photoshop.

Printed in China by Toppan Leefung Printing Ltd., Dongguan City, Guangdong Province

ISBN 978-1-250-61835-1 (paperback)
10 9 8 7 6 5 4 3

ISBN 978-1-250-61836-8 (hardcover)
10 9 8 7 6 5 4 3 2 1

Don't miss your next favorite book from First Second!
For the latest updates go to firstsecondnewsletter.com and sign up for our enewsletter.

First, a confession: I was not at Stonewall on June 28, 1969. Even though I was a twenty-year-old "out" college student who lived in New Jersey and spent a great deal of time in Greenwich Village socializing and hanging out with gay friends, I did not happen to be there that fateful night. I was probably with friends, somewhere farther uptown in Manhattan, seeing a movie and having a hamburger after. If only world-shaking events could be scheduled and announced in advance, I certainly would have been at the Stonewall Inn.

That night was an explosion of passion, excitement, rage, and anger. And as is often the case with defining moments in history, it might have seemed to come out of nowhere—but was the result of long-simmering problems.

STONEWALL
INN
HOMOSEXUAL

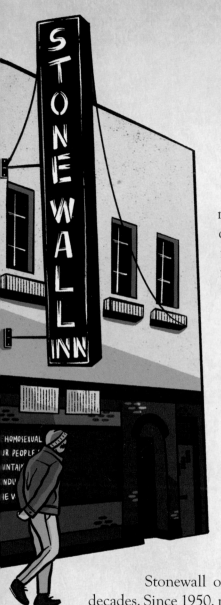

The Stonewall riots, which some more accurately prefer to call uprisings or insurrections—as they were political in nature—became the most important moment in contemporary LGBT history. They were revolutionary, completely changing how we think. In that moment, LGBT people began to see themselves as a powerful political force capable of changing society for the better. For many LGBT people, it was the first time they could truly be open about who they wanted to date, how they wanted to dress, and how they wanted to live their lives. They saw that "coming out"—as whoever you really were—was not only okay, but also necessary if they were to push for a more equitable world.

The explosion of energy that put Stonewall on the map had been simmering for decades. Since 1950, national groups such as the Mattachine Society and Daughters of Bilitis had promoted community and safety for gay men and lesbians, at times organizing protests to bring attention to injustice. Beginning in 1965 and lasting until 1969, the Annual Reminders were a series of pickets held every July 4 in front of Philadelphia's

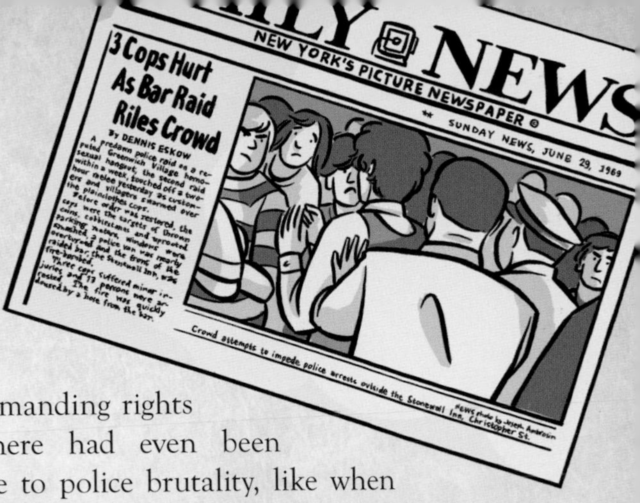
NEW YORK'S PICTURE NEWSPAPER ©
SUNDAY NEWS, JUNE 29, 1969
3 Cops Hurt As Bar Raid Riles Crowd
By DENNIS ESKOW
A predawn police raid on a reputed Greenwich Village homosexual hangout, the second raid within a week, touched off a two-hour melee yesterday as customers and villagers swarmed over the plainclothes cops.
Before order was restored, the cops were the targets of thrown coins, cobblestones and uprooted parking meters, windows were smashed, a police van was nearly overturned and the front of the raided bar, the Stonewall Inn, was fire-bombed.
Three cops suffered minor injuries and 13 persons were arrested. The fire was quickly doused by a hose from the bar.
Crowd attempts to impede police arrests outside the Stonewall Inn, Christopher St.
NEWS photo by Joseph Ambrosin

Independence Hall demanding rights for homosexuals. There had even been spontaneous resistance to police brutality, like when men who cross-dressed—known as transvestites at the time—battled with police harassing them at Compton's Cafeteria, in San Francisco's Tenderloin district in August 1966.

These are all important events in the struggle for LGBT rights. So what made the events at Stonewall so different? Part of the answer is the unique historical climate in which these events occurred. The 1960s were a time of incredible political and social change in the United States. You couldn't miss it! Headlines in every newspaper shouted out that America was changing—and old ideas were being challenged. The counterculture, musical groups such as the Rolling Stones and the Beatles, liberated American youth through celebration of new sexual freedoms, hippies, and more easily available, although still-illegal, marijuana. Radical feminism demanded that women be free to choose their own lives rather than live in the shadow of men. Grassroots action groups such as the Black Panthers and the Young Lords, a Latinx activist group, engaged in community organizing, fought discrimination, and battled police brutality. During this same time, hundreds of thousands of American citizens began protesting the U.S. government's war in Vietnam, which was killing thousands of U.S. soldiers and millions of Vietnamese people.

All across our country, people were fighting for their sexual freedom; for liberation from misogynist attitudes and laws; and against pervasive racial violence, discrimination, and a war that was universally condemned by most other countries. So on that summer night in 1969, the angry crowd at the Stonewall Inn was very aware of the battles being fought. In fact, many had participated in at least one of them—and the people saw their fight that night as part of the radical changes that illuminated the American landscape calling out for new freedoms. At marches, banners and posters proclaimed the words of Martin Luther King Jr.: "No one is free until we are all free."

The rest of the country also saw Stonewall as part of a larger liberation movement to make America freer and safer for many more people. Days after the Stonewall riots, many activists met and formed the Gay Liberation Front. I may have missed the uprising at the Stonewall Inn, but I immediately began attending Gay Liberation Front meetings and have been involved in LGBT politics and writing ever since.

The changes over the past half century have also been monumental. Queer people no longer have to live quietly. We don't have to meet at gay bars in order to find someone to date. We can do so in public, at local coffee shops, and, of course, online. There are now gay-straight alliances in middle schools and high schools, where young people can get support and make friends. The unethical and inhumane practice of so-called conversion therapy is now banned in twenty states and more will do so eventually. Same-sex marriage is finally legal in the United States, and romantic acts between people of the same gender are no longer crimes, as had been the case since the foundation of our country.

Despite all the progress, there is still a lot more to be done! Many states still allow discrimination against LGBT people. Violence against lesbians and gay men is ever present and on the rise. Violence against trans people—particularly trans women of color—is reaching epidemic proportions. As much as things have improved, not all schools, workplaces— or even parents—are as accepting as they should be.

The message of Stonewall in 1969, and now, is that if we want to see change in the world, we must fight. But there is another message that is equally important that this book beautifully illustrates. We must acknowledge our history, reflect on the people who came before us, preserve their stories, and pass them along. As James Baldwin, an African American author and gay man, wrote in 1965, "the great force of history comes from the fact that we carry it within us, are unconsciously controlled by it in many ways, and history is literally present in all that we do." Everything you do and say now to make the world a better place will be history—as important as anything that happened at Stonewall.

—**Michael Bronski,**
Harvard professor and author of
A Queer History of the United States for Young People

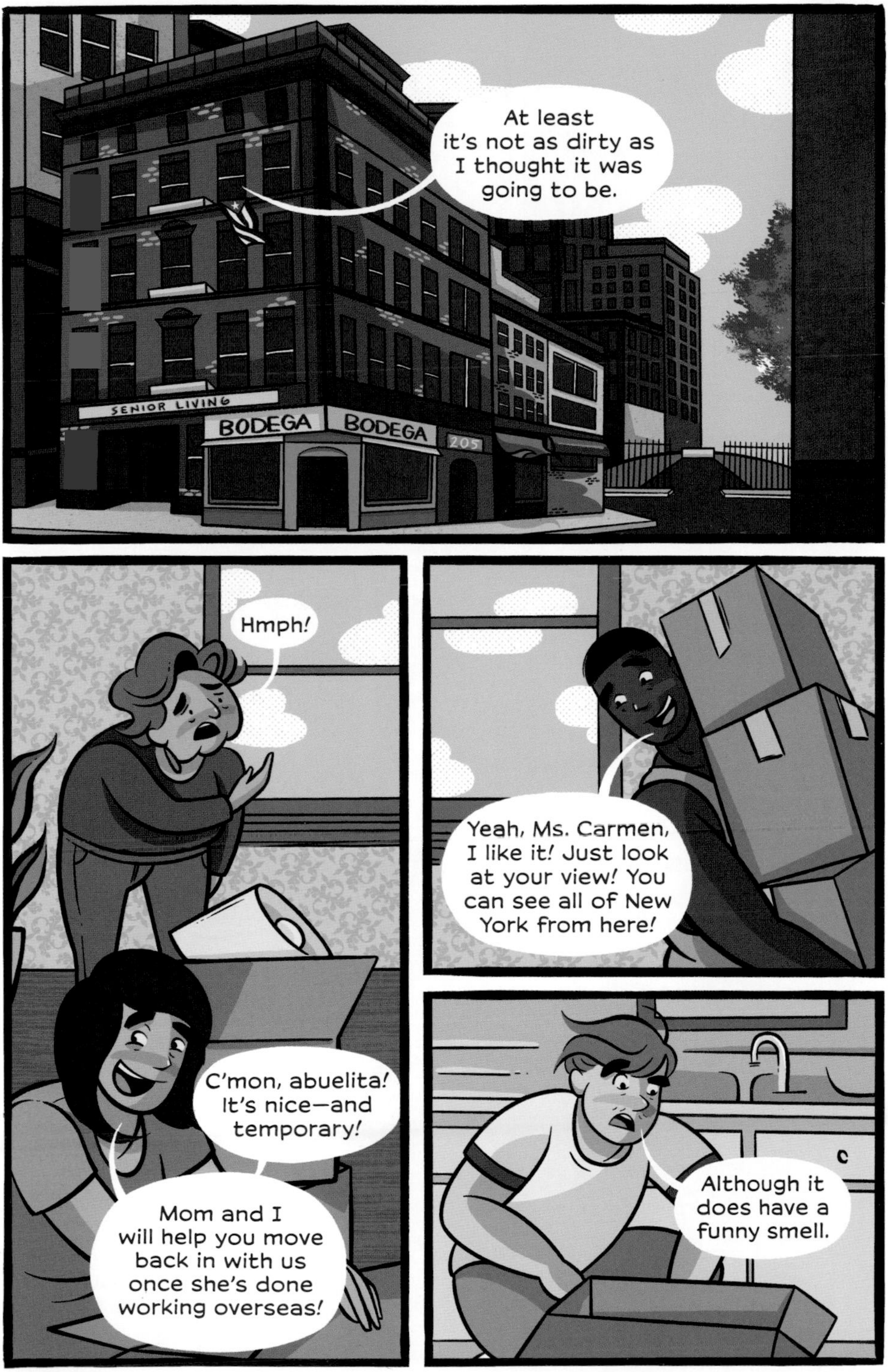
At least it's not as dirty as I thought it was going to be.
SENIOR LIVING
BODEGA
BODEGA
205
Hmph!
Yeah, Ms. Carmen, I like it! Just look at your view! You can see all of New York from here!
C'mon, abuelita! It's nice—and temporary!
Mom and I will help you move back in with us once she's done working overseas!
Although it does have a funny smell.

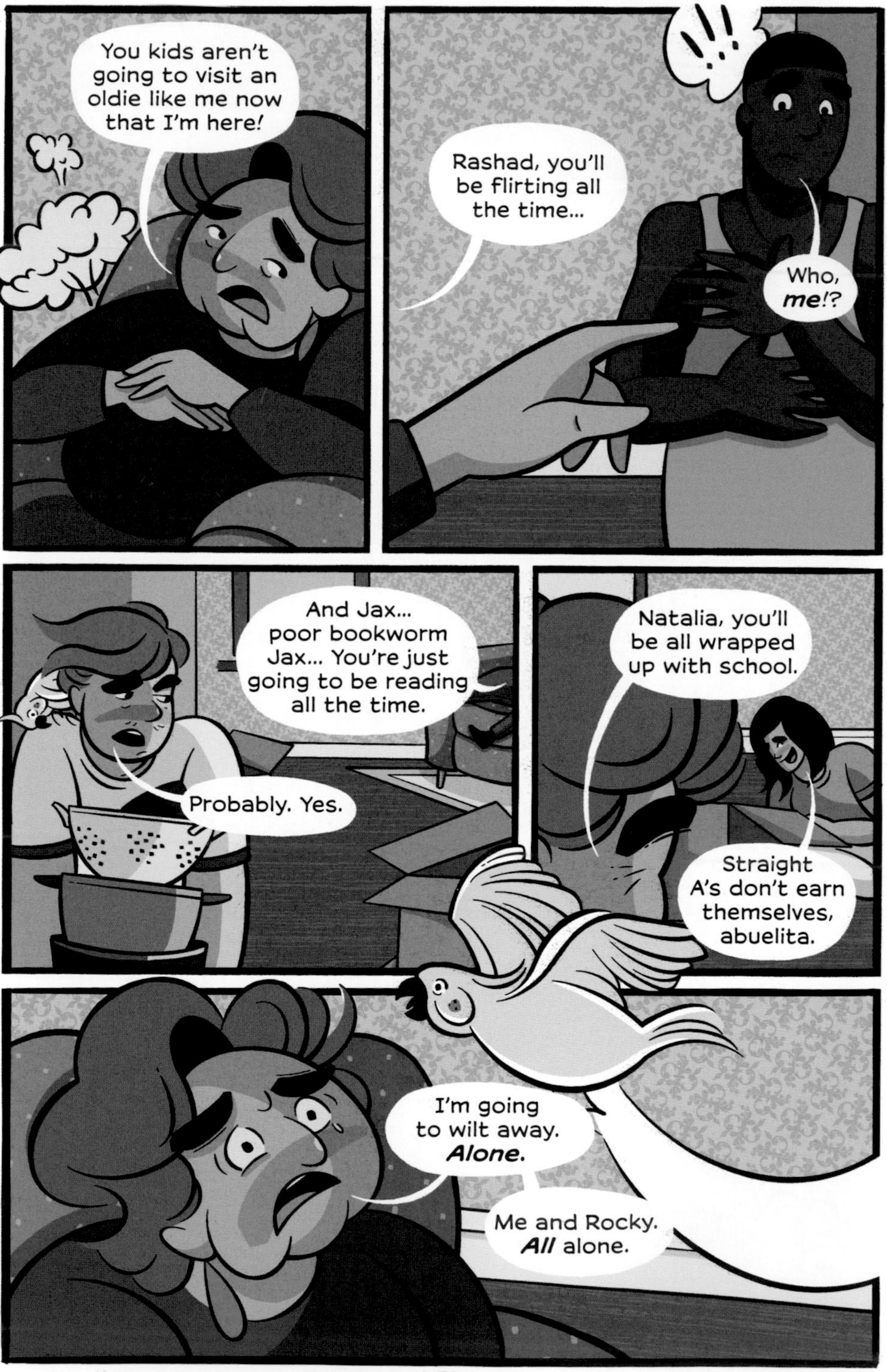
You kids aren't going to visit an oldie like me now that I'm here!
!!
Rashad, you'll be flirting all the time...
Who, *me*!?
And Jax... poor bookworm Jax... You're just going to be reading all the time.
Probably. Yes.
Natalia, you'll be all wrapped up with school.
Straight A's don't earn themselves, abuelita.
I'm going to wilt away. ***Alone.***
Me and Rocky. ***All*** alone.

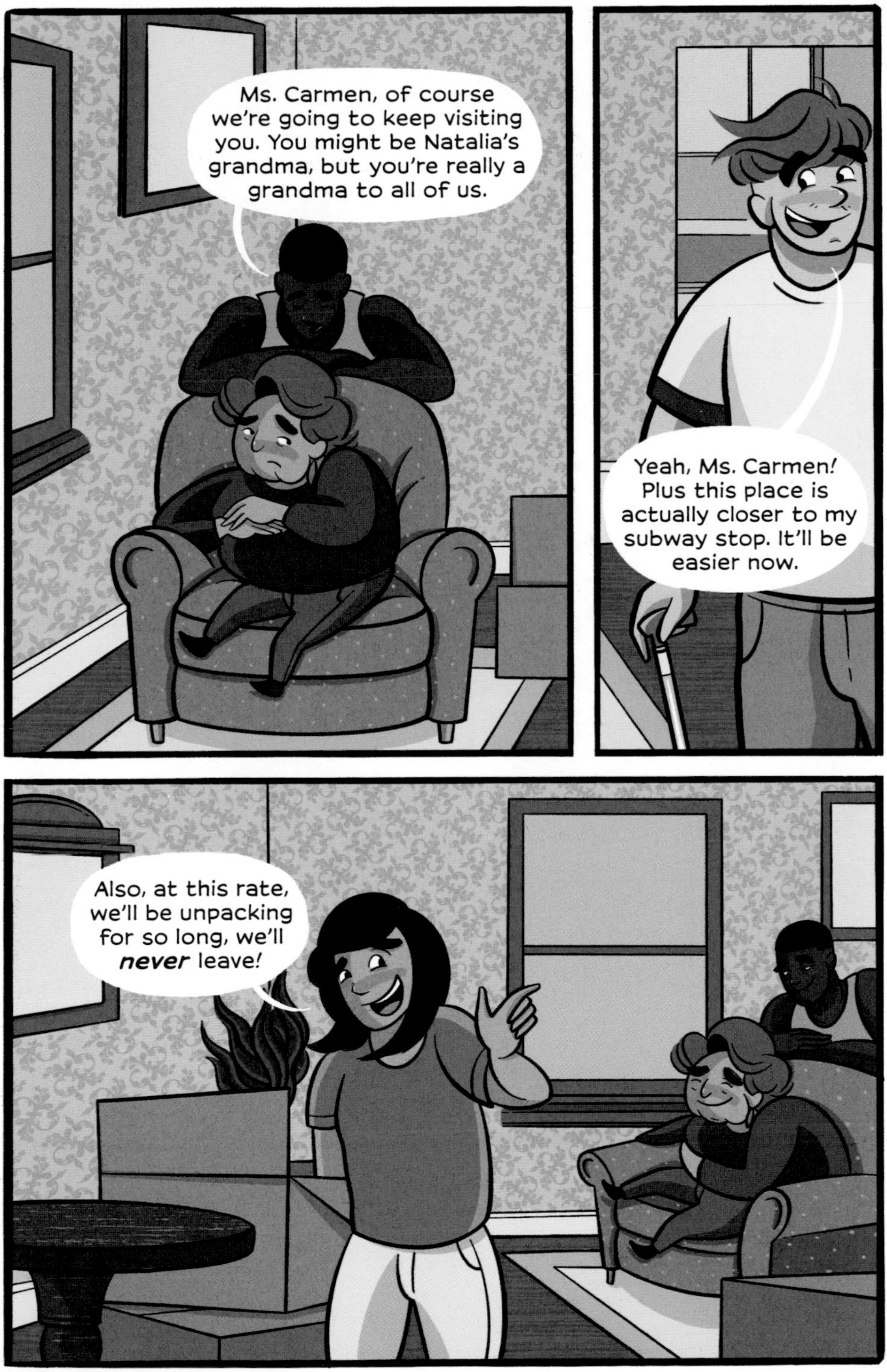
Ms. Carmen, of course we're going to keep visiting you. You might be Natalia's grandma, but you're really a grandma to all of us.
Yeah, Ms. Carmen! Plus this place is actually closer to my subway stop. It'll be easier now.
Also, at this rate, we'll be unpacking for so long, we'll ***never*** leave!

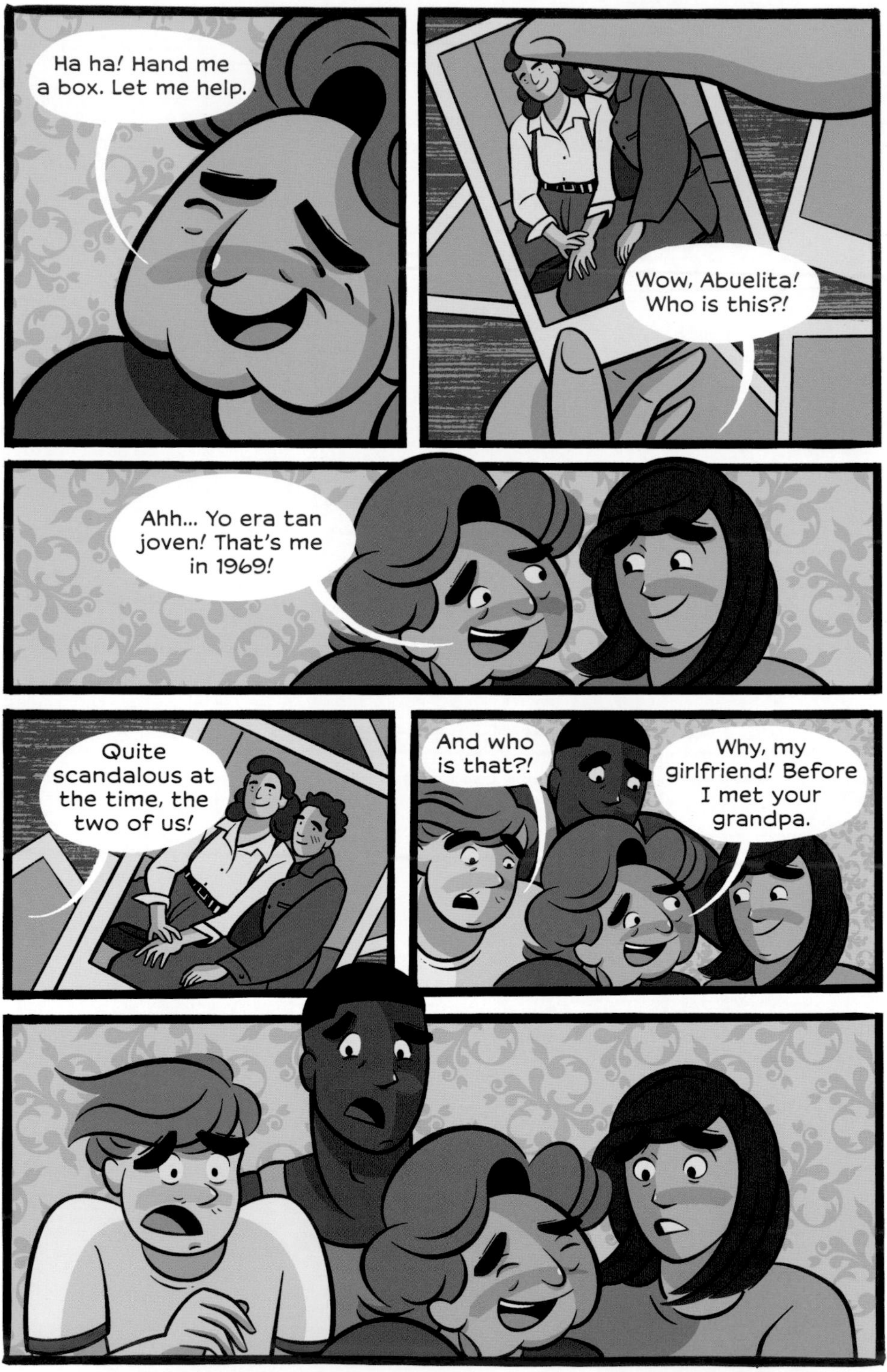
Ha ha! Hand me a box. Let me help.
Wow, Abuelita! Who is this?!
Ahh... Yo era tan joven! That's me in 1969!
Quite scandalous at the time, the two of us!
And who is that?!
Why, my girlfriend! Before I met your grandpa.

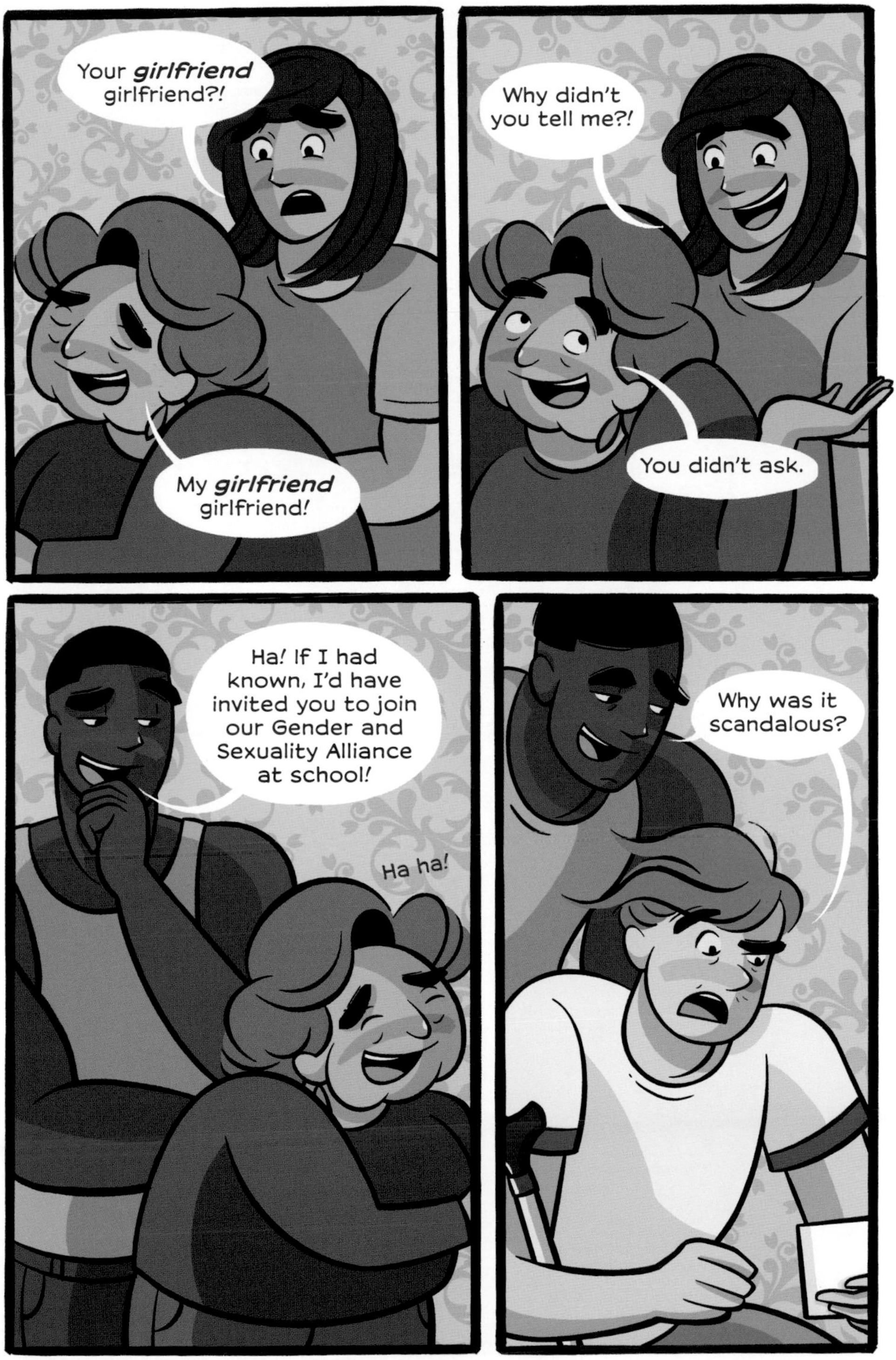
Your *girlfriend* girlfriend?!
My *girlfriend* girlfriend!
Why didn't you tell me?!
You didn't ask.
Ha! If I had known, I'd have invited you to join our Gender and Sexuality Alliance at school!
Ha ha!
Why was it scandalous?

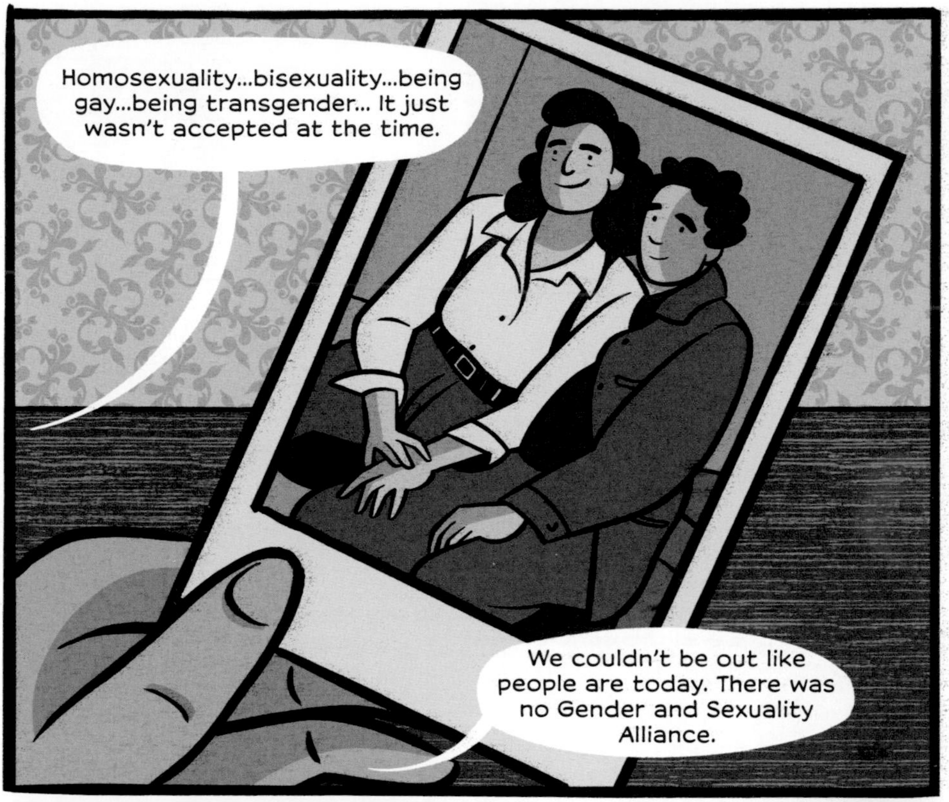
Homosexuality...bisexuality...being gay...being transgender... It just wasn't accepted at the time.
We couldn't be out like people are today. There was no Gender and Sexuality Alliance.

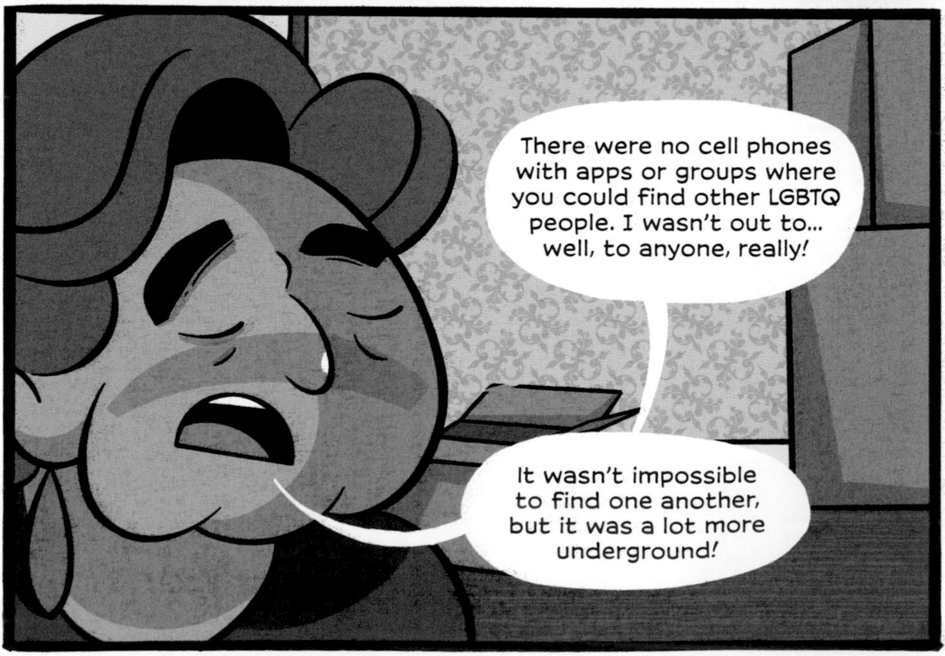
There were no cell phones with apps or groups where you could find other LGBTQ people. I wasn't out to... well, to anyone, really!
It wasn't impossible to find one another, but it was a lot more underground!

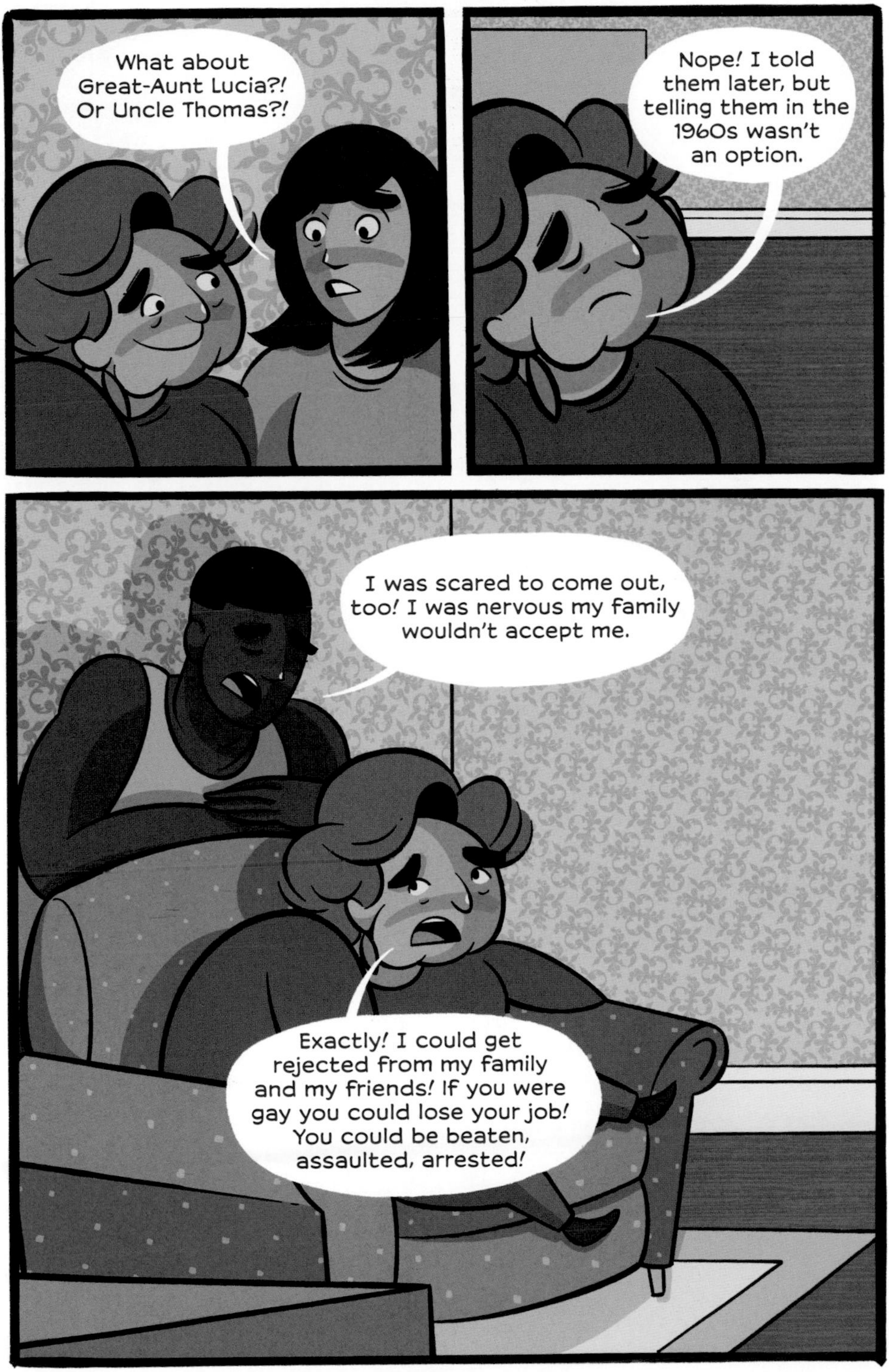
What about Great-Aunt Lucia?! Or Uncle Thomas?!
Nope! I told them later, but telling them in the 1960s wasn't an option.
I was scared to come out, too! I was nervous my family wouldn't accept me.
Exactly! I could get rejected from my family and my friends! If you were gay you could lose your job! You could be beaten, assaulted, arrested!

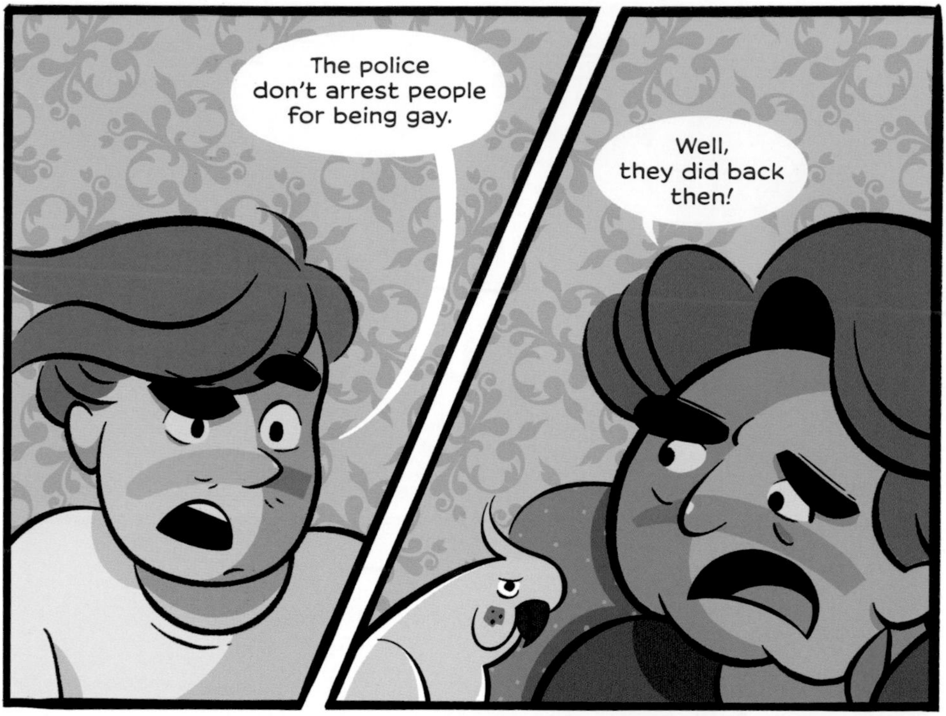

The police don't arrest people for being gay.
Well, they did back then!

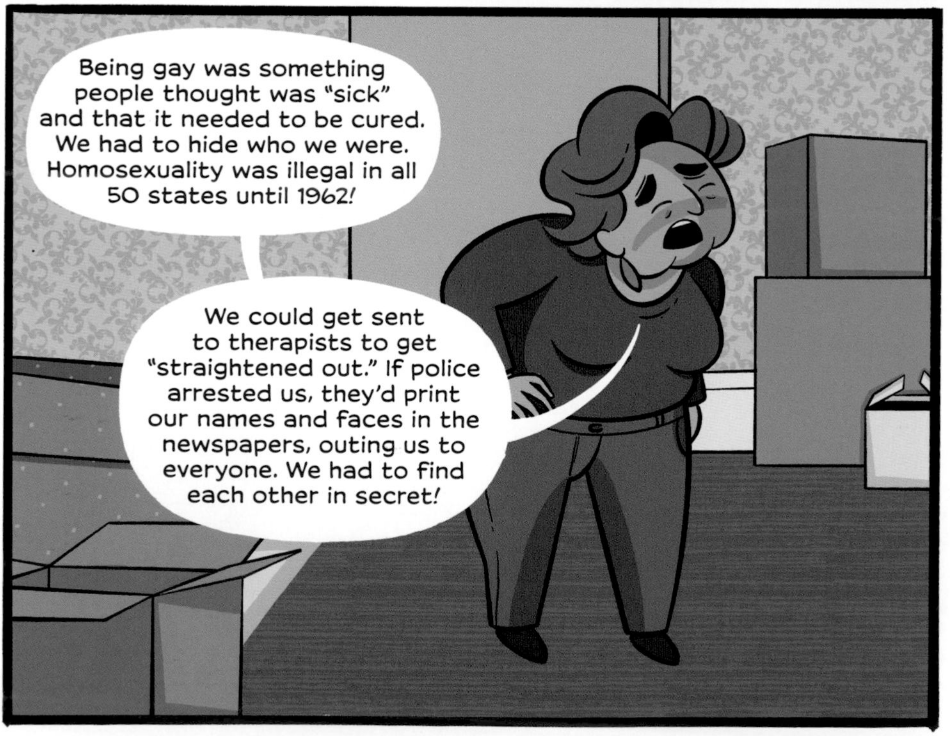

Being gay was something people thought was "sick" and that it needed to be cured. We had to hide who we were. Homosexuality was illegal in all 50 states until 1962!
We could get sent to therapists to get "straightened out." If police arrested us, they'd print our names and faces in the newspapers, outing us to everyone. We had to find each other in secret!

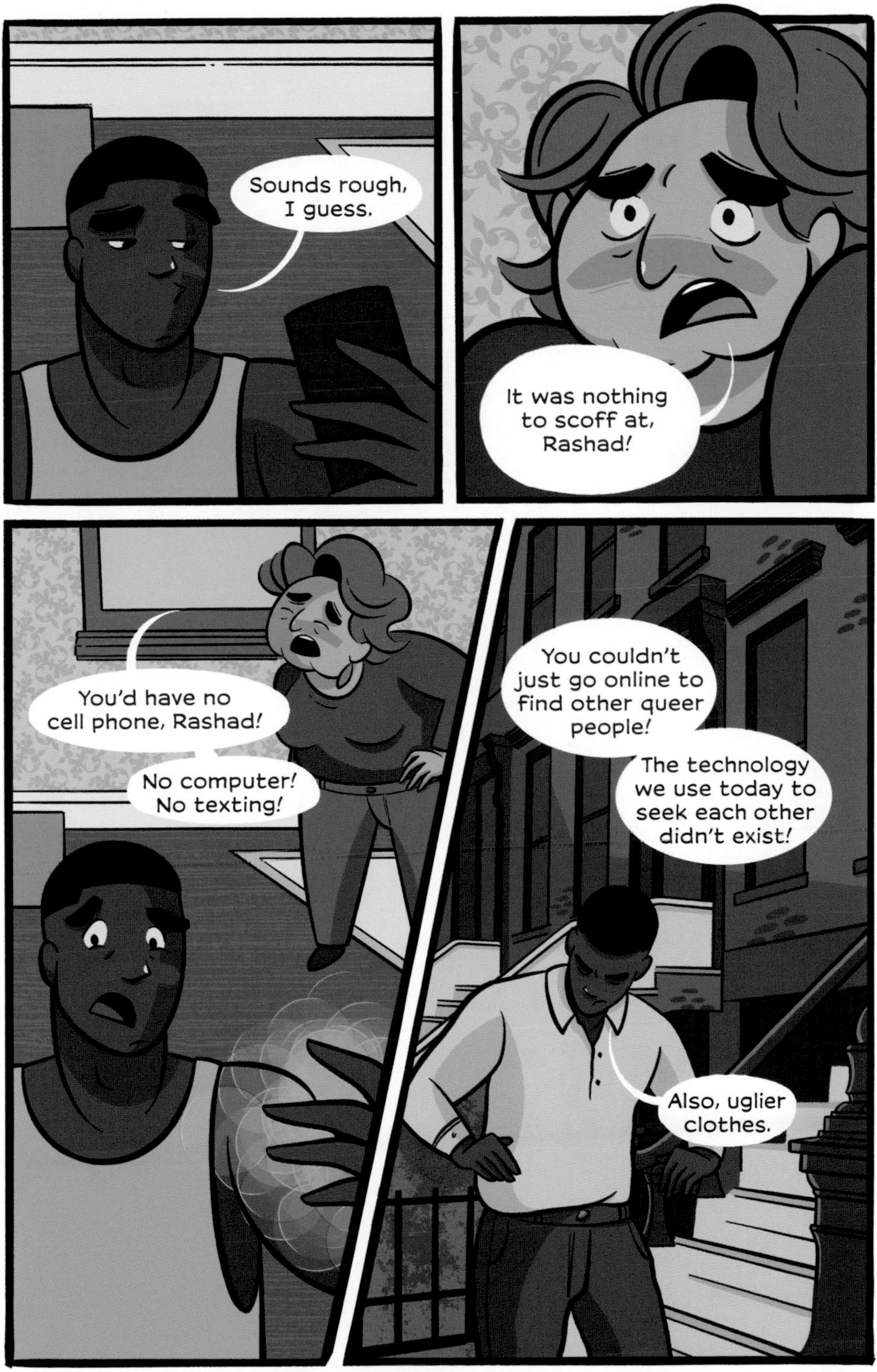
Sounds rough, I guess.
It was nothing to scoff at, Rashad!
You'd have no cell phone, Rashad!
No computer! No texting!
You couldn't just go online to find other queer people!
The technology we use today to seek each other didn't exist!
Also, uglier clothes.

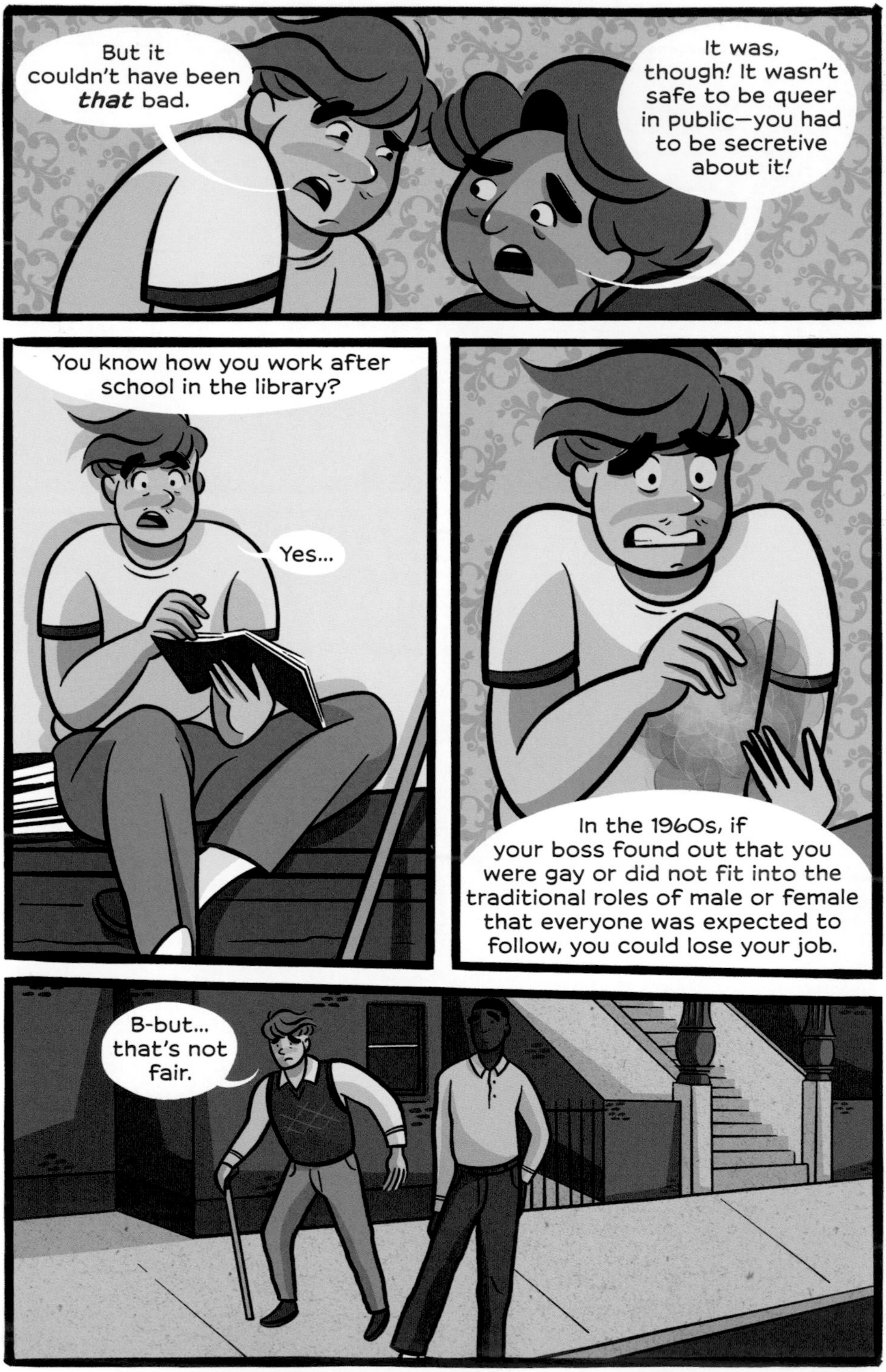
But it couldn't have been ***that*** bad.
It was, though! It wasn't safe to be queer in public—you had to be secretive about it!
You know how you work after school in the library?
Yes...
In the 1960s, if your boss found out that you were gay or did not fit into the traditional roles of male or female that everyone was expected to follow, you could lose your job.
B-but... that's not fair.

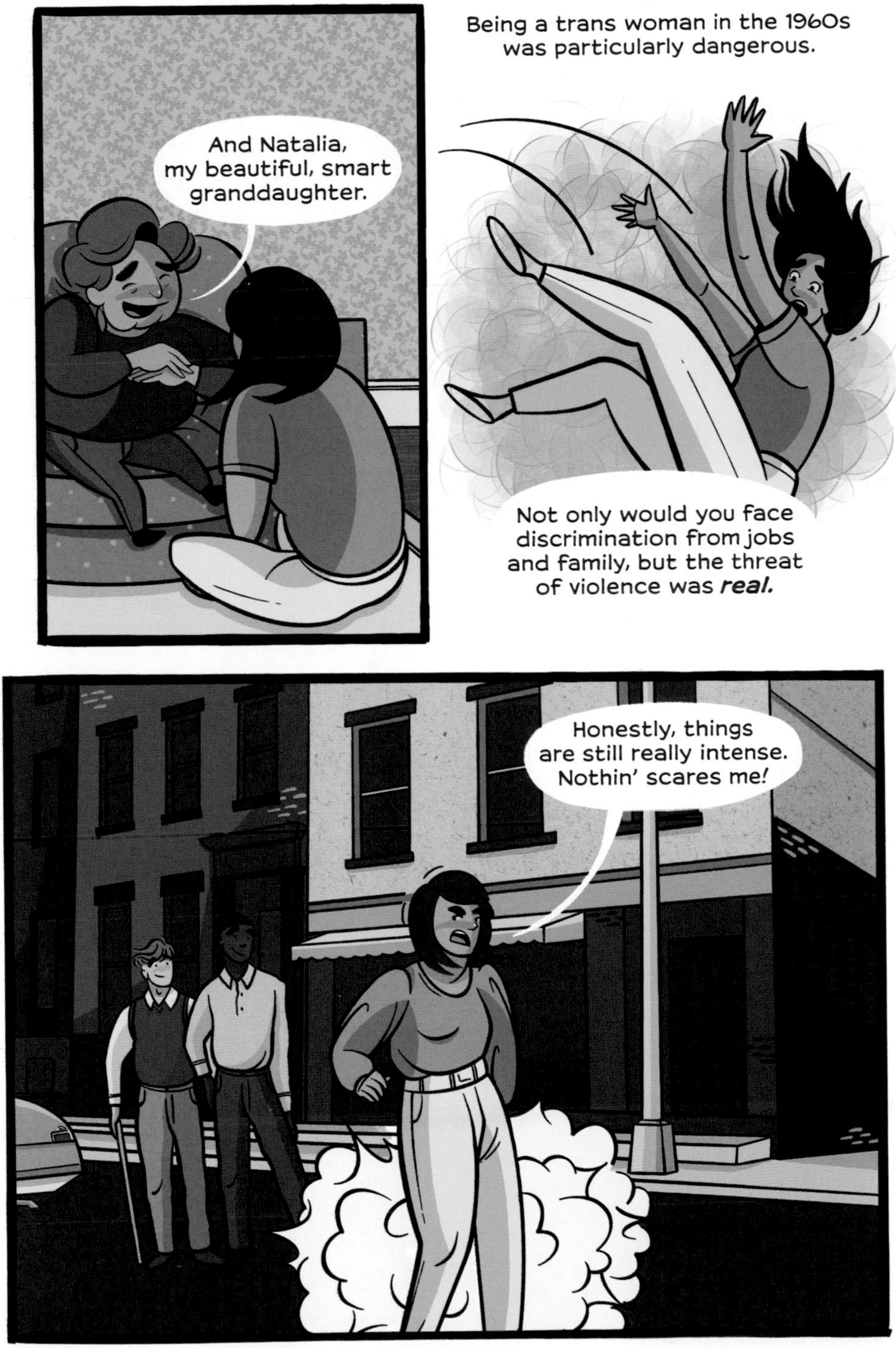
And Natalia, my beautiful, smart granddaughter.
Being a trans woman in the 1960s was particularly dangerous.
Not only would you face discrimination from jobs and family, but the threat of violence was ***real.***
Honestly, things are still really intense. Nothin' scares me!

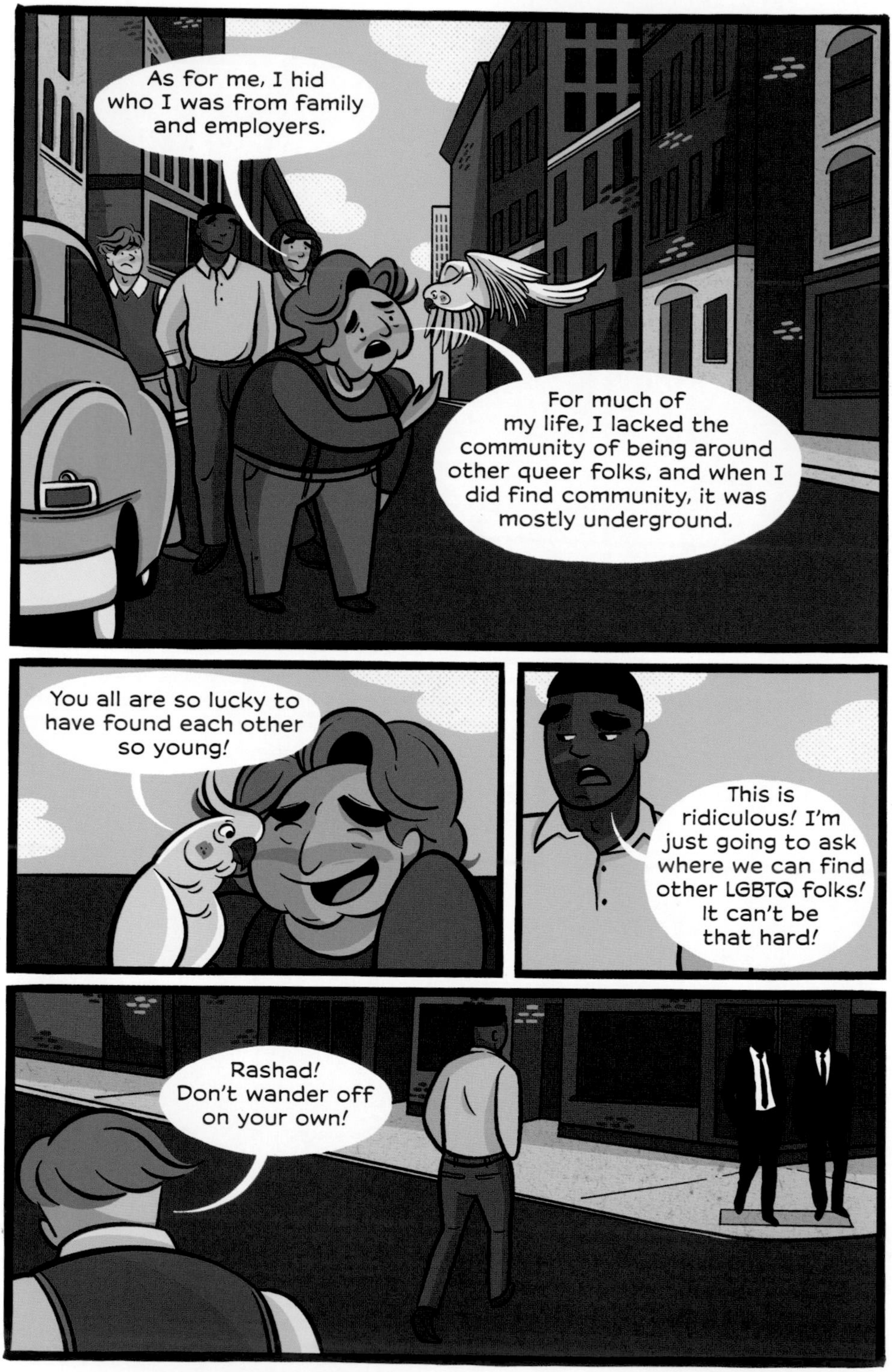
As for me, I hid who I was from family and employers.
For much of my life, I lacked the community of being around other queer folks, and when I did find community, it was mostly underground.
You all are so lucky to have found each other so young!
This is ridiculous! I'm just going to ask where we can find other LGBTQ folks! It can't be that hard!
Rashad! Don't wander off on your own!

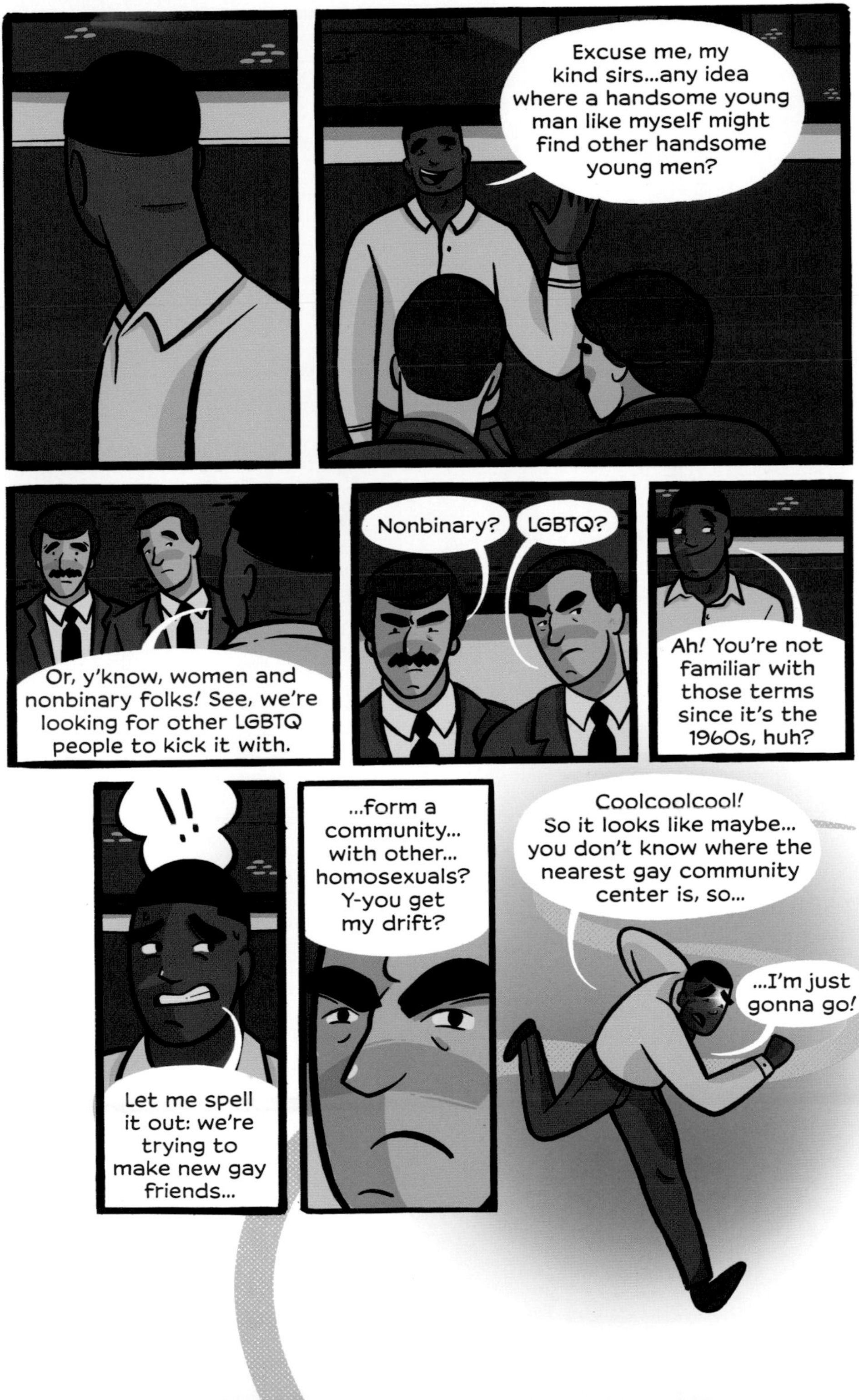
Excuse me, my kind sirs...any idea where a handsome young man like myself might find other handsome young men?
Or, y'know, women and nonbinary folks! See, we're looking for other LGBTQ people to kick it with.
Nonbinary?
LGBTQ?
Ah! You're not familiar with those terms since it's the 1960s, huh?
!!
Let me spell it out: we're trying to make new gay friends...
...form a community... with other... homosexuals? Y-you get my drift?
Coolcoolcool! So it looks like maybe... you don't know where the nearest gay community center is, so...
...I'm just gonna go!

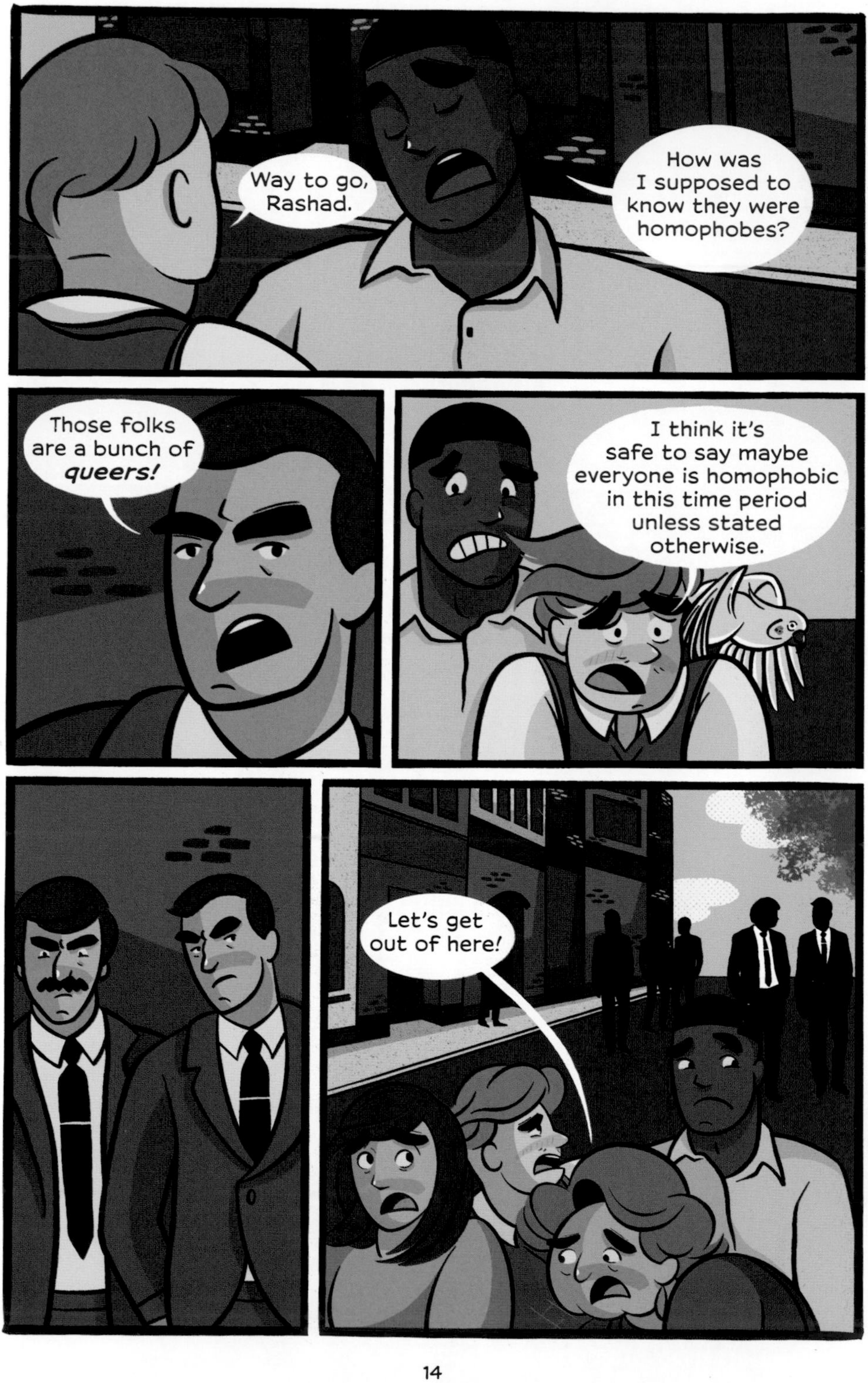

Way to go, Rashad.
How was I supposed to know they were homophobes?
Those folks are a bunch of *queers!*
I think it's safe to say maybe everyone is homophobic in this time period unless stated otherwise.
Let's get out of here!

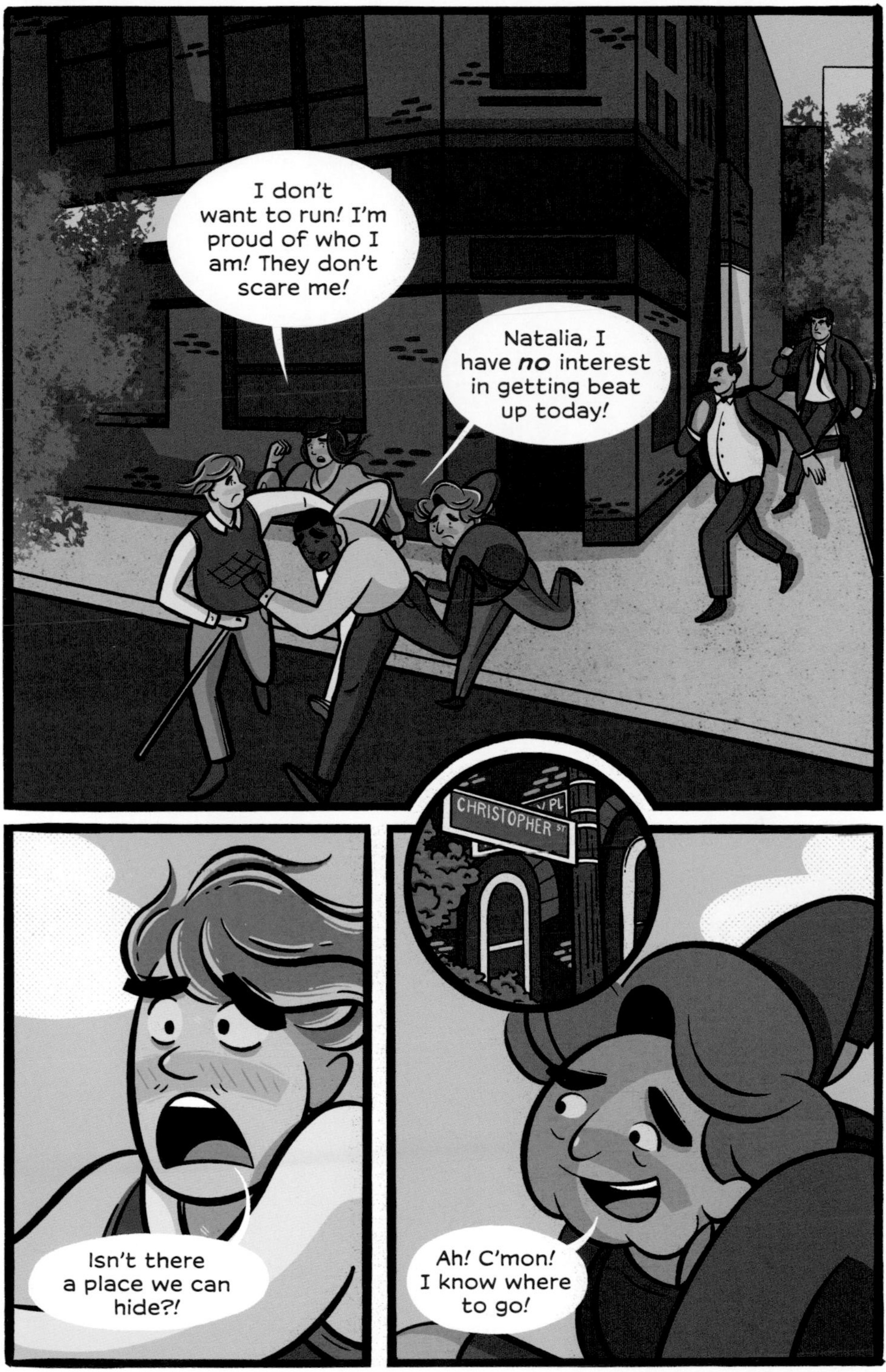
I don't want to run! I'm proud of who I am! They don't scare me!
Natalia, I have ***no*** interest in getting beat up today!
CHRISTOPHER ST
Isn't there a place we can hide?!
Ah! C'mon! I know where to go!

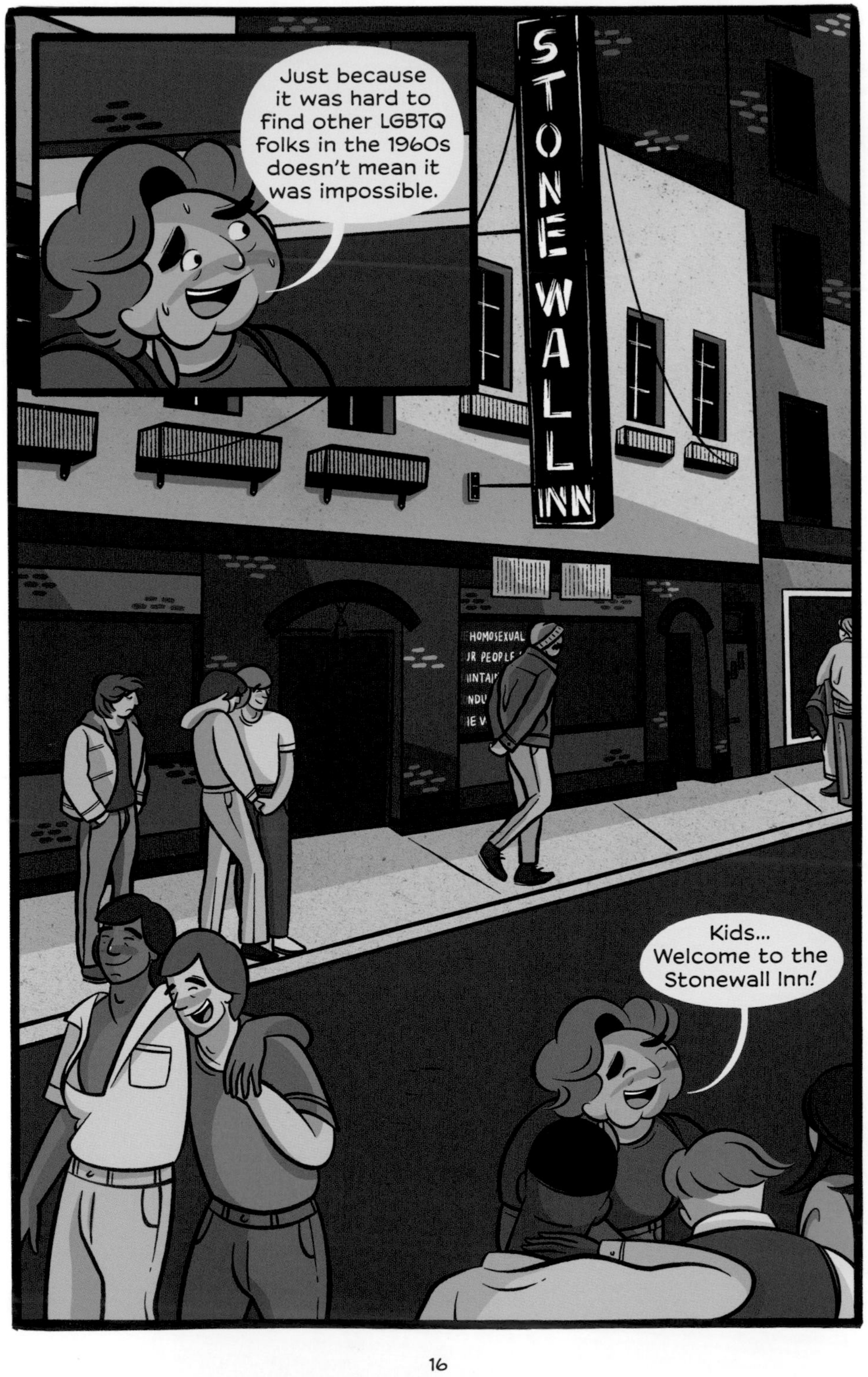
Just because it was hard to find other LGBTQ folks in the 1960s doesn't mean it was impossible.
STONEWALL INN
HOMOSEXUAL
Kids... Welcome to the Stonewall Inn!

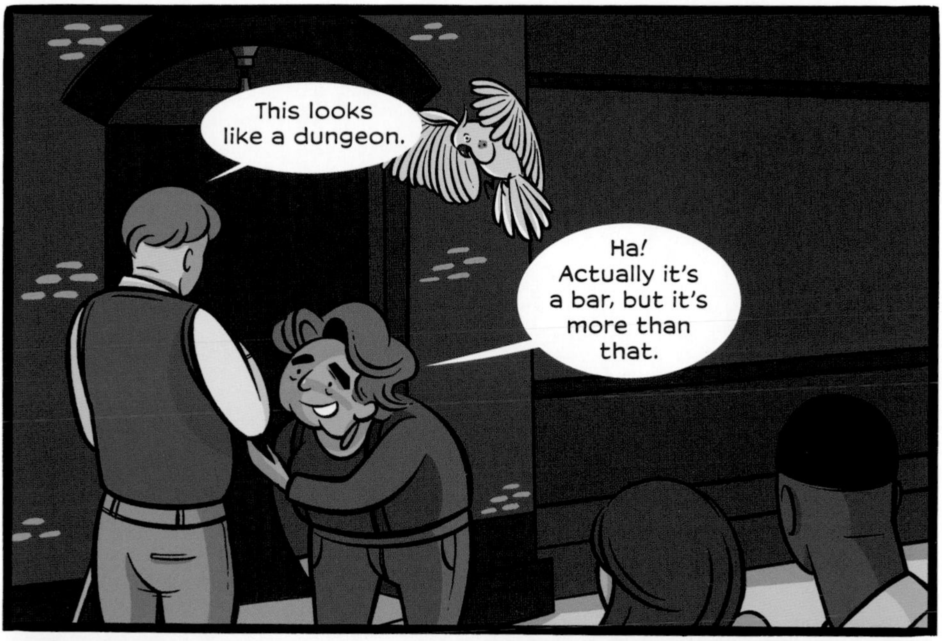
This looks like a dungeon.
Ha! Actually it's a bar, but it's more than that.

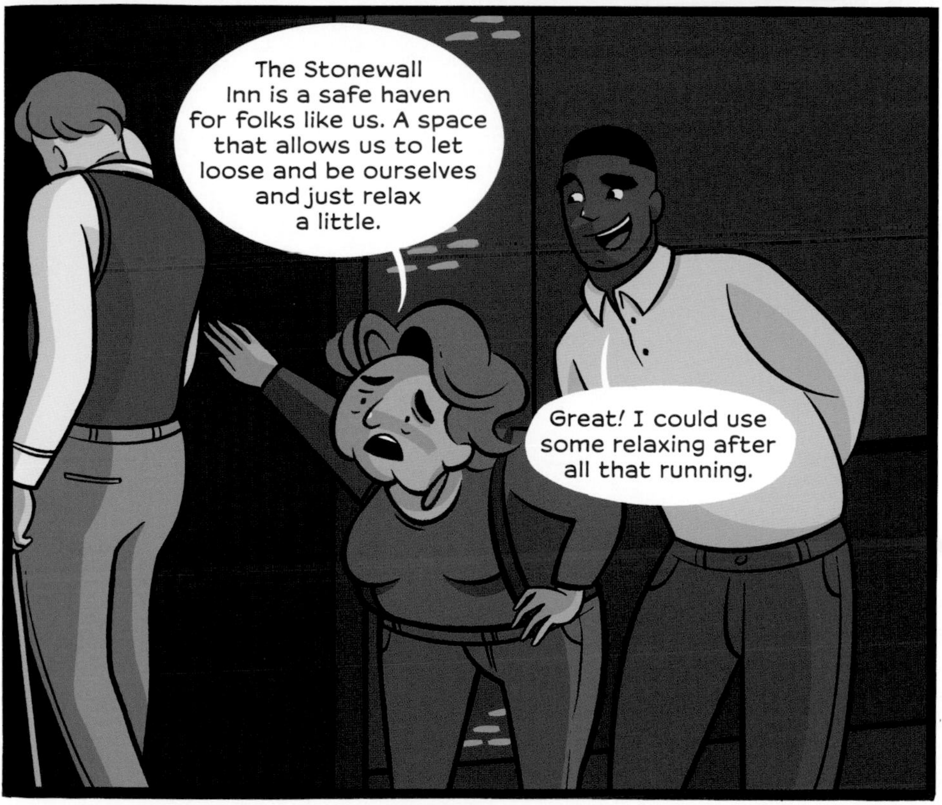
The Stonewall Inn is a safe haven for folks like us. A space that allows us to let loose and be ourselves and just relax a little.
Great! I could use some relaxing after all that running.

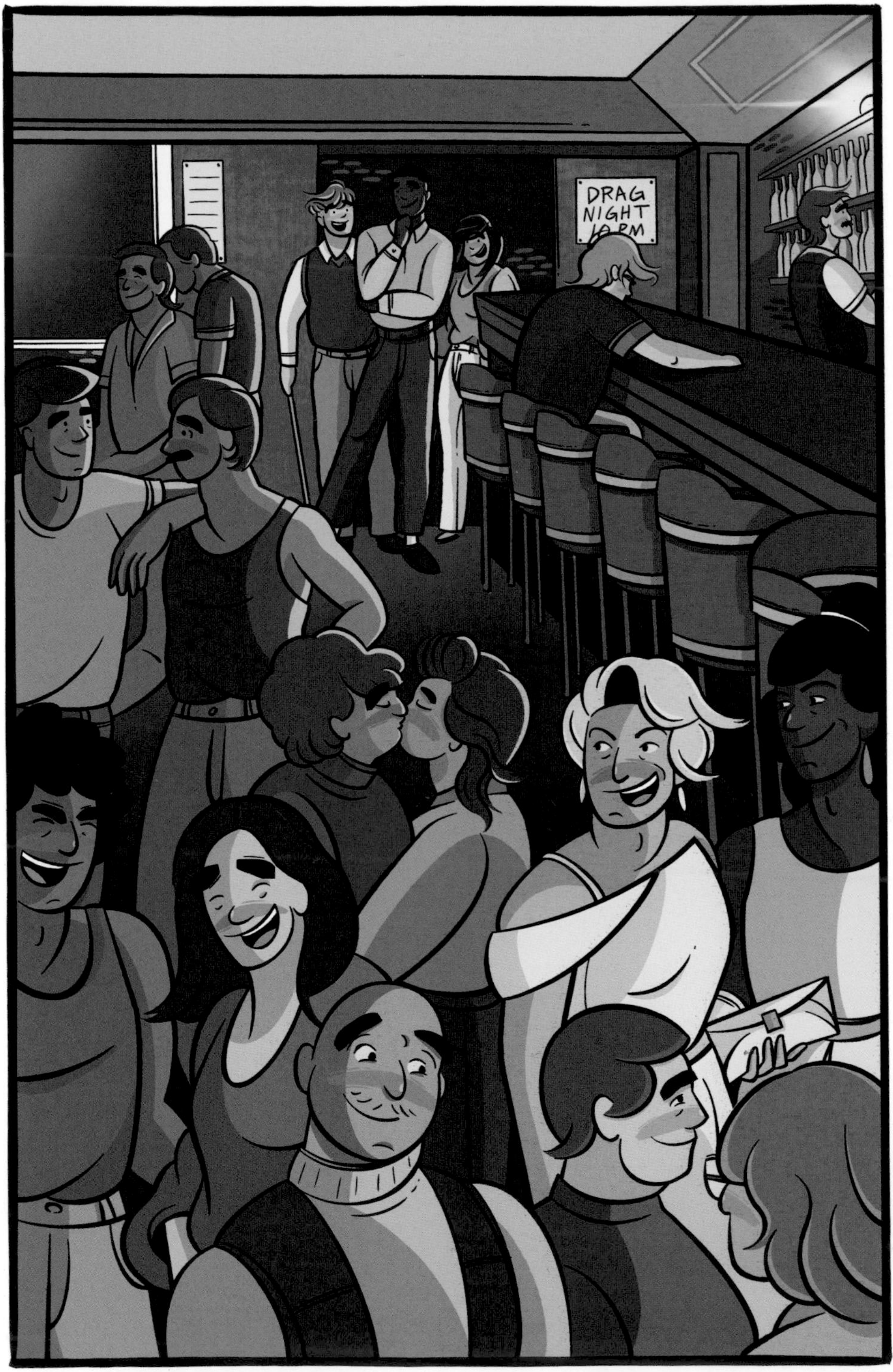
DRAG
NIGHT
10 PM

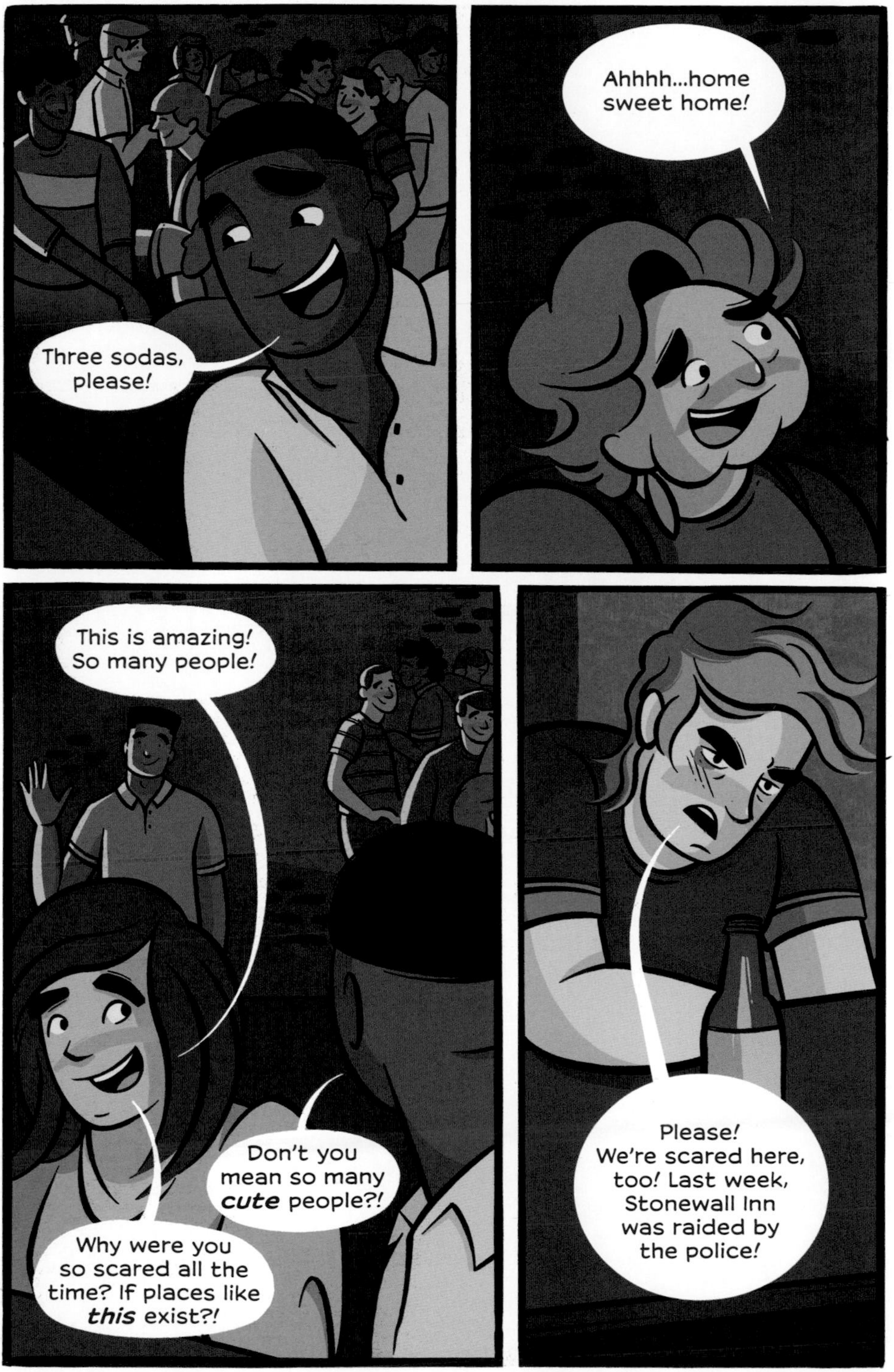
Three sodas, please!
Ahhhh...home sweet home!
This is amazing! So many people!
Why were you so scared all the time? If places like *this* exist?!
Don't you mean so many *cute* people?!
Please! We're scared here, too! Last week, Stonewall Inn was raided by the police!

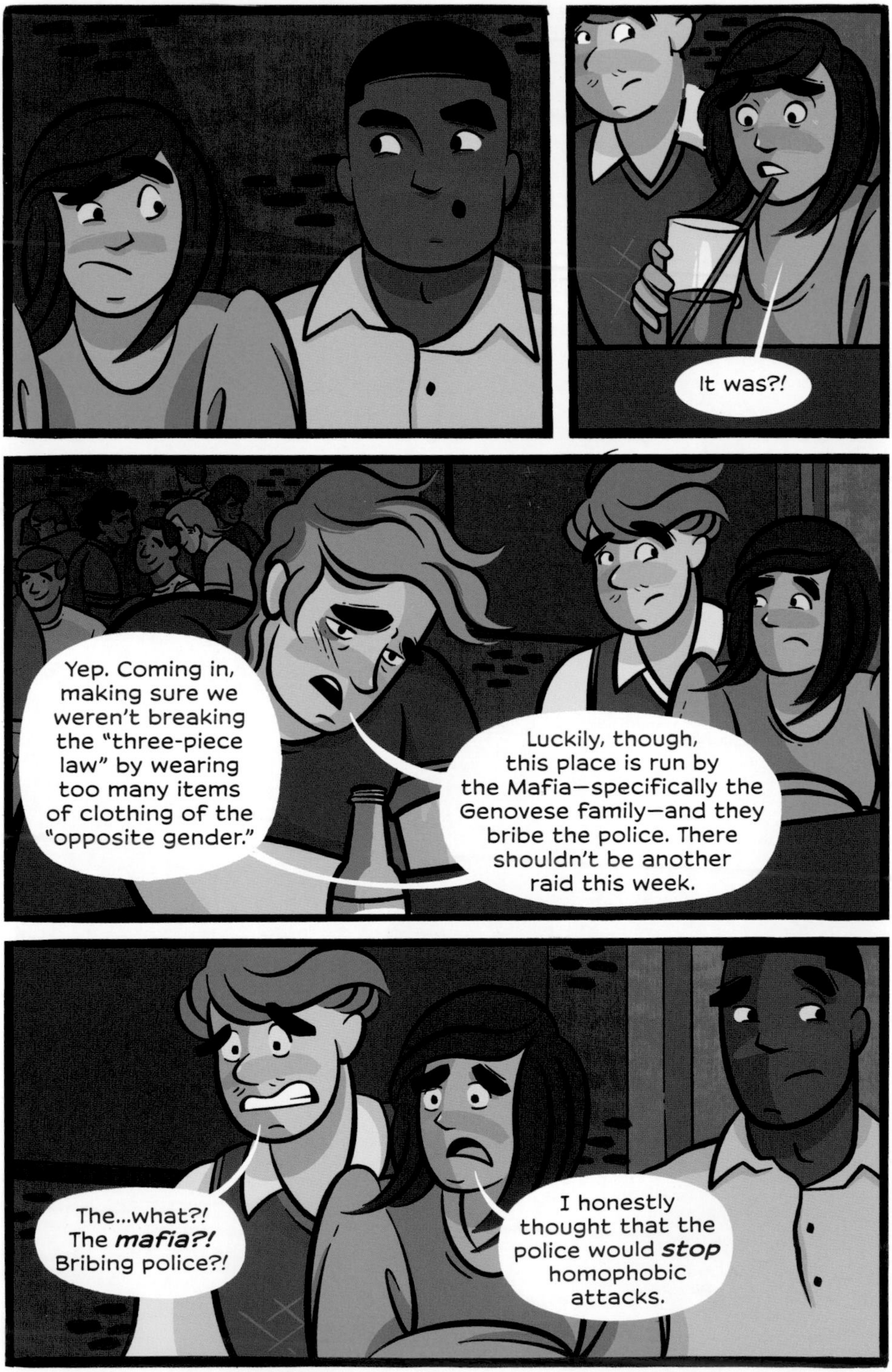
It was?!
Yep. Coming in, making sure we weren't breaking the "three-piece law" by wearing too many items of clothing of the "opposite gender."
Luckily, though, this place is run by the Mafia—specifically the Genovese family—and they bribe the police. There shouldn't be another raid this week.
The...what?! The *mafia?!* Bribing police?!
I honestly thought that the police would *stop* homophobic attacks.

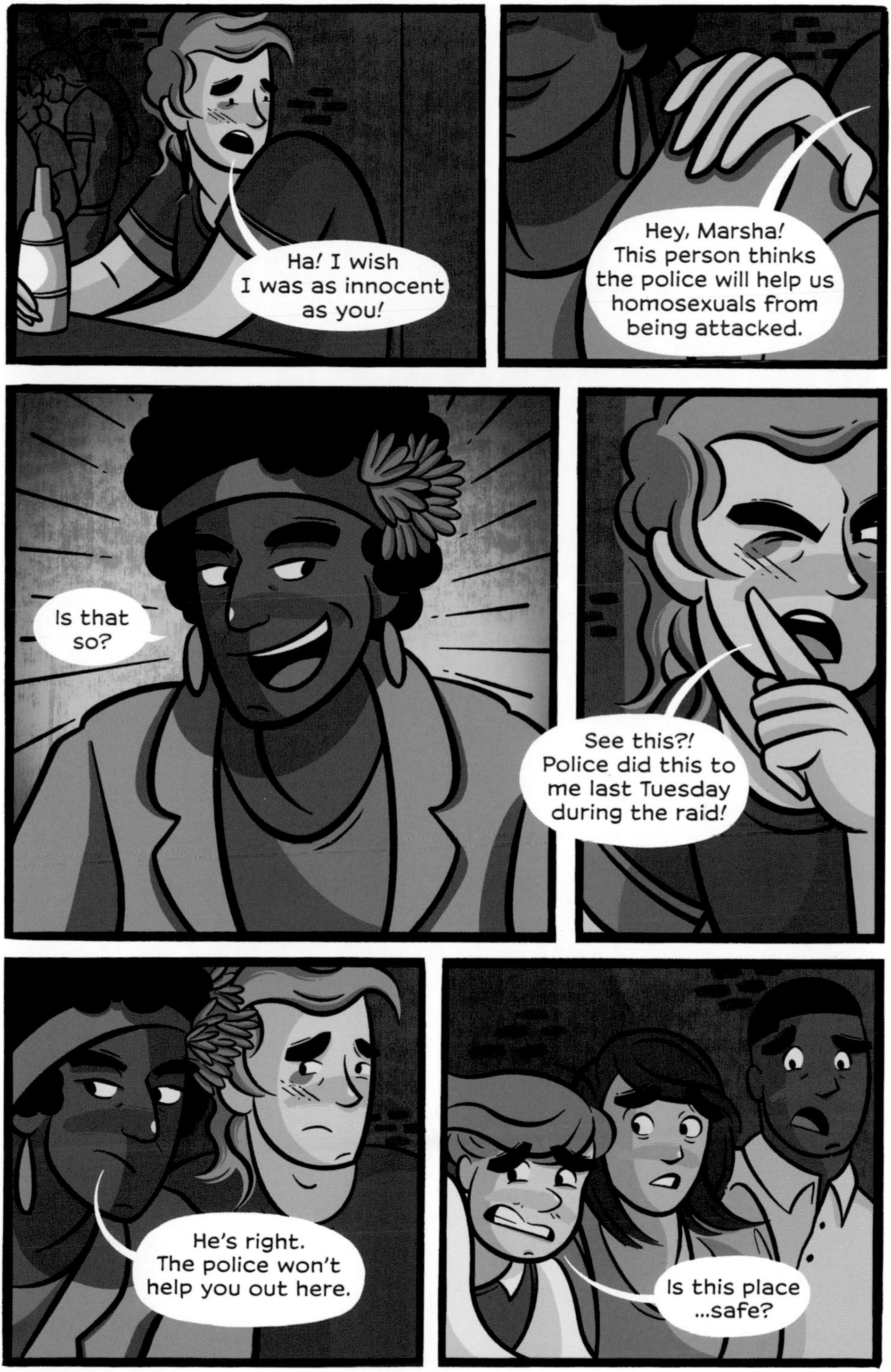
Ha! I wish I was as innocent as you!
Hey, Marsha! This person thinks the police will help us homosexuals from being attacked.
Is that so?
See this?! Police did this to me last Tuesday during the raid!
He's right. The police won't help you out here.
Is this place ...safe?

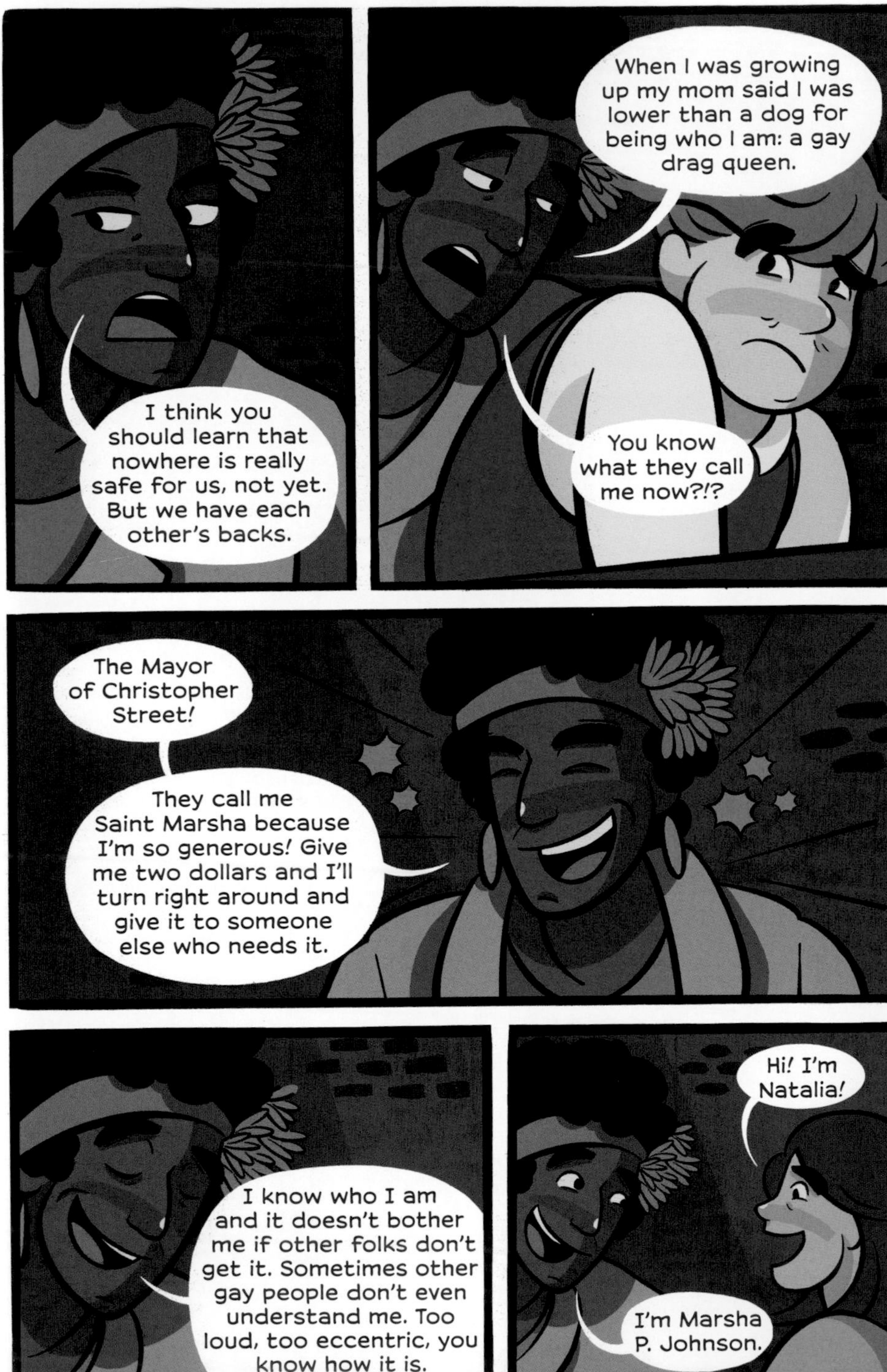
I think you should learn that nowhere is really safe for us, not yet. But we have each other's backs.
When I was growing up my mom said I was lower than a dog for being who I am: a gay drag queen.
You know what they call me now?!?
The Mayor of Christopher Street!
They call me Saint Marsha because I'm so generous! Give me two dollars and I'll turn right around and give it to someone else who needs it.
I know who I am and it doesn't bother me if other folks don't get it. Sometimes other gay people don't even understand me. Too loud, too eccentric, you know how it is.
Hi! I'm Natalia!
I'm Marsha P. Johnson.

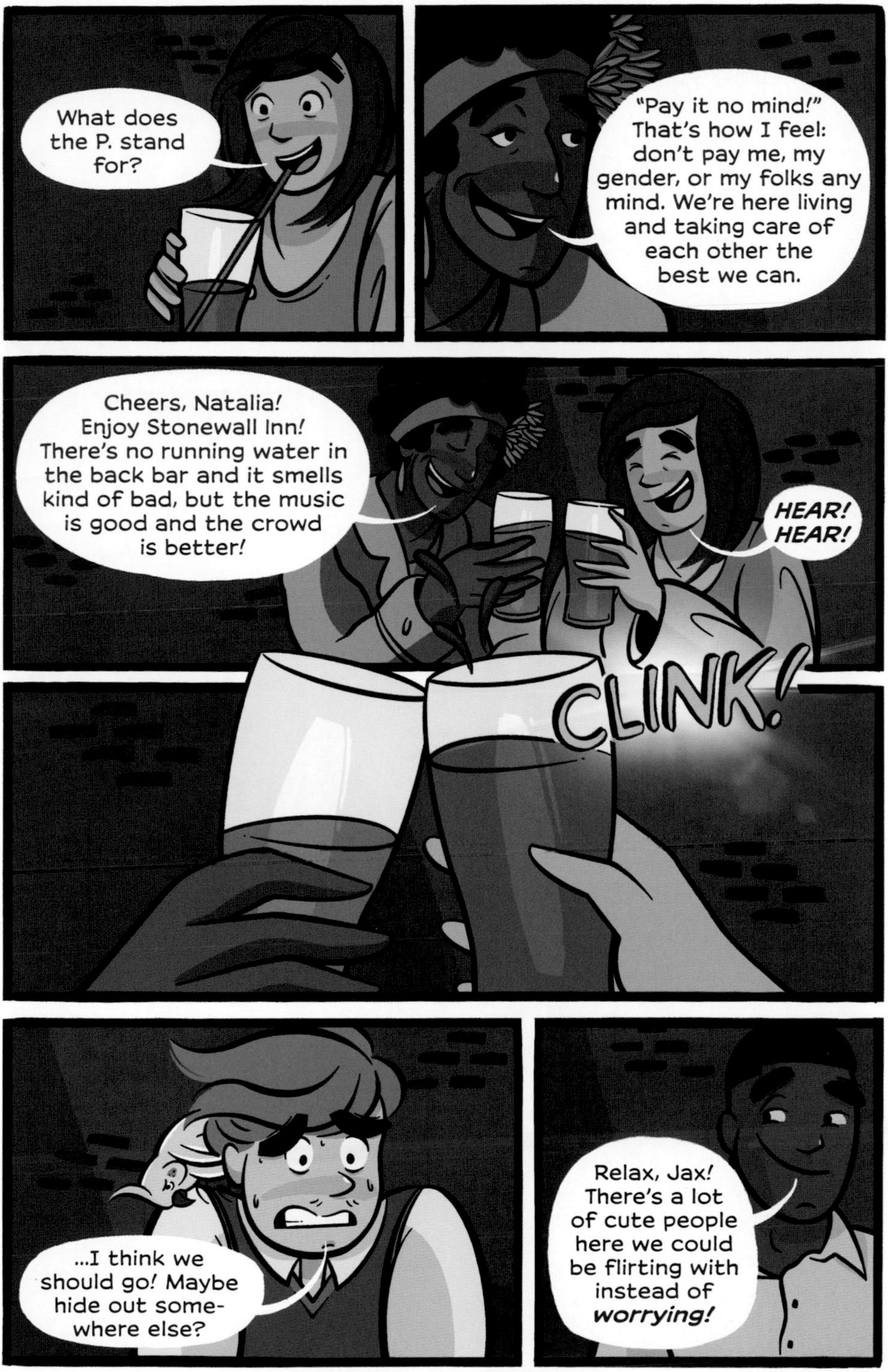

What does the P. stand for?
"Pay it no mind!" That's how I feel: don't pay me, my gender, or my folks any mind. We're here living and taking care of each other the best we can.
Cheers, Natalia! Enjoy Stonewall Inn! There's no running water in the back bar and it smells kind of bad, but the music is good and the crowd is better!
HEAR! HEAR!
CLINK!
...I think we should go! Maybe hide out some-where else?
Relax, Jax! There's a lot of cute people here we could be flirting with instead of *worrying!*

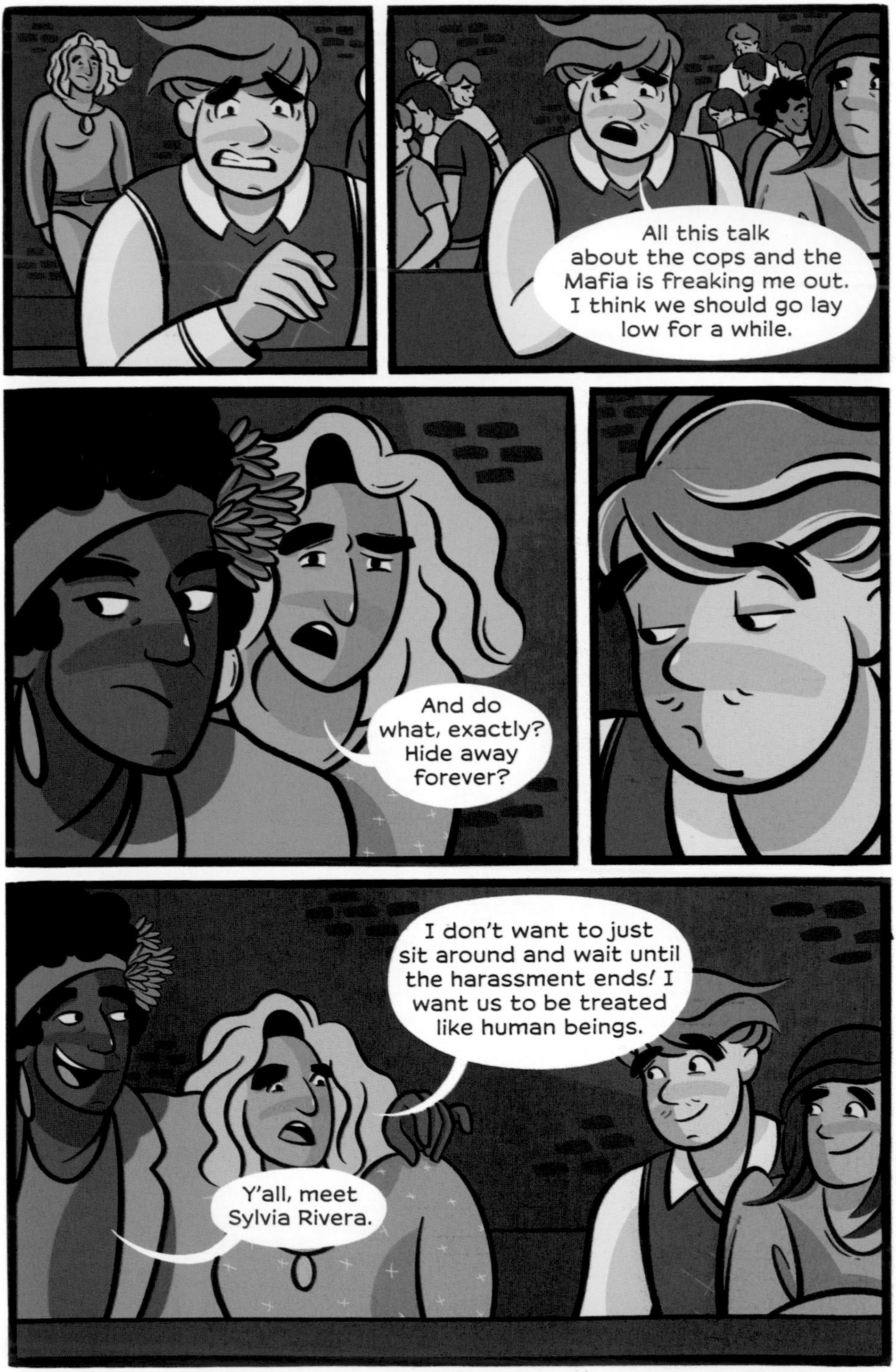
All this talk about the cops and the Mafia is freaking me out. I think we should go lay low for a while.
And do what, exactly? Hide away forever?
I don't want to just sit around and wait until the harassment ends! I want us to be treated like human beings.
Y'all, meet Sylvia Rivera.

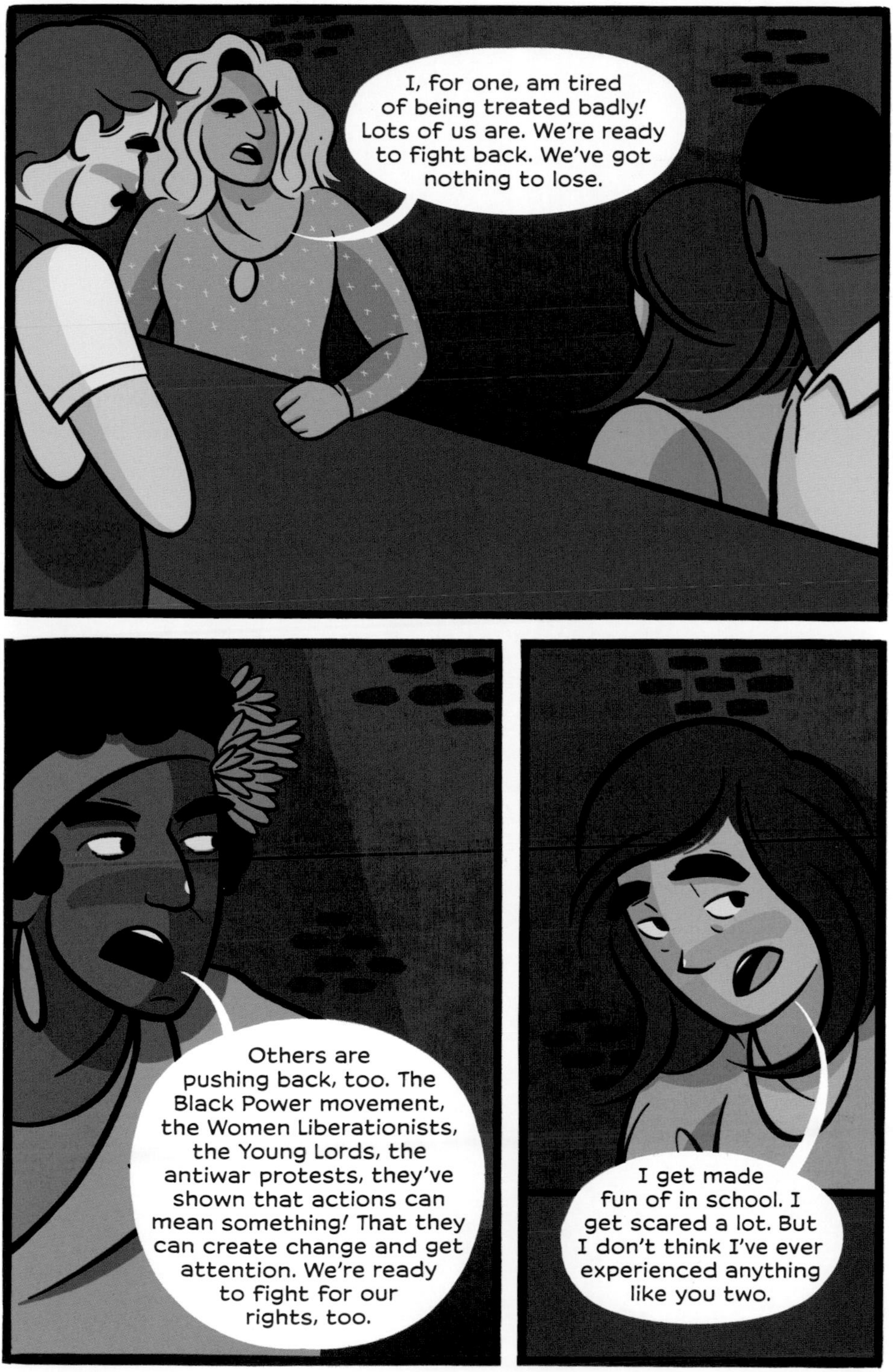
I, for one, am tired of being treated badly! Lots of us are. We're ready to fight back. We've got nothing to lose.
Others are pushing back, too. The Black Power movement, the Women Liberationists, the Young Lords, the antiwar protests, they've shown that actions can mean something! That they can create change and get attention. We're ready to fight for our rights, too.
I get made fun of in school. I get scared a lot. But I don't think I've ever experienced anything like you two.

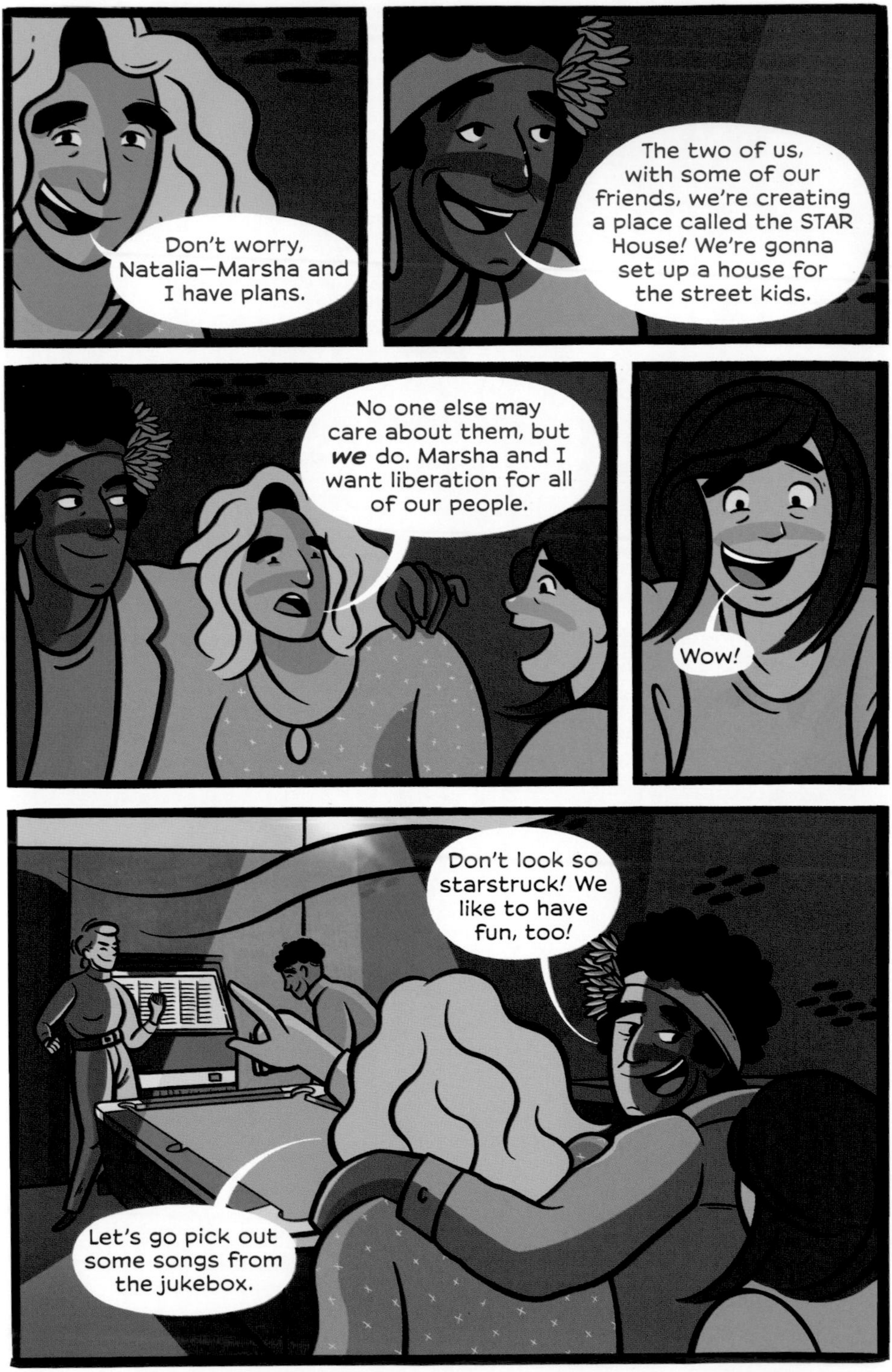
Don't worry, Natalia—Marsha and I have plans.
The two of us, with some of our friends, we're creating a place called the STAR House! We're gonna set up a house for the street kids.
No one else may care about them, but **we** do. Marsha and I want liberation for all of our people.
Wow!
Don't look so starstruck! We like to have fun, too!
Let's go pick out some songs from the jukebox.

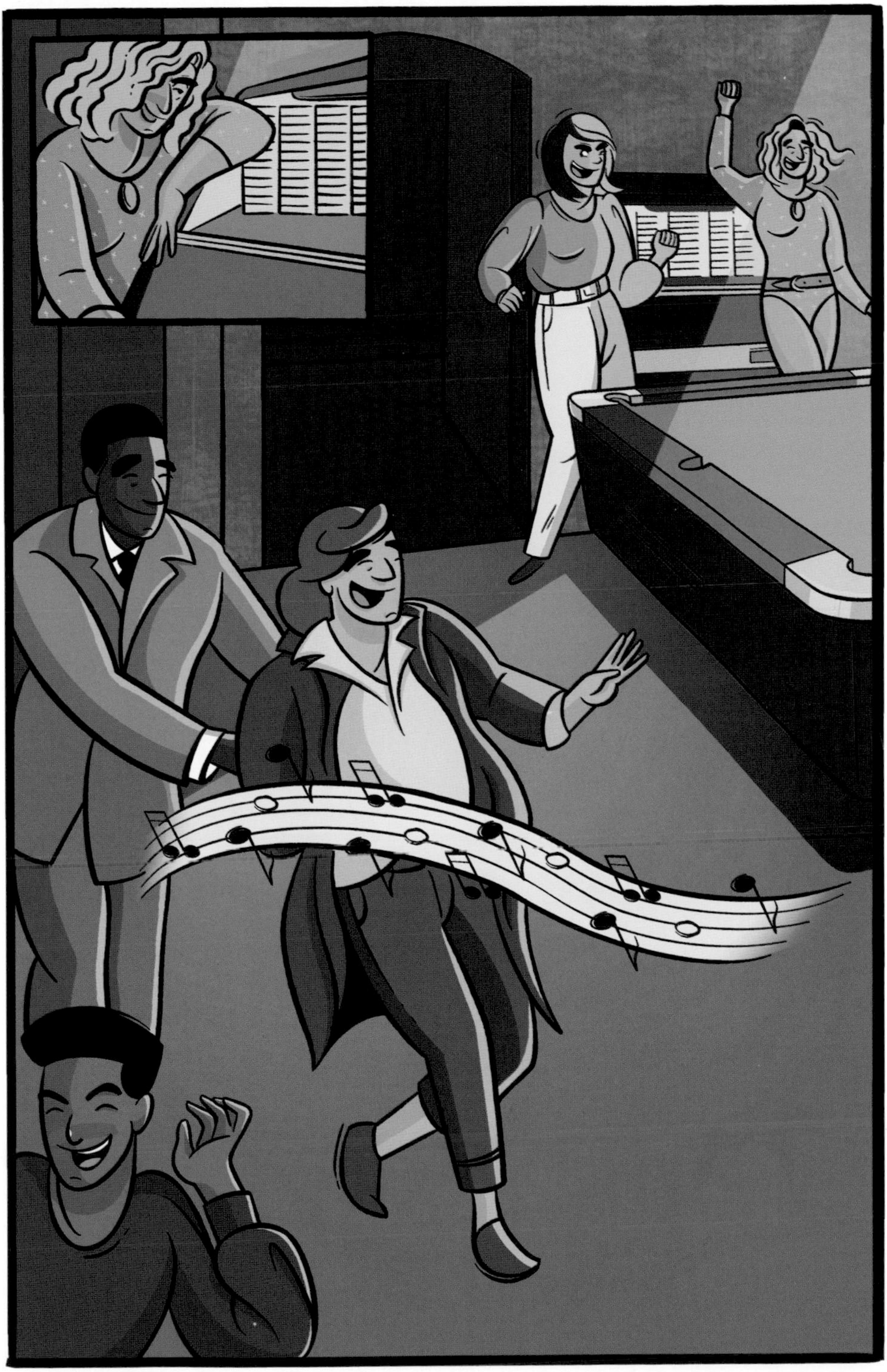

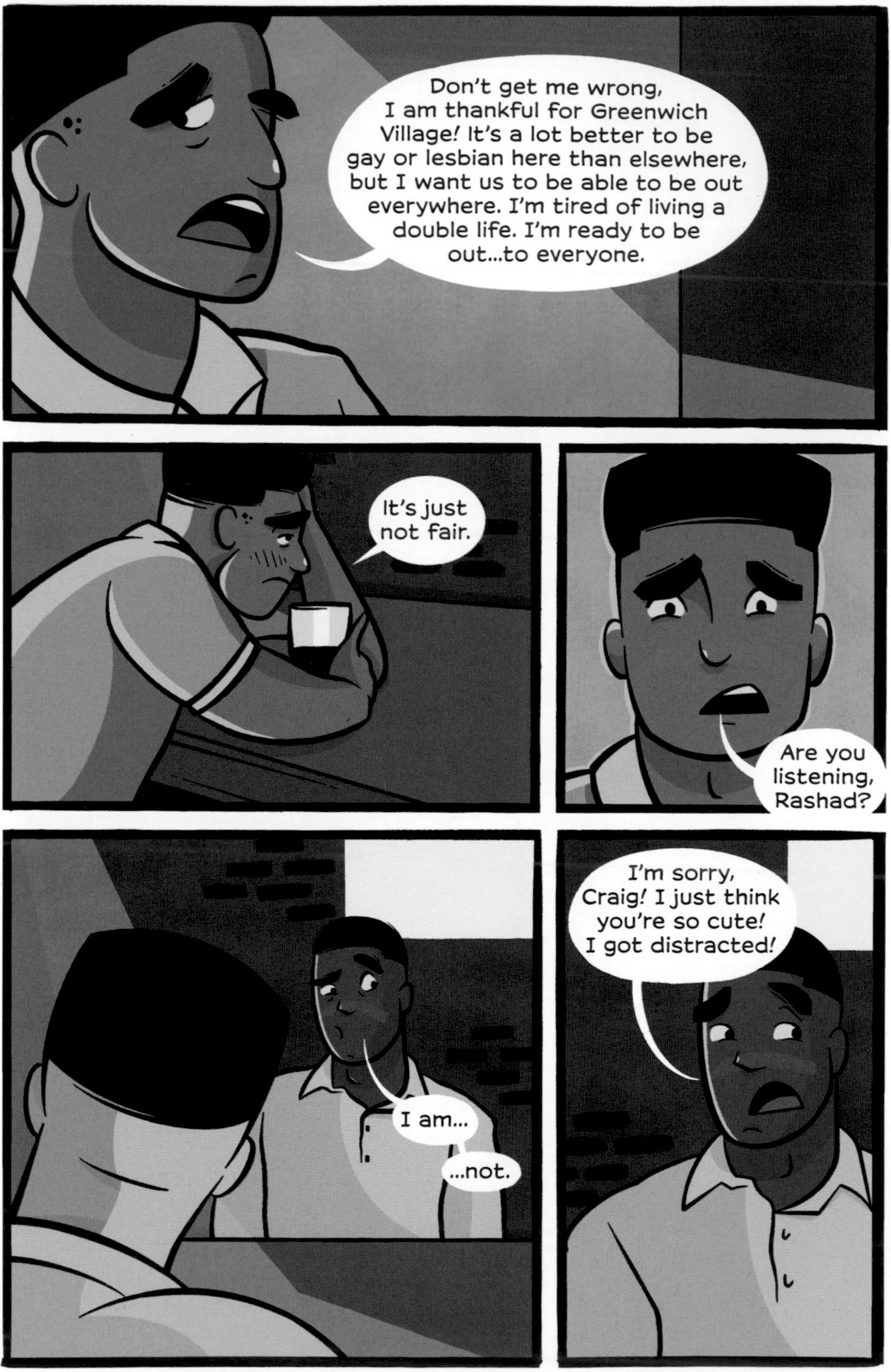
Don't get me wrong, I am thankful for Greenwich Village! It's a lot better to be gay or lesbian here than elsewhere, but I want us to be able to be out everywhere. I'm tired of living a double life. I'm ready to be out...to everyone.
It's just not fair.
Are you listening, Rashad?
I am...
...not.
I'm sorry, Craig! I just think you're so cute! I got distracted!

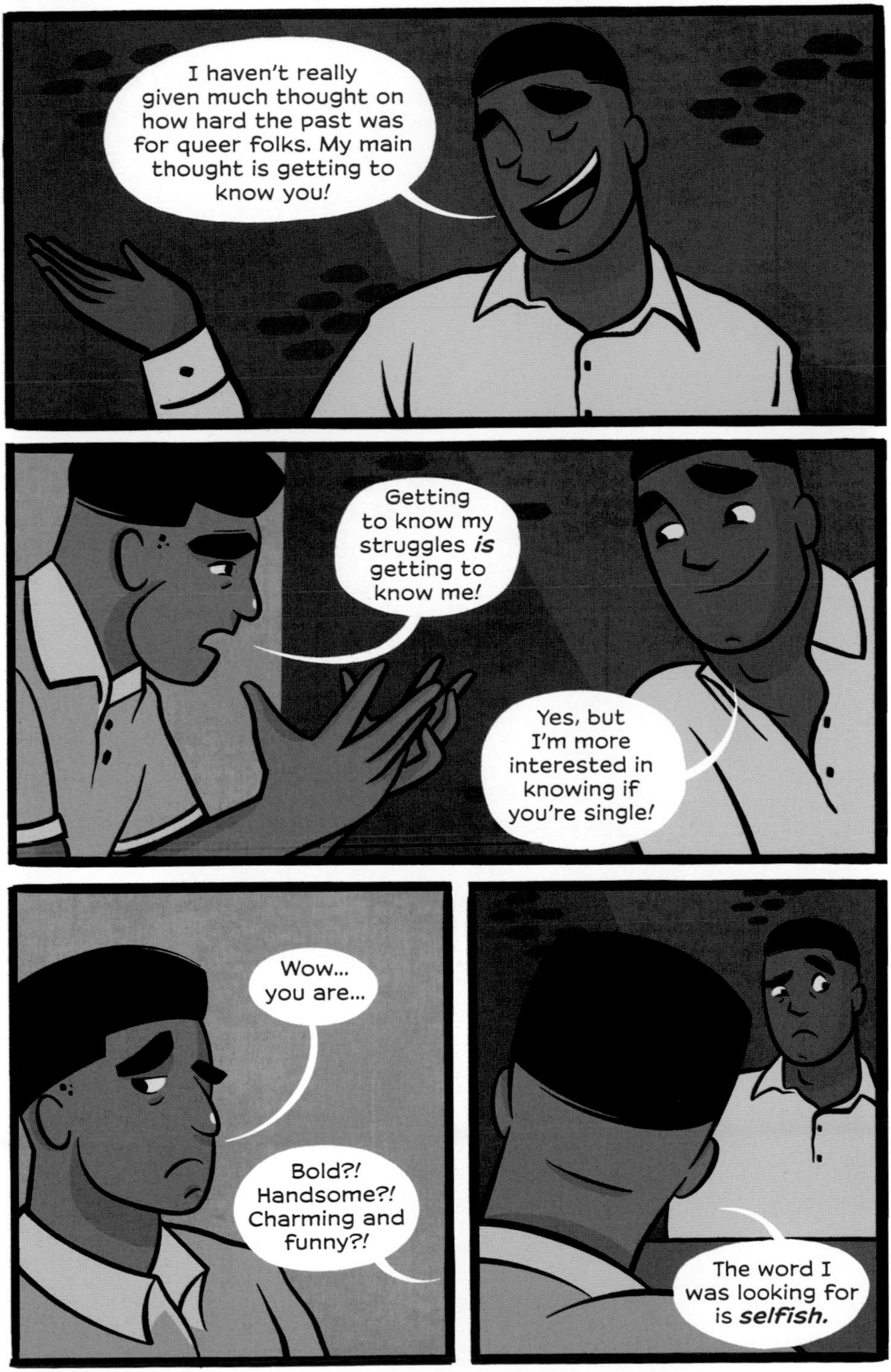
I haven't really given much thought on how hard the past was for queer folks. My main thought is getting to know you!
Getting to know my struggles *is* getting to know me!
Yes, but I'm more interested in knowing if you're single!
Wow... you are...
Bold?! Handsome?! Charming and funny?!
The word I was looking for is ***selfish.***

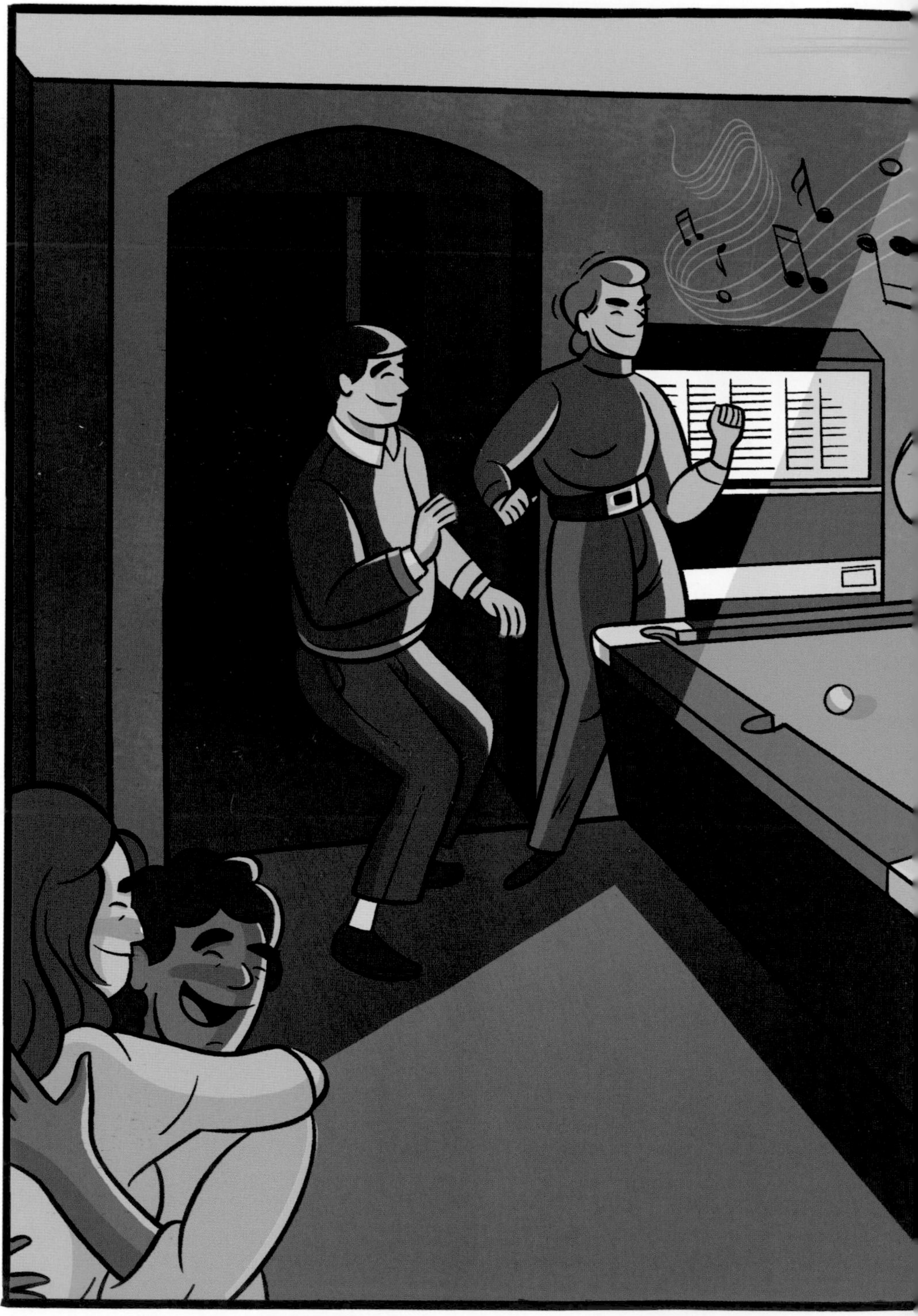

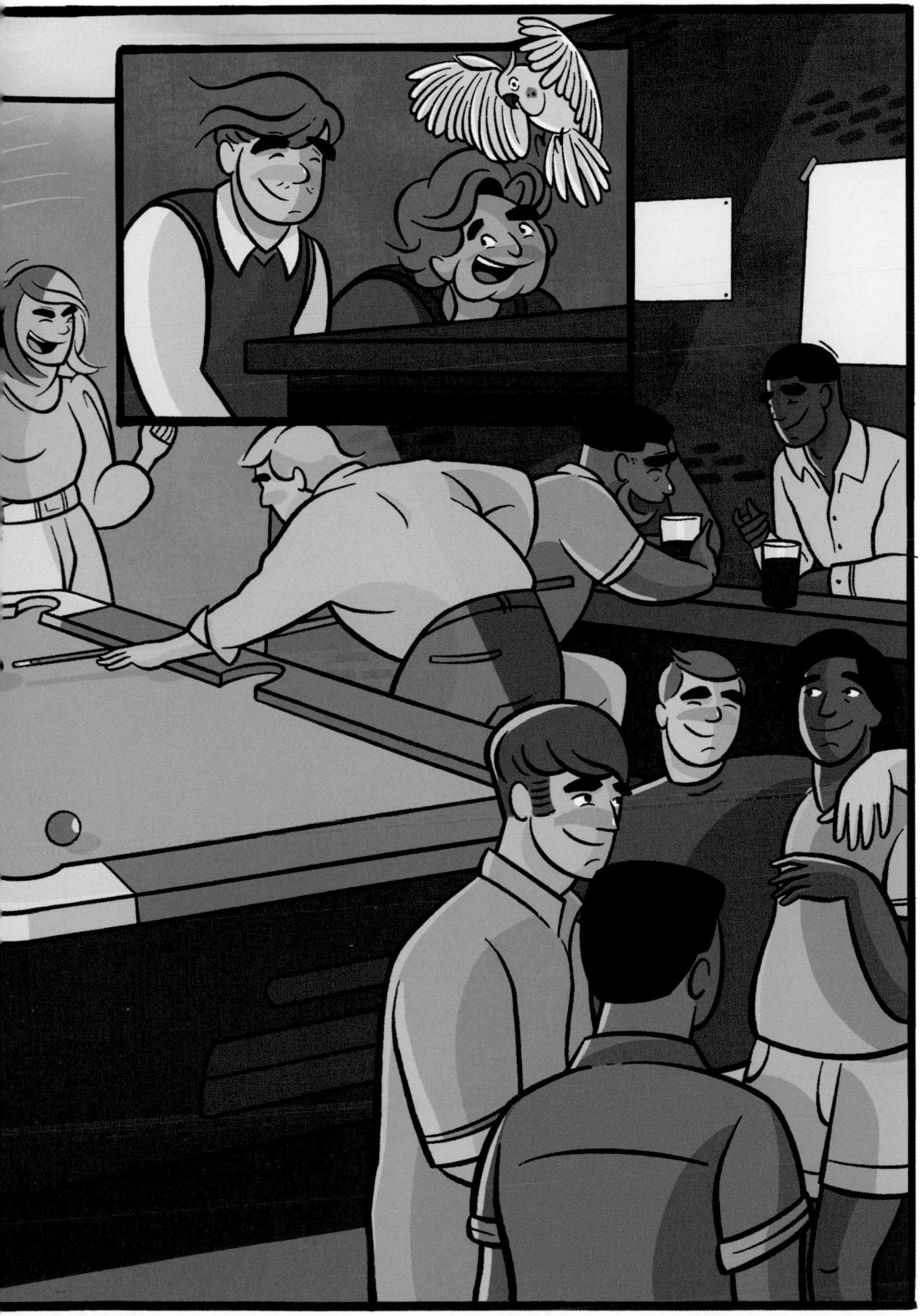

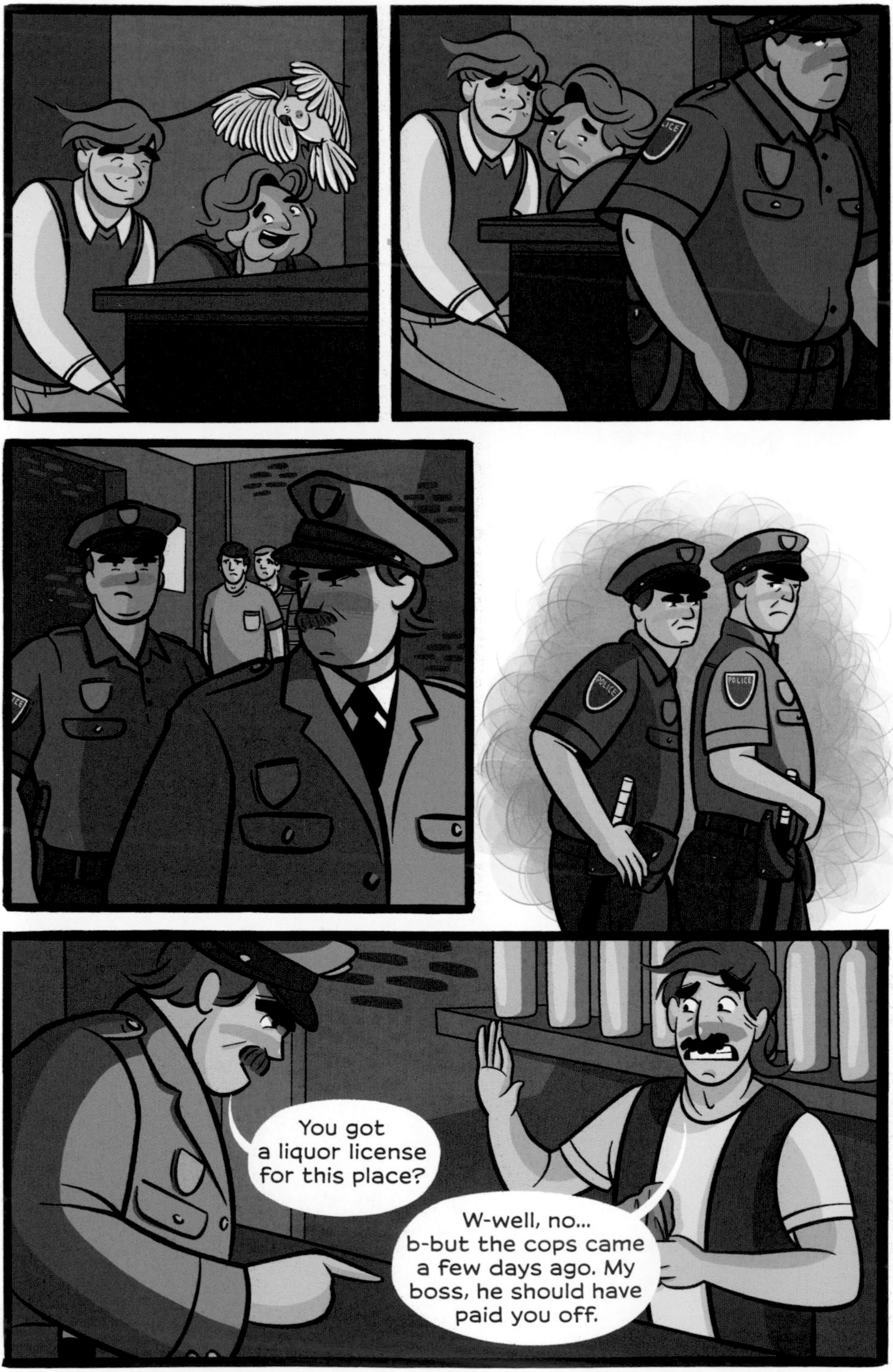
POLICE
POLICE
You got a liquor license for this place?
W-well, no... b-but the cops came a few days ago. My boss, he should have paid you off.

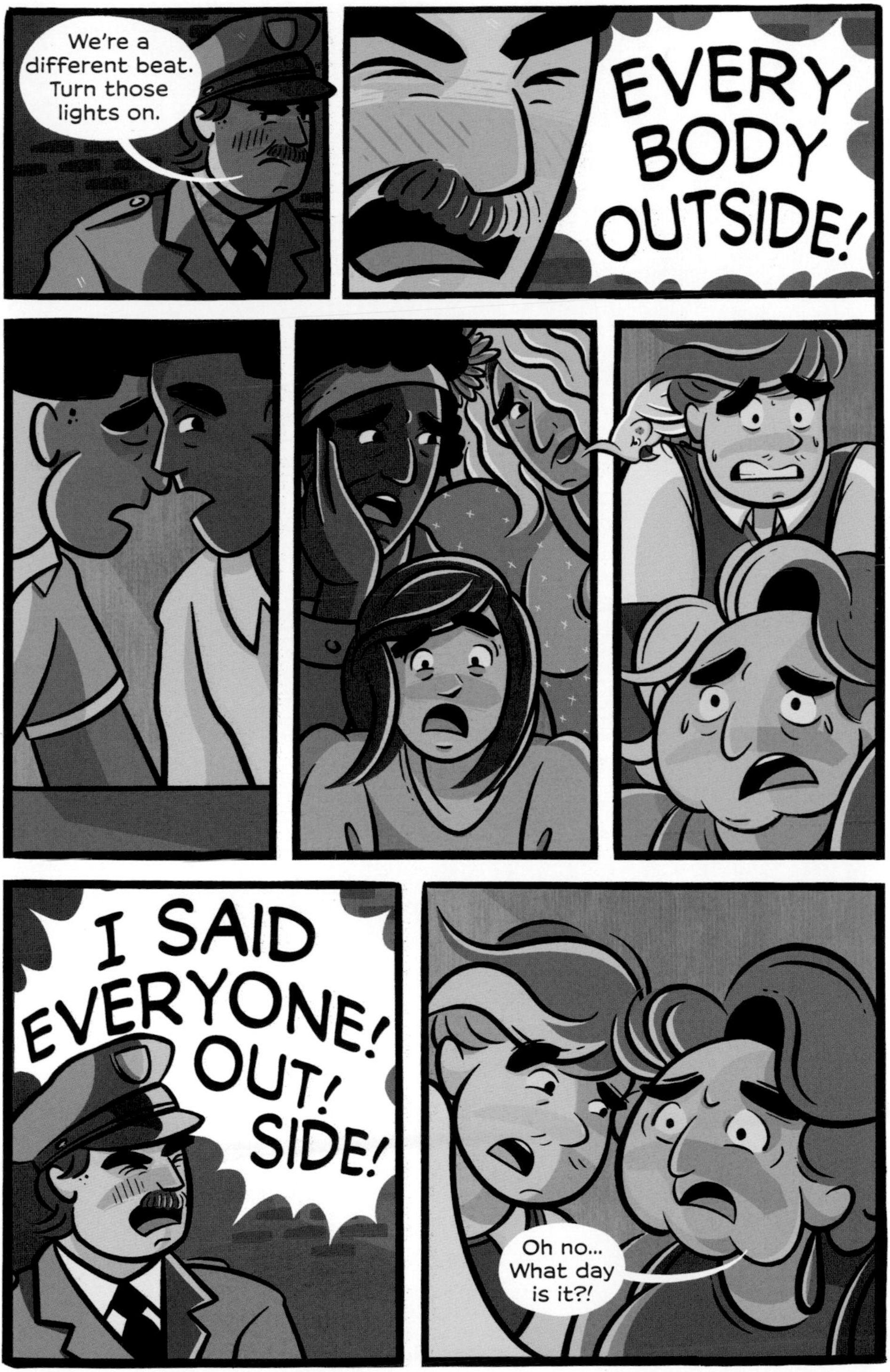
We're a different beat. Turn those lights on.
EVERY BODY OUTSIDE!
I SAID EVERYONE! OUT! SIDE!
Oh no... What day is it?!

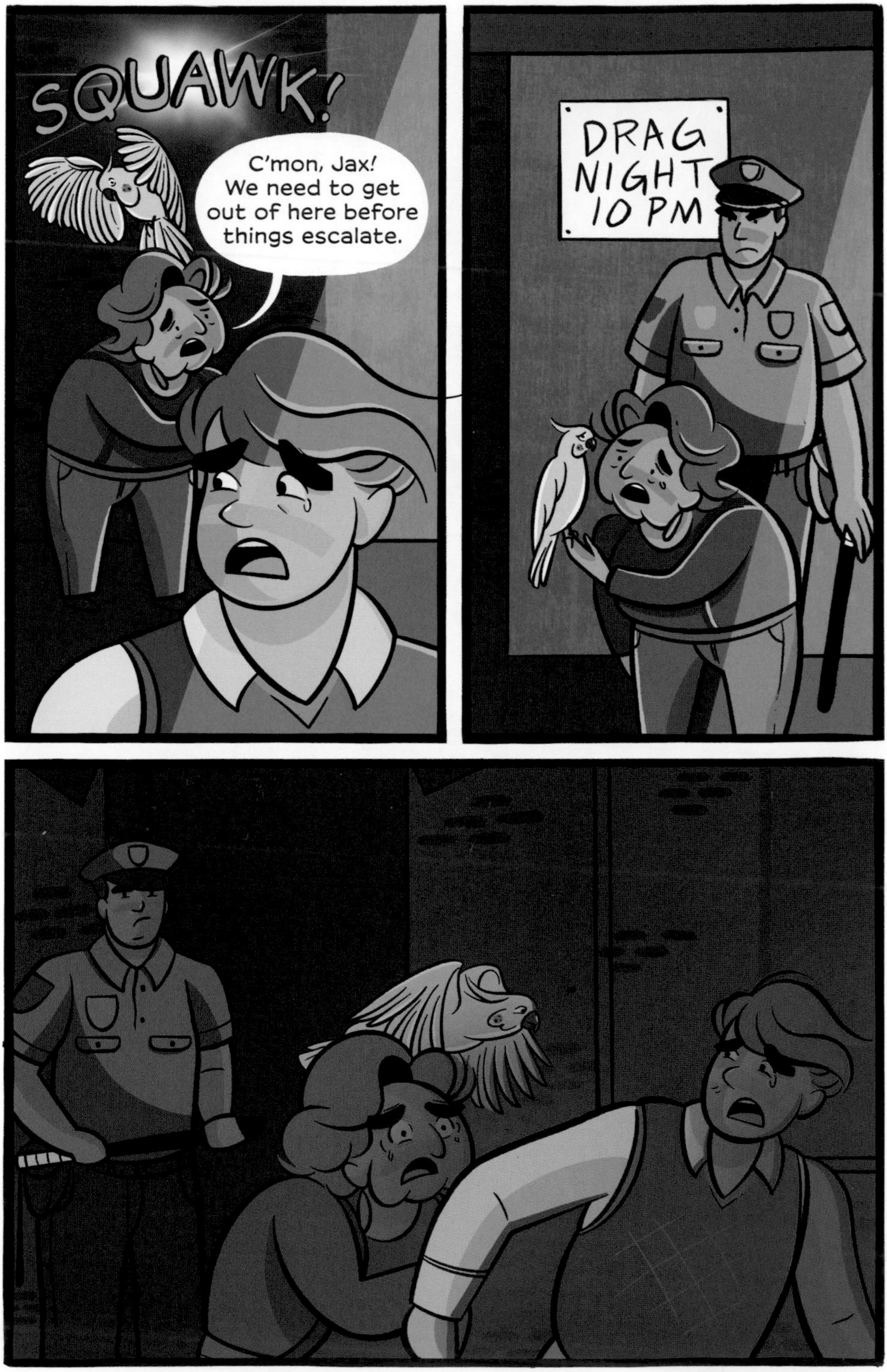
SQUAWK!
C'mon, Jax! We need to get out of here before things escalate.
DRAG NIGHT 10 PM

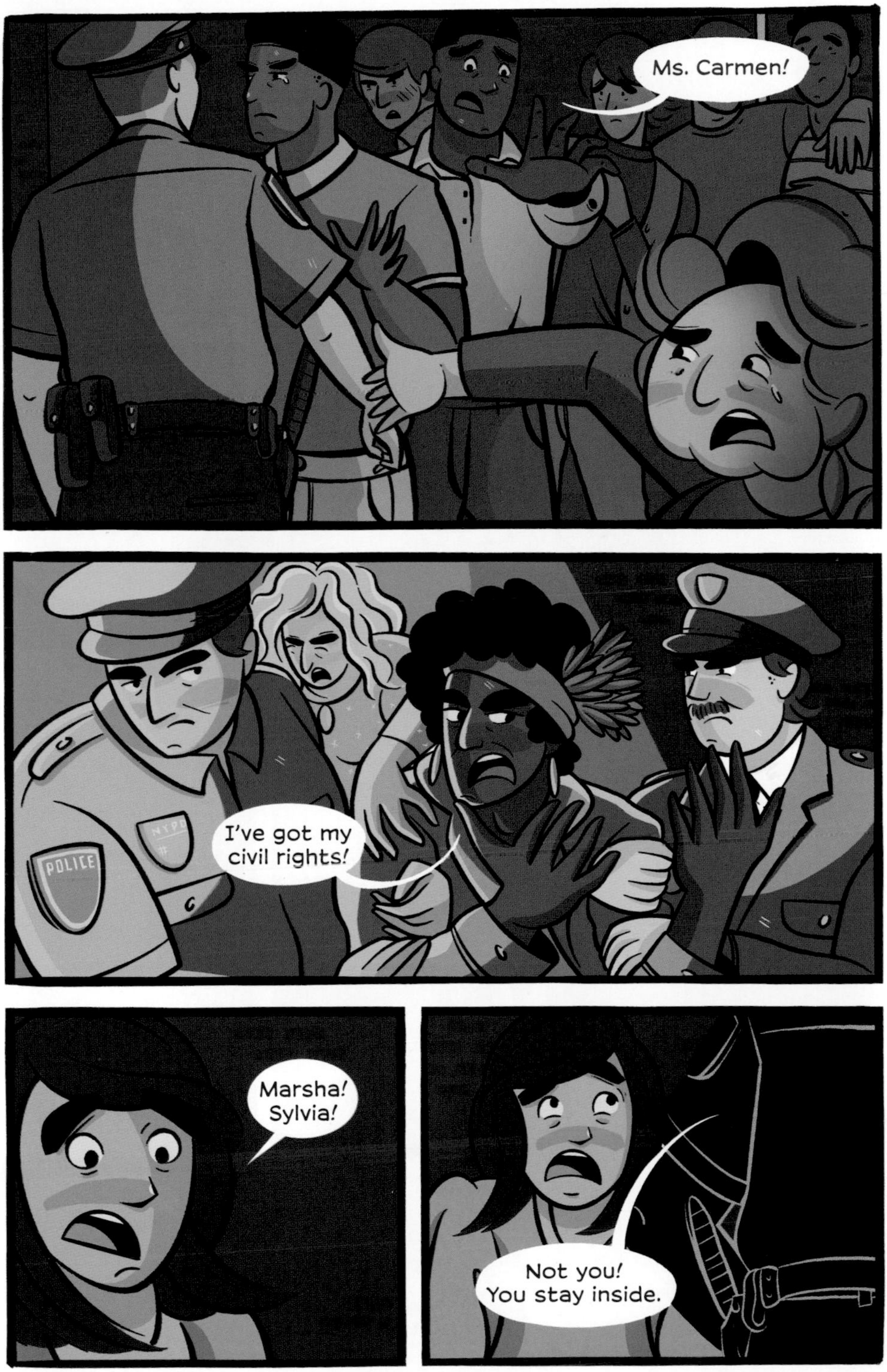
Ms. Carmen!
I've got my civil rights!
Marsha! Sylvia!
Not you! You stay inside.

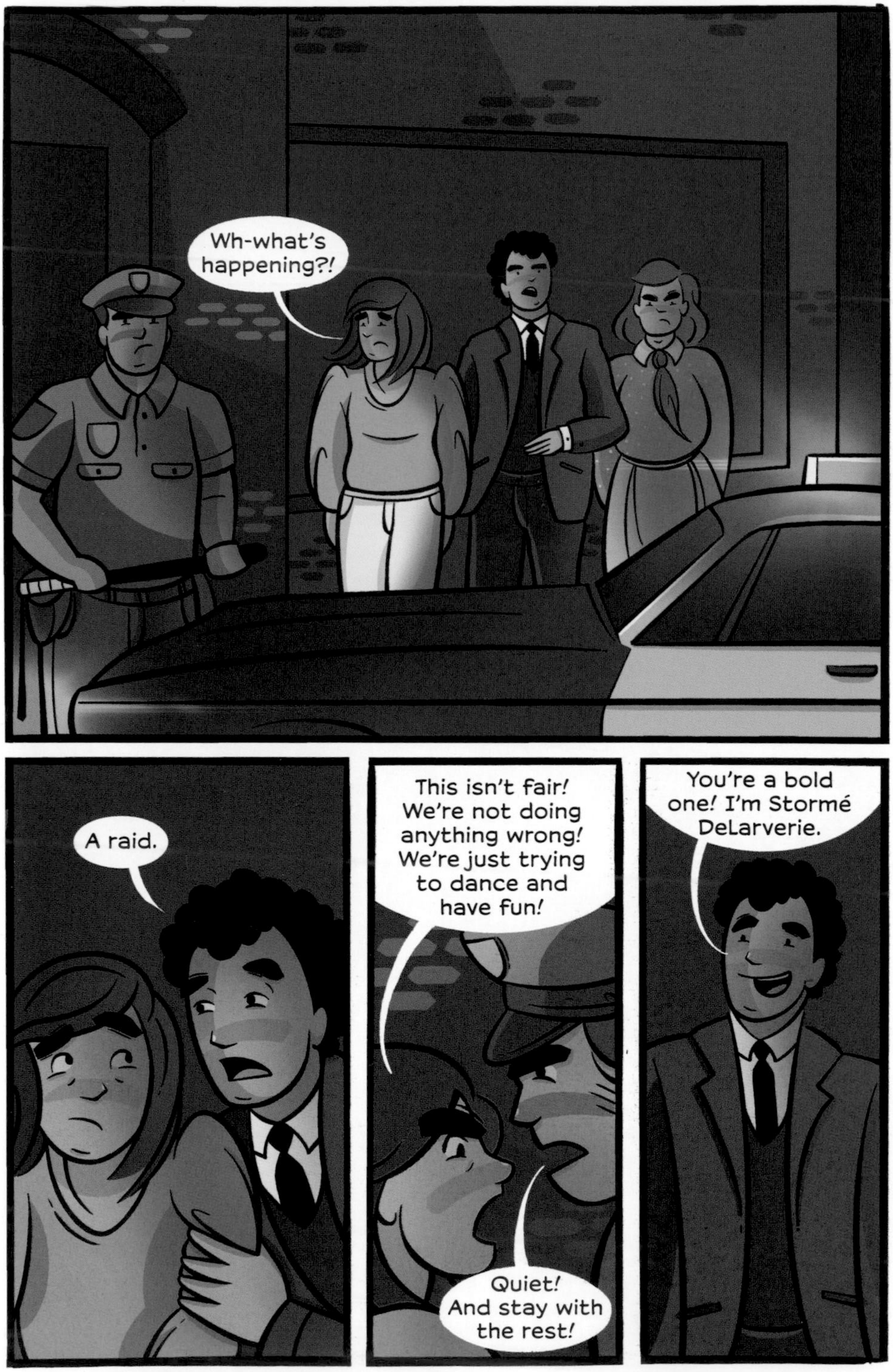
Wh-what's happening?!
A raid.
This isn't fair! We're not doing anything wrong! We're just trying to dance and have fun!
Quiet! And stay with the rest!
You're a bold one! I'm Stormé DeLarverie.

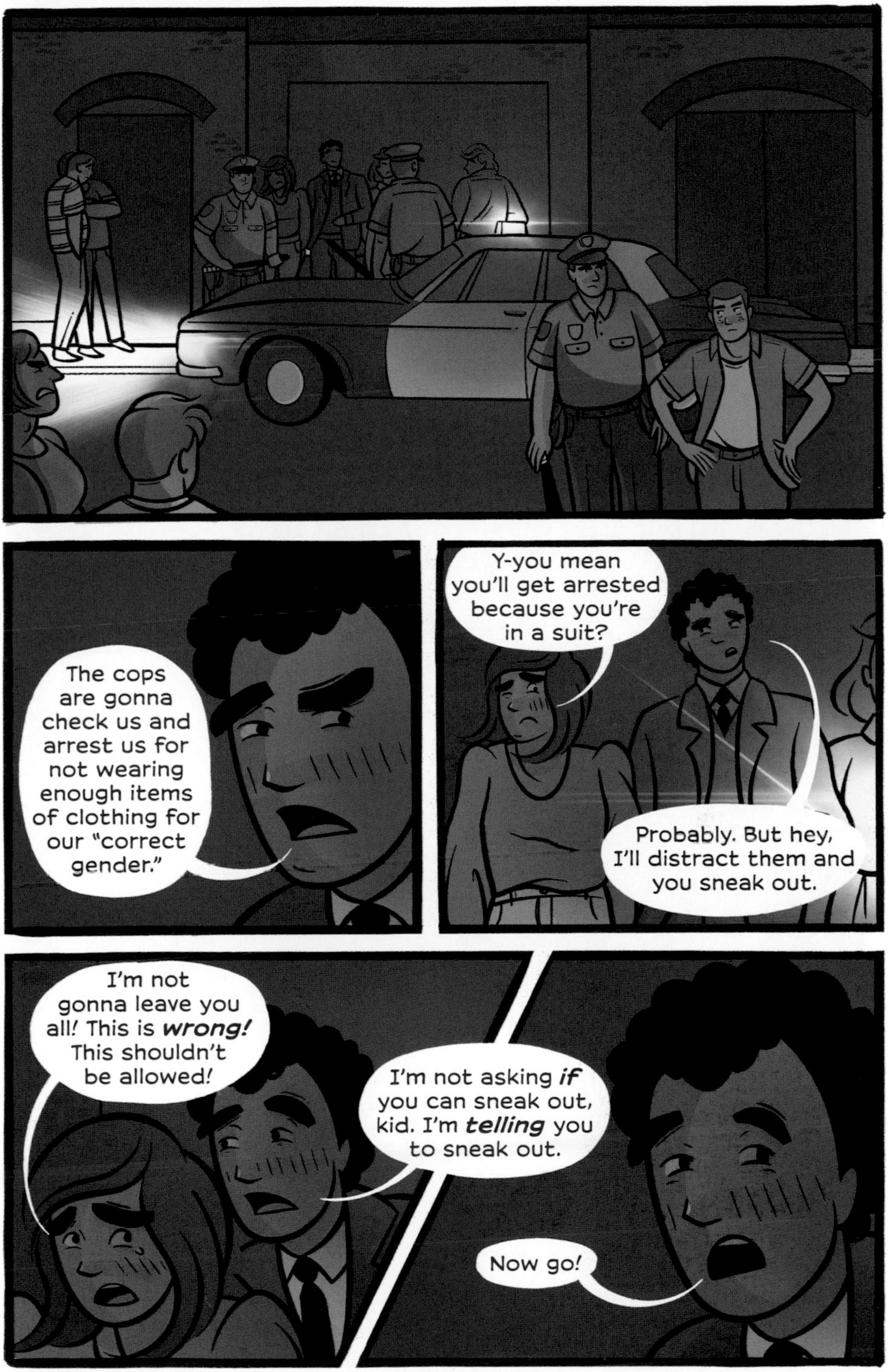
The cops are gonna check us and arrest us for not wearing enough items of clothing for our "correct gender."
Y-you mean you'll get arrested because you're in a suit?
Probably. But hey, I'll distract them and you sneak out.
I'm not gonna leave you all! This is ***wrong!*** This shouldn't be allowed!
I'm not asking ***if*** you can sneak out, kid. I'm ***telling*** you to sneak out.
Now go!

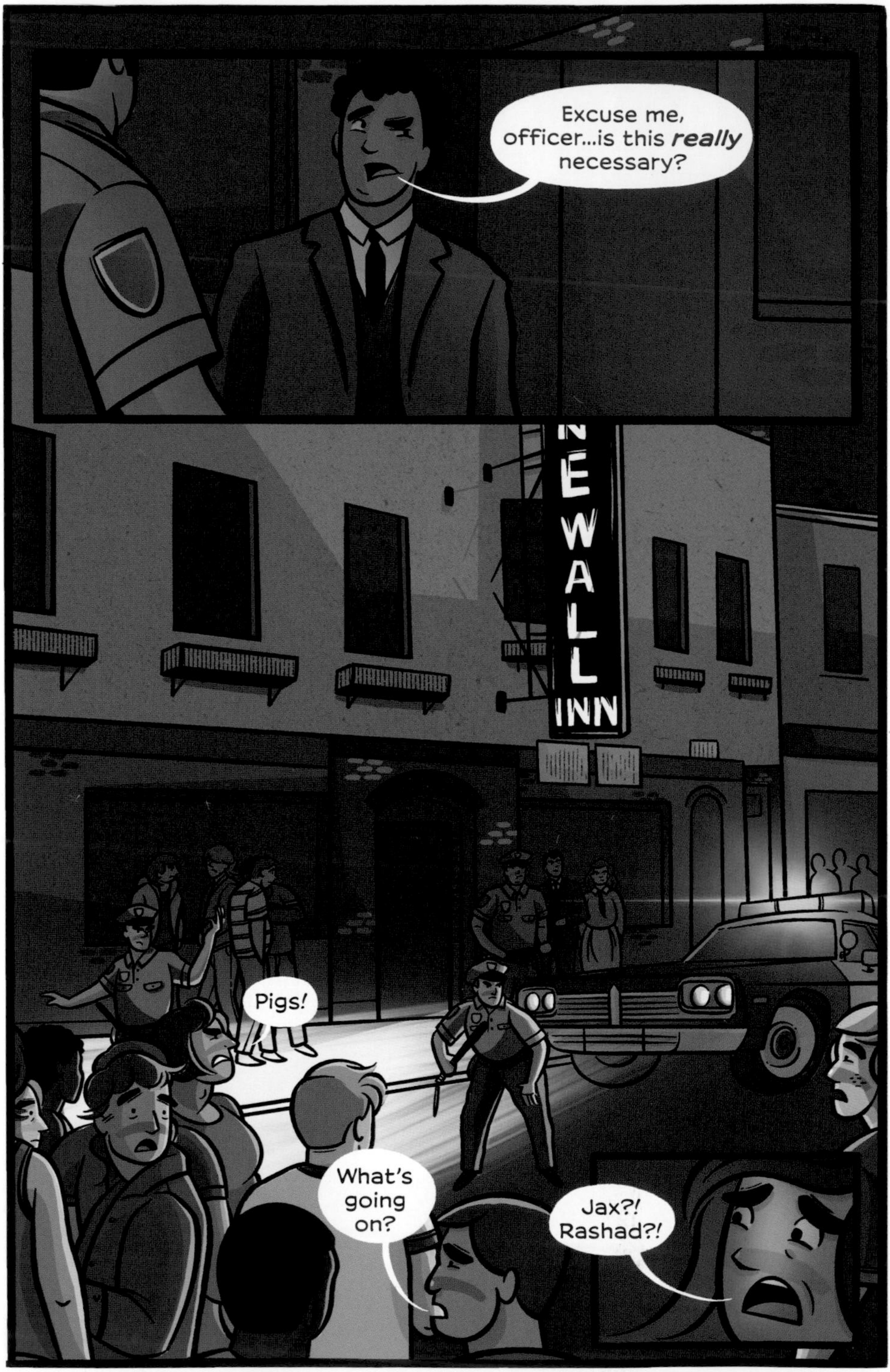
Excuse me, officer...is this *really* necessary?
NEWALL INN
Pigs!
What's going on?
Jax?! Rashad?!

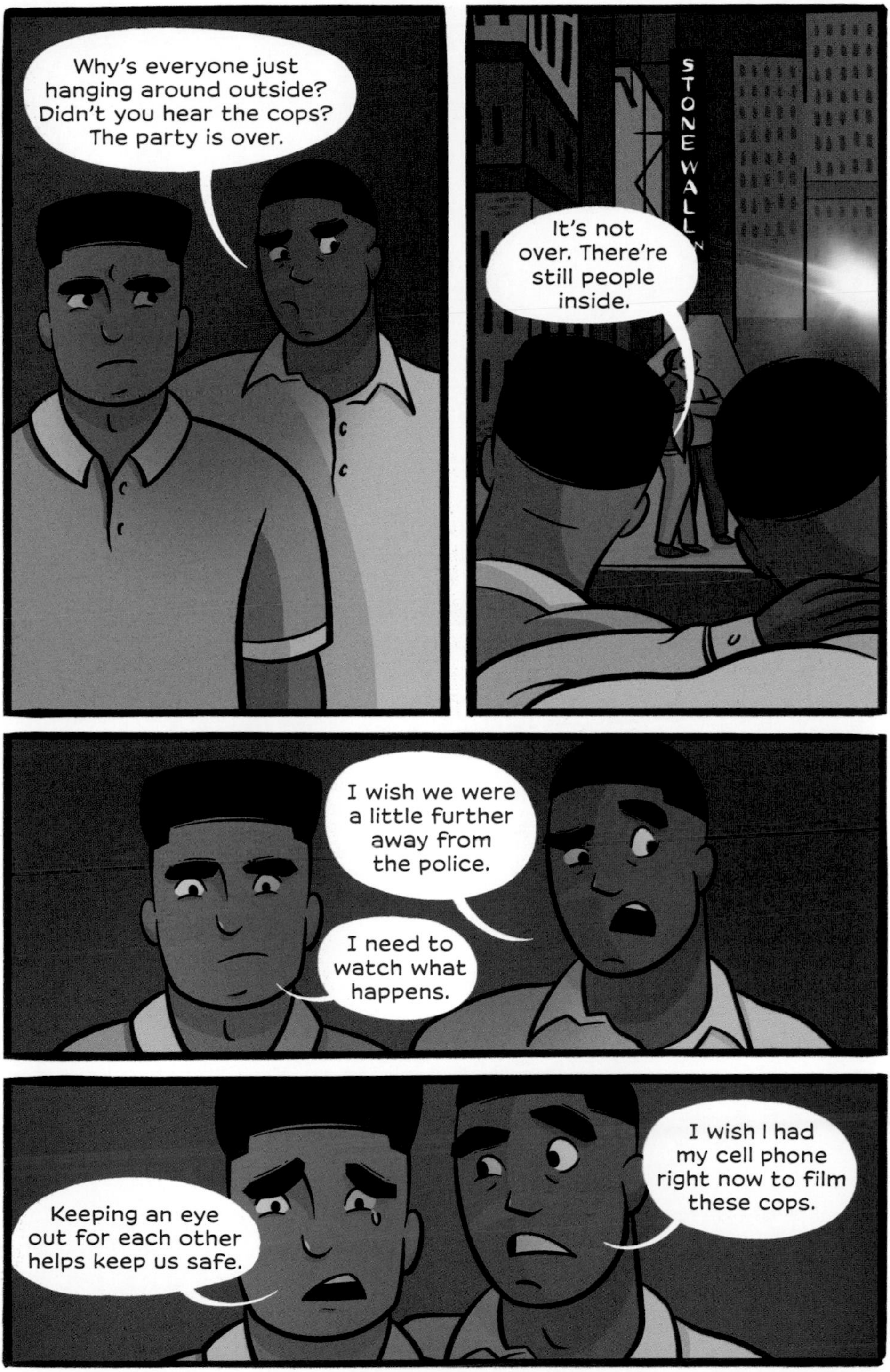
Why's everyone just hanging around outside? Didn't you hear the cops? The party is over.
STONEWALL
It's not over. There're still people inside.
I wish we were a little further away from the police.
I need to watch what happens.
I wish I had my cell phone right now to film these cops.
Keeping an eye out for each other helps keep us safe.

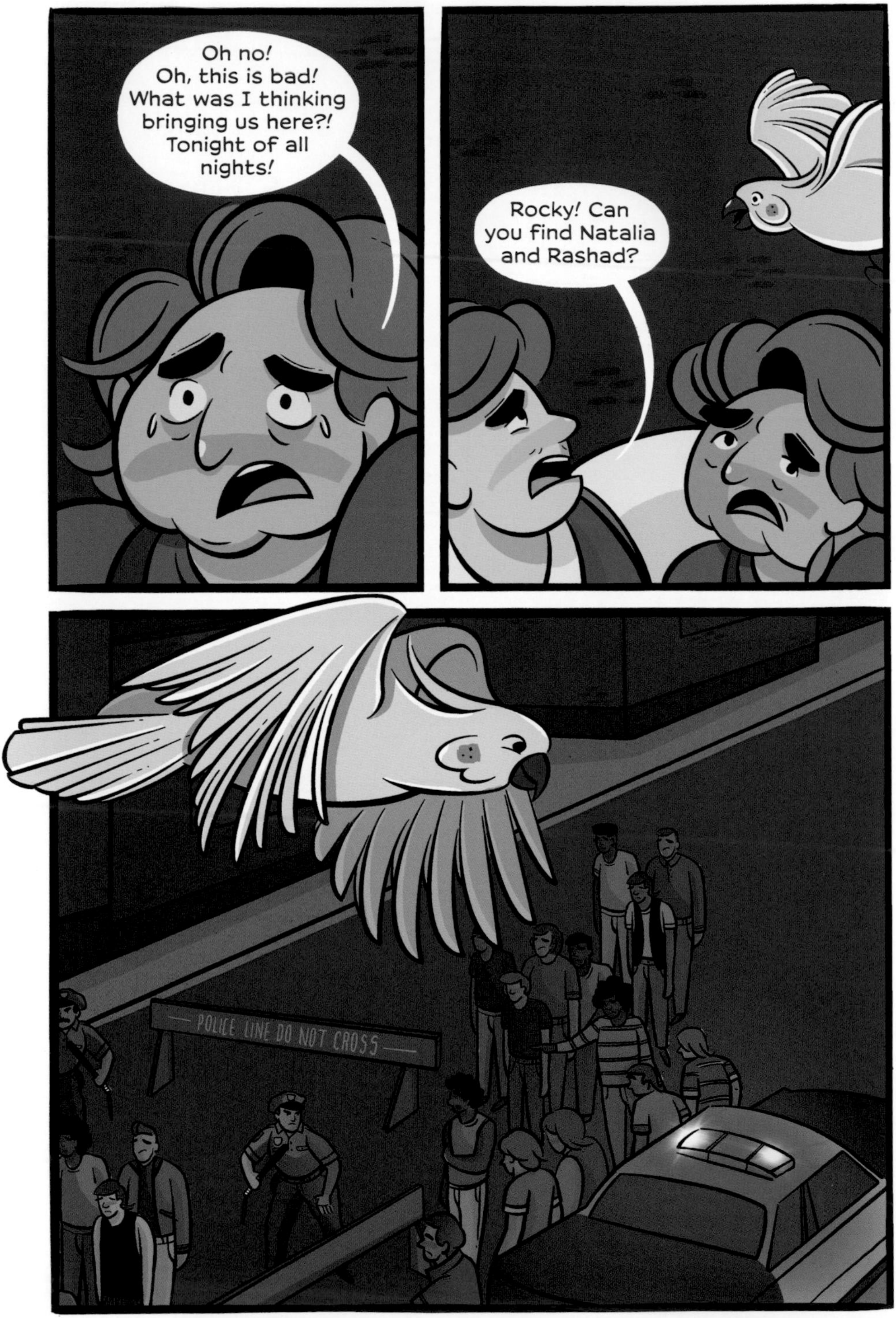
Oh no!
Oh, this is bad!
What was I thinking
bringing us here?!
Tonight of all
nights!
Rocky! Can
you find Natalia
and Rashad?
POLICE LINE DO NOT CROSS

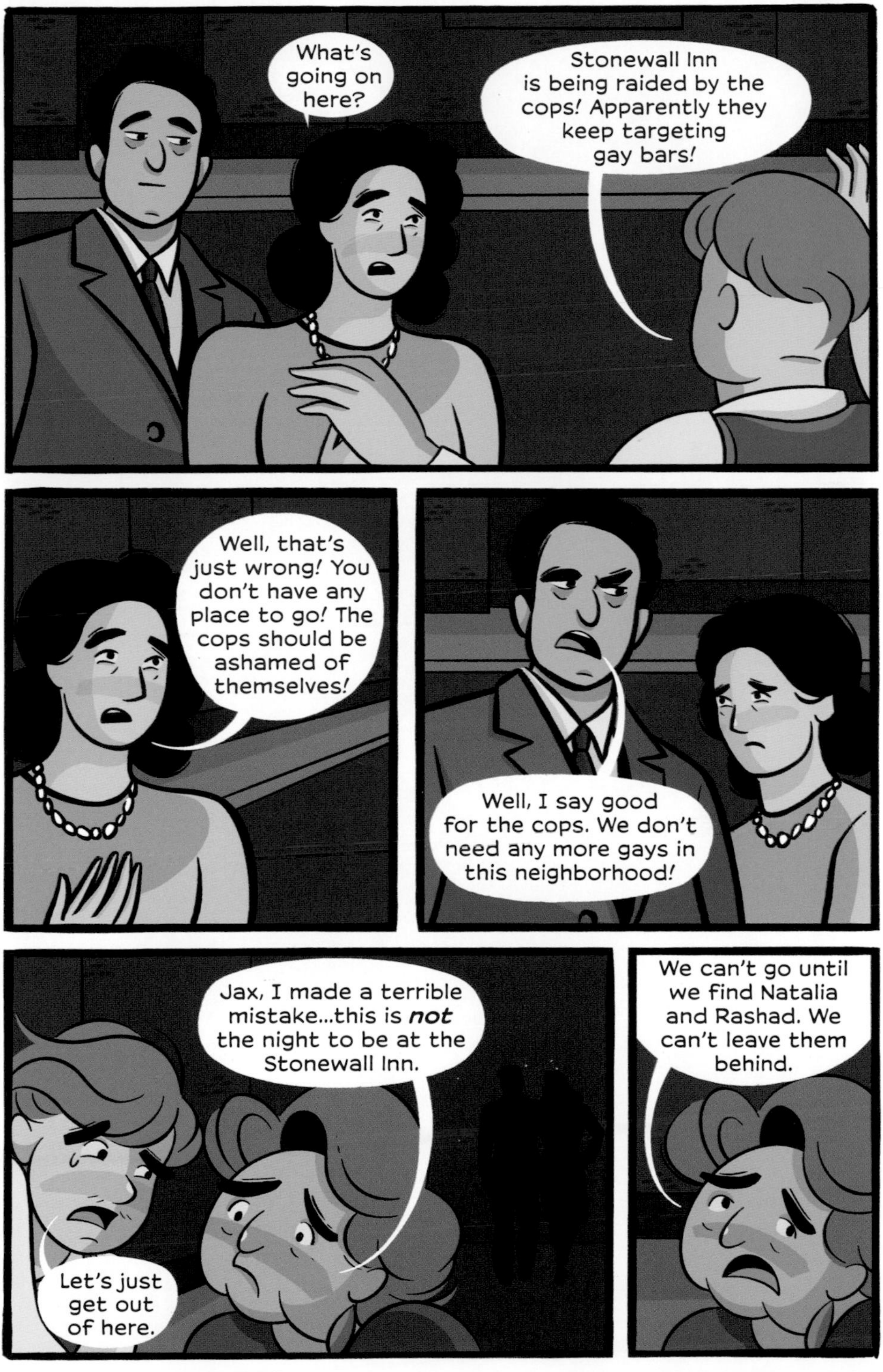
What's going on here?
Stonewall Inn is being raided by the cops! Apparently they keep targeting gay bars!
Well, that's just wrong! You don't have any place to go! The cops should be ashamed of themselves!
Well, I say good for the cops. We don't need any more gays in this neighborhood!
Jax, I made a terrible mistake...this is ***not*** the night to be at the Stonewall Inn.
Let's just get out of here.
We can't go until we find Natalia and Rashad. We can't leave them behind.

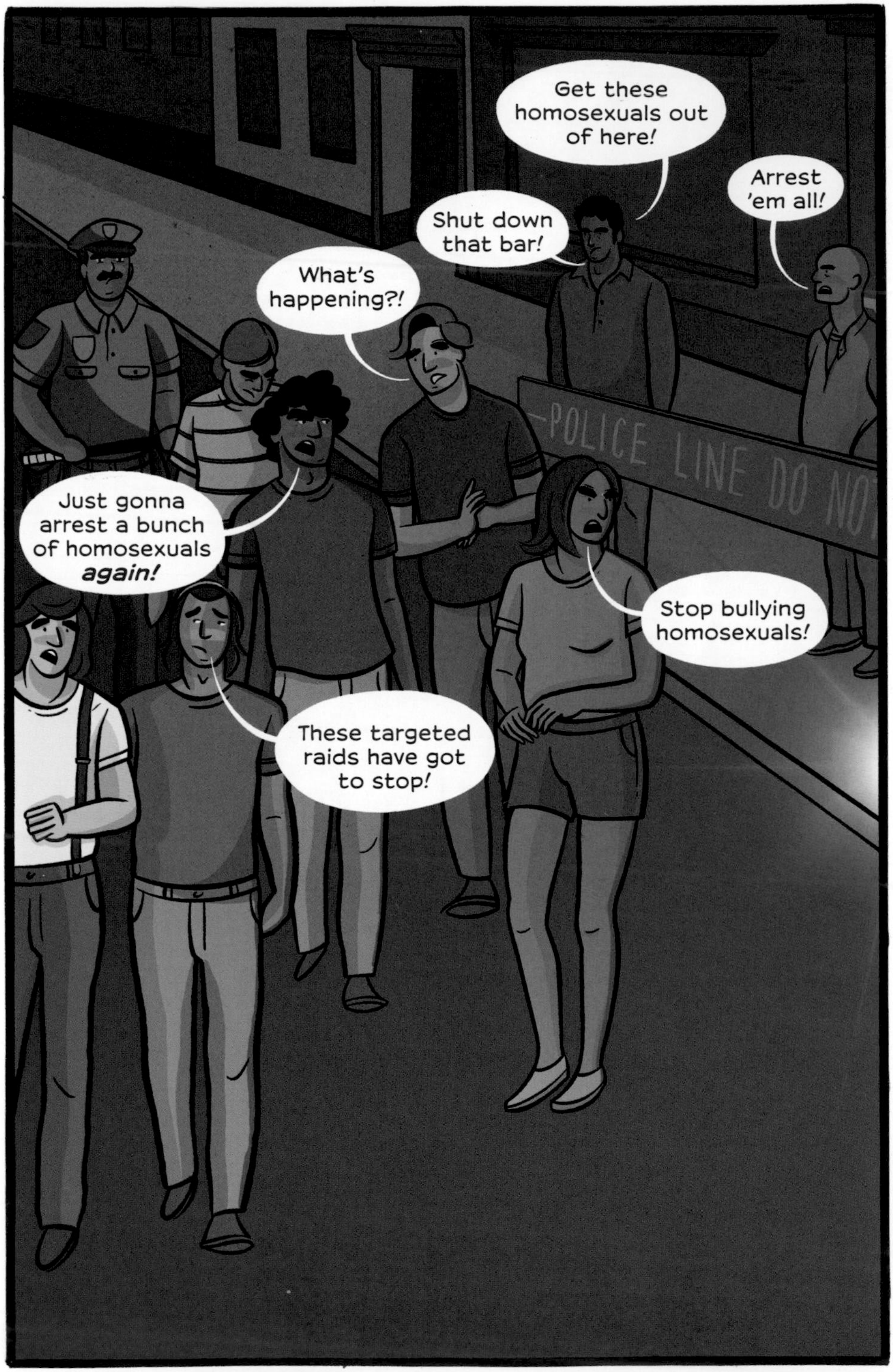
Get these homosexuals out of here!
Arrest 'em all!
Shut down that bar!
What's happening?!
Just gonna arrest a bunch of homosexuals ***again!***
Stop bullying homosexuals!
These targeted raids have got to stop!
POLICE LINE DO NO

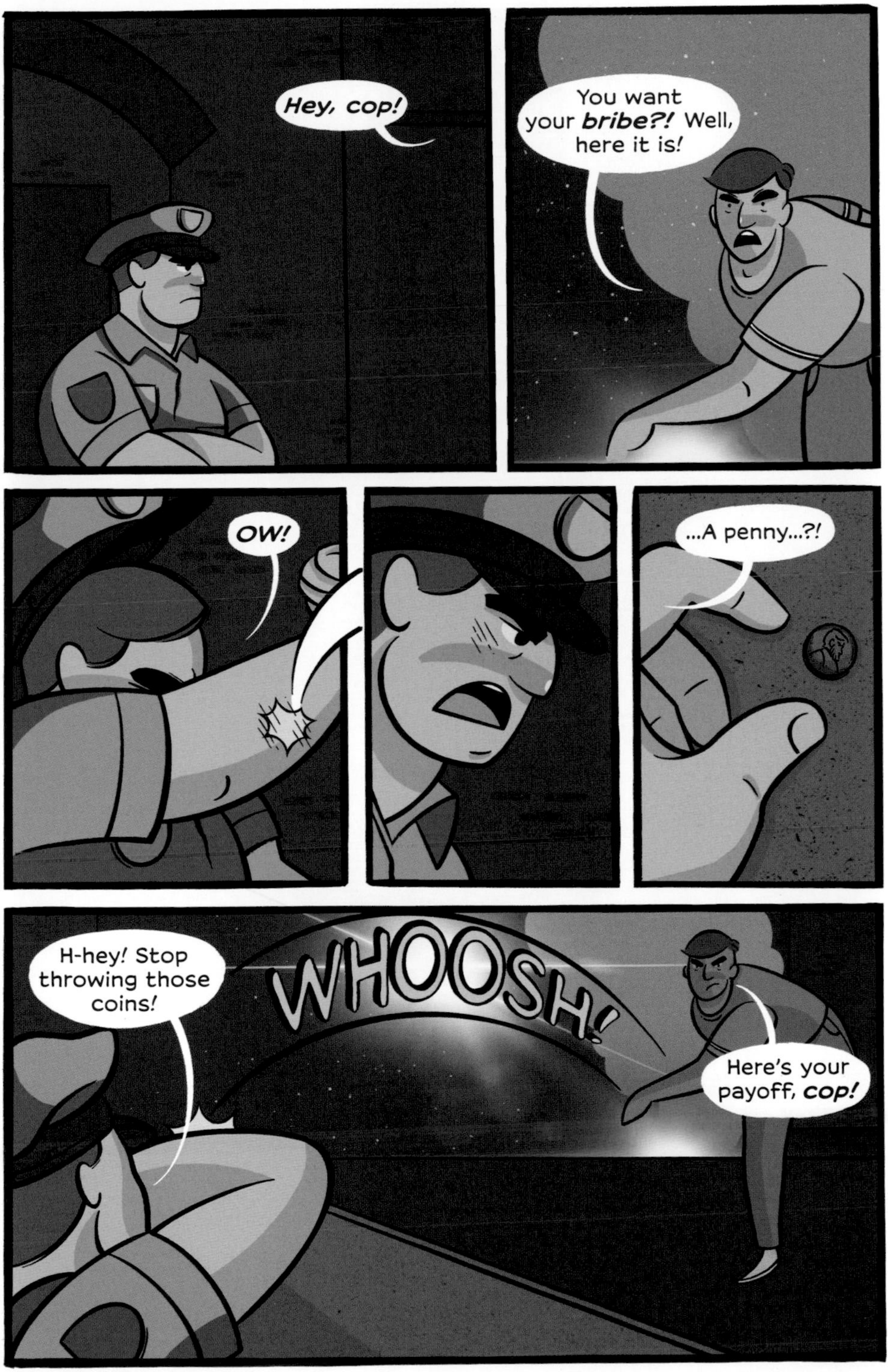
Hey, cop!
You want your *bribe?!* Well, here it is!
OW!
...A penny...?!
H-hey! Stop throwing those coins!
WHOOSH!
Here's your payoff, *cop!*

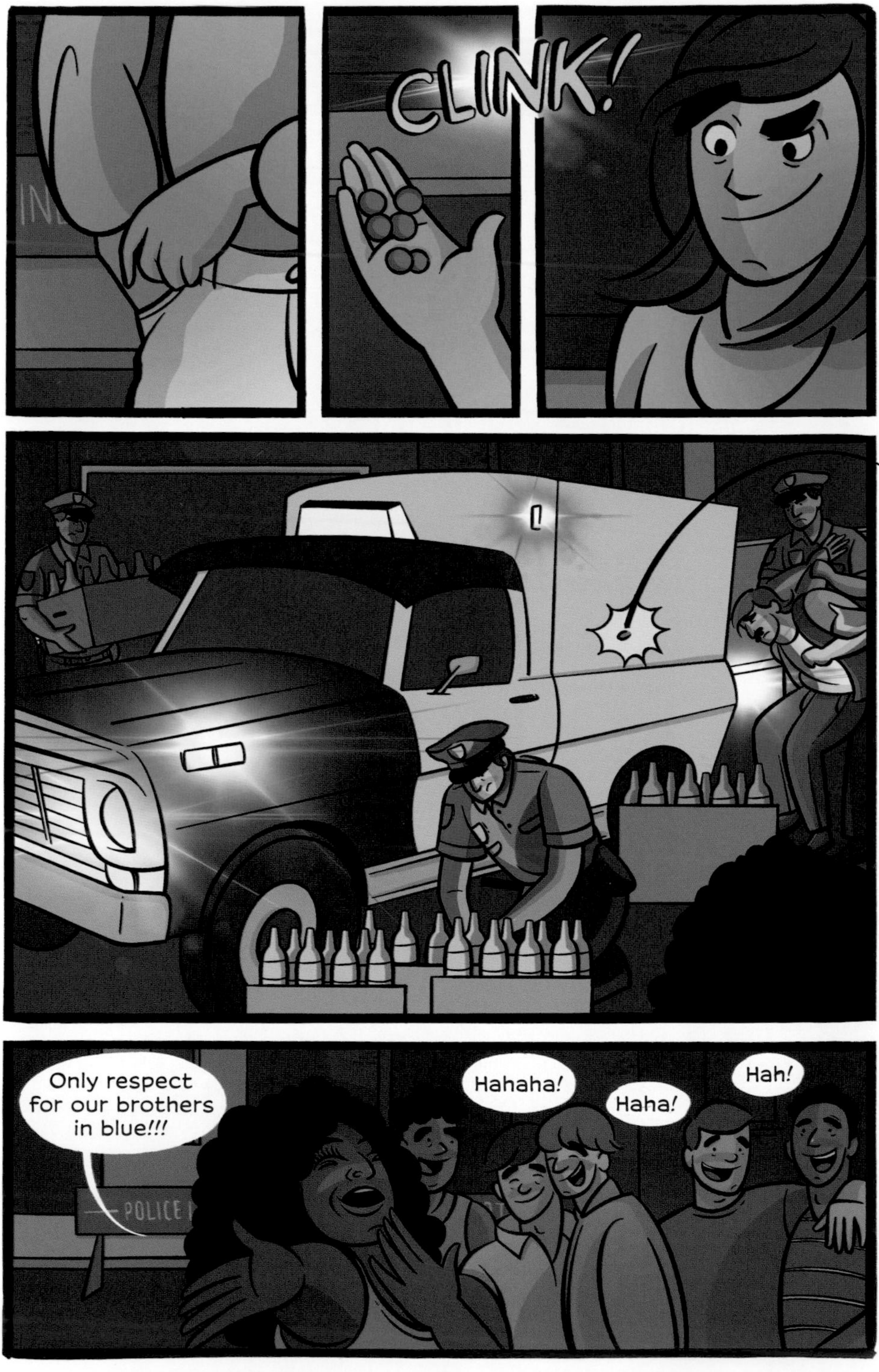
CLINK!
Only respect for our brothers in blue!!!
Hahaha!
Haha!
Hah!

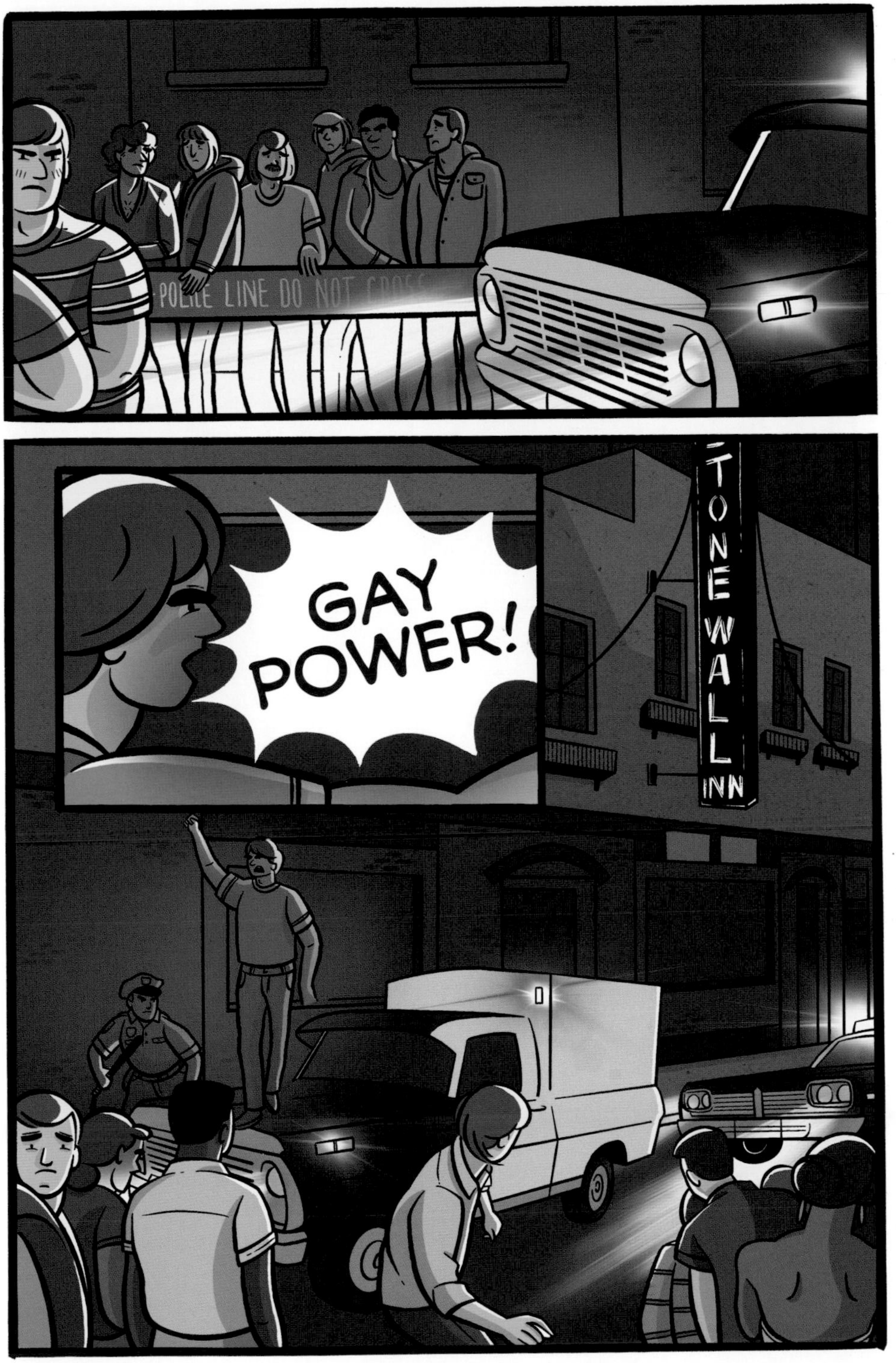
POLICE LINE DO NOT
GAY POWER!
STONEWALL INN

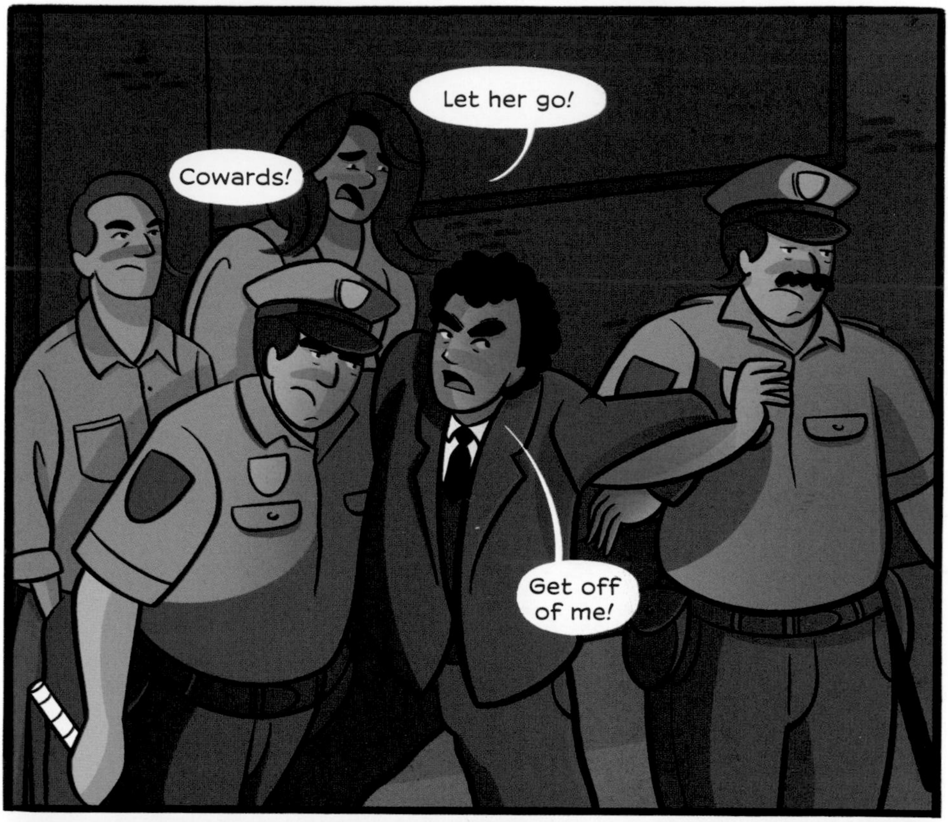
Cowards!
Let her go!
Get off of me!

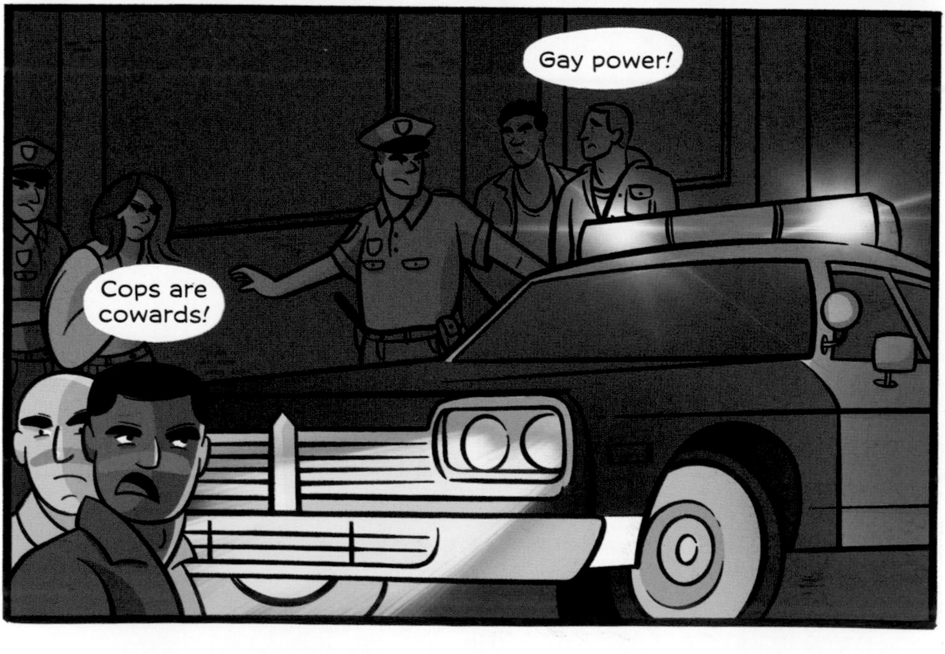
Gay power!
Cops are cowards!

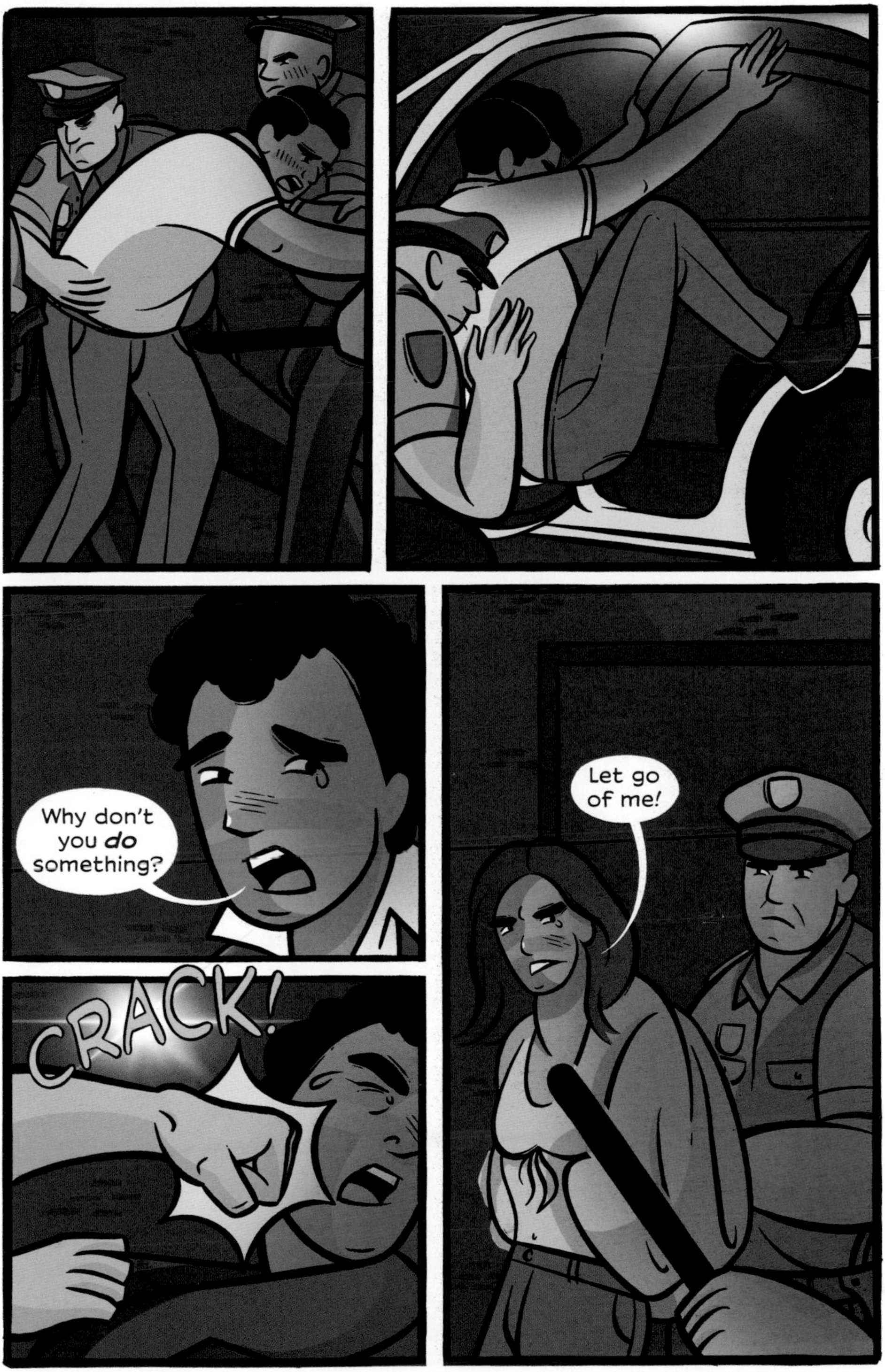
Why don't you *do* something?
Let go of me!
CRACK!

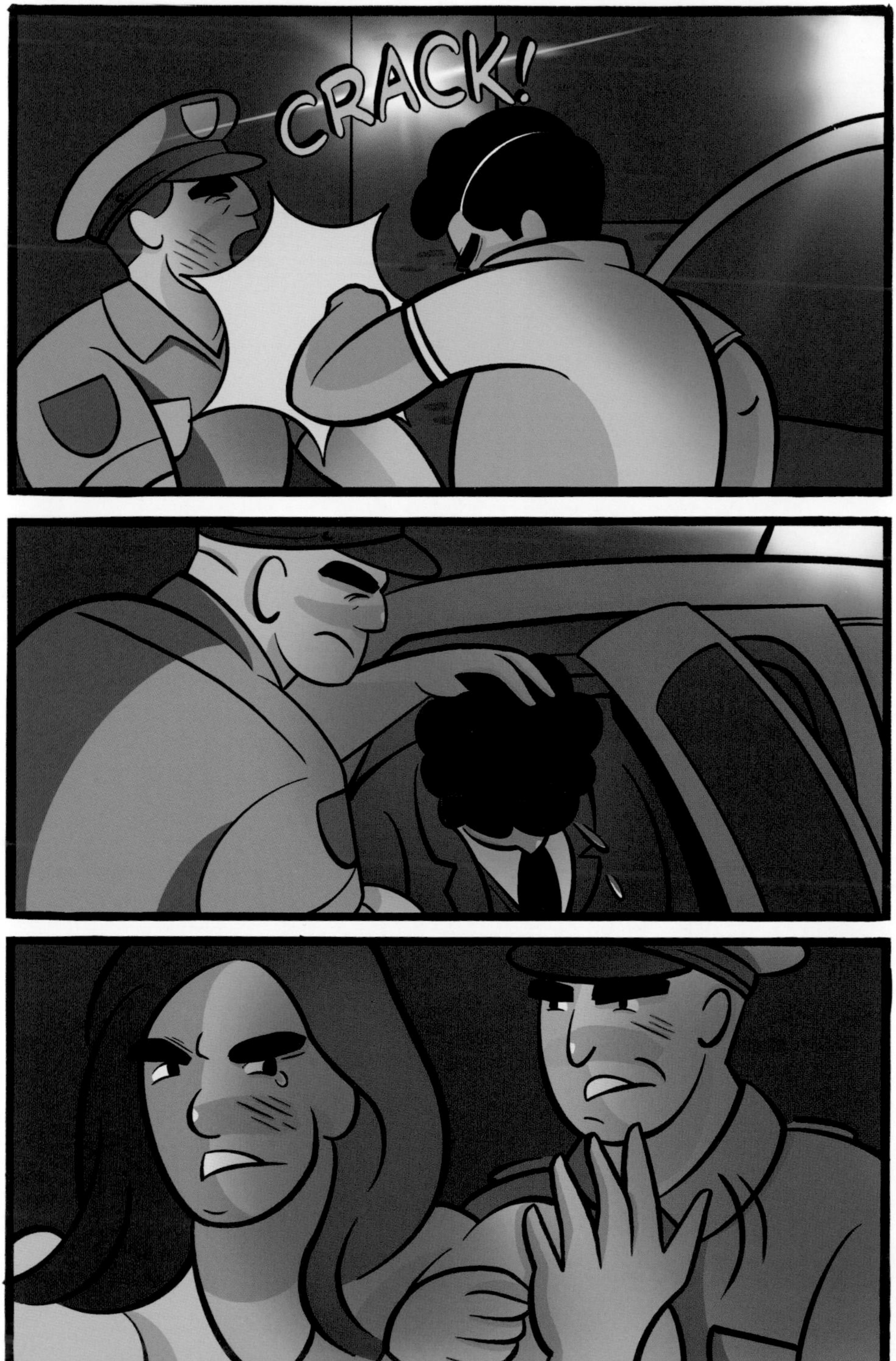
CRACK!

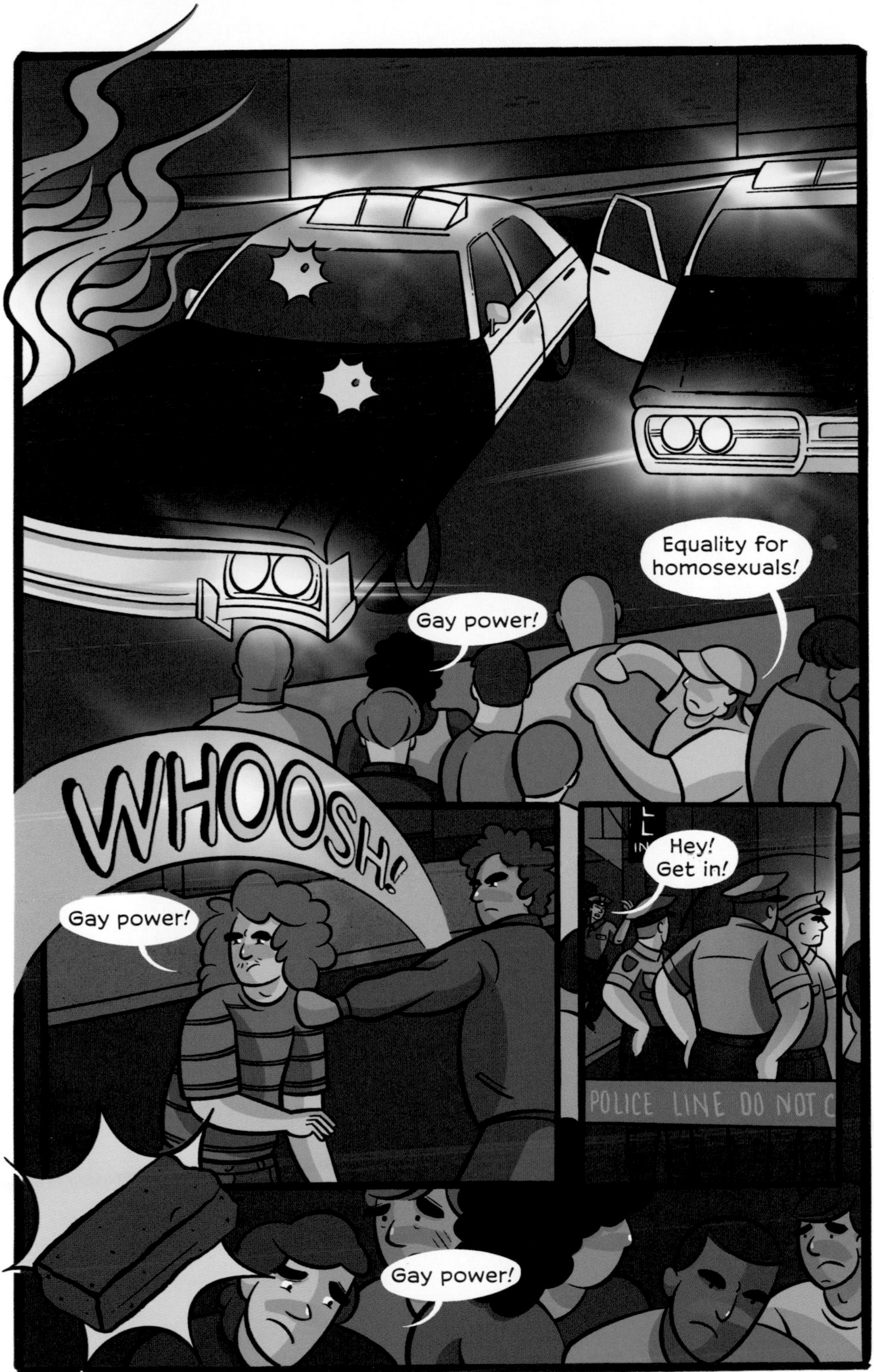

Equality for homosexuals!
Gay power!
WHOOSH!
Gay power!
Hey! Get in!
POLICE LINE DO NOT C
Gay power!

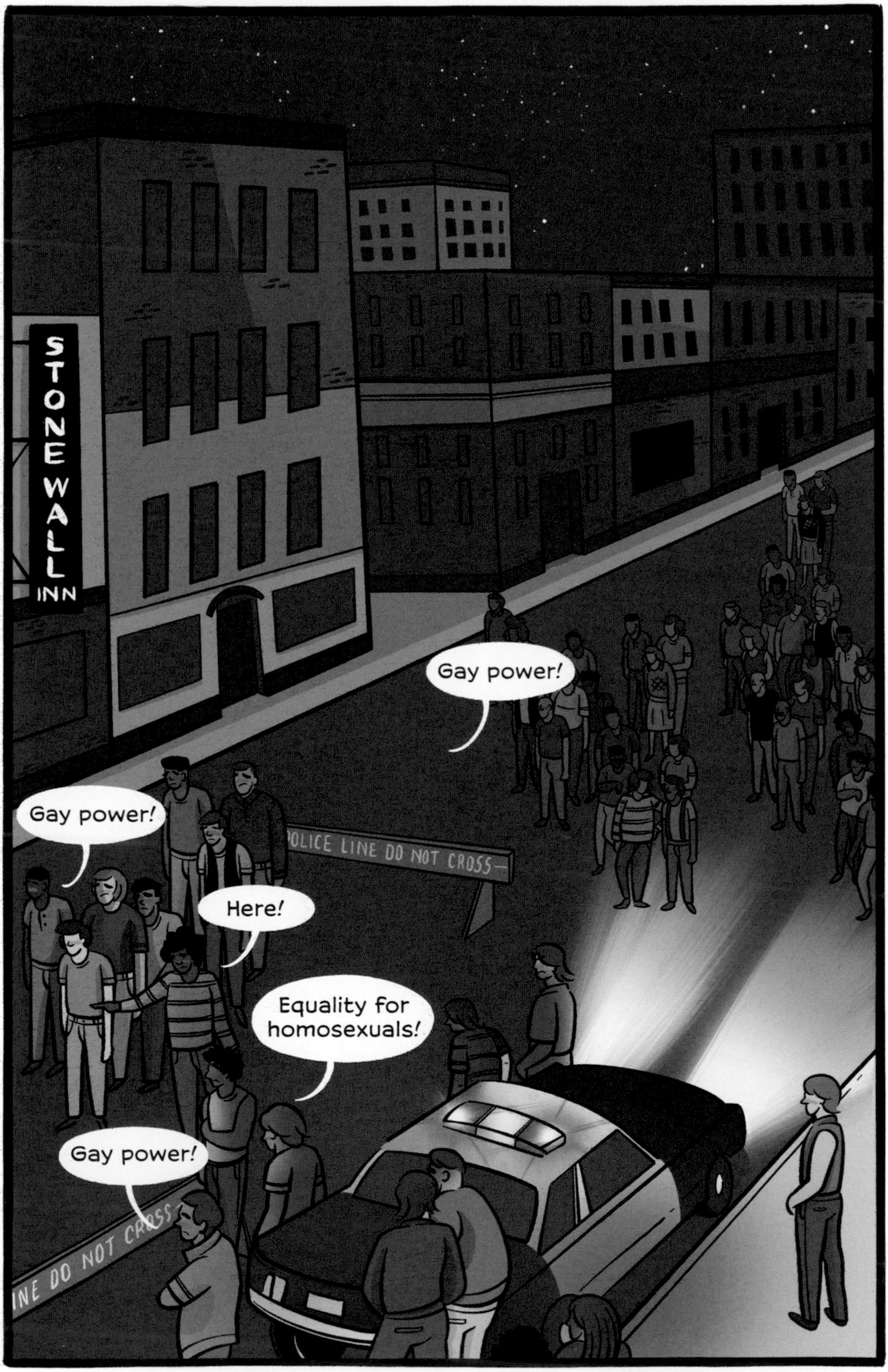
STONEWALL INN
Gay power!
Gay power!
POLICE LINE DO NOT CROSS
Here!
Equality for homosexuals!
Gay power!
LINE DO NOT CROSS

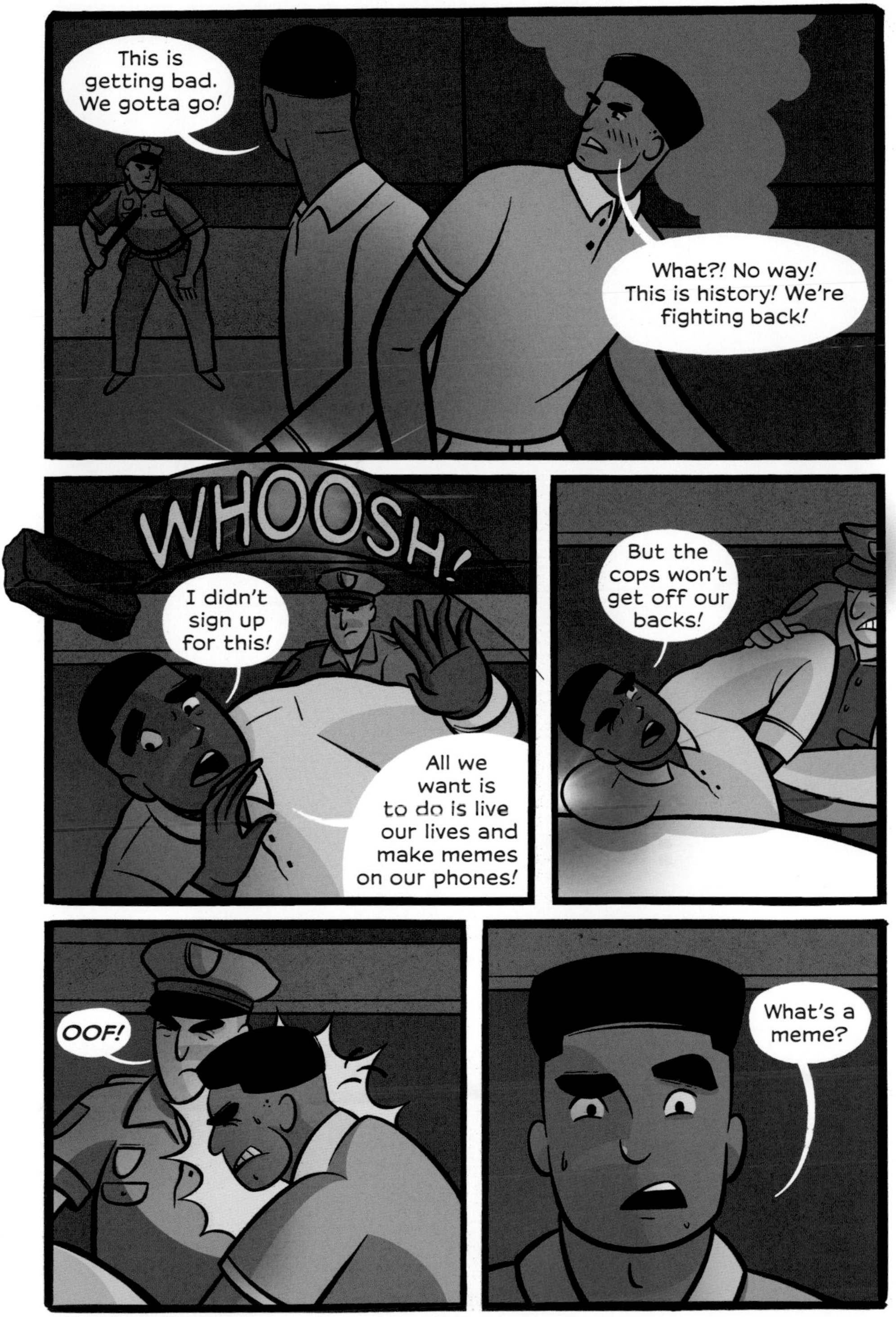
This is getting bad. We gotta go!
What?! No way! This is history! We're fighting back!
WHOOSH!
I didn't sign up for this!
All we want is to do is live our lives and make memes on our phones!
But the cops won't get off our backs!
OOF!
What's a meme?

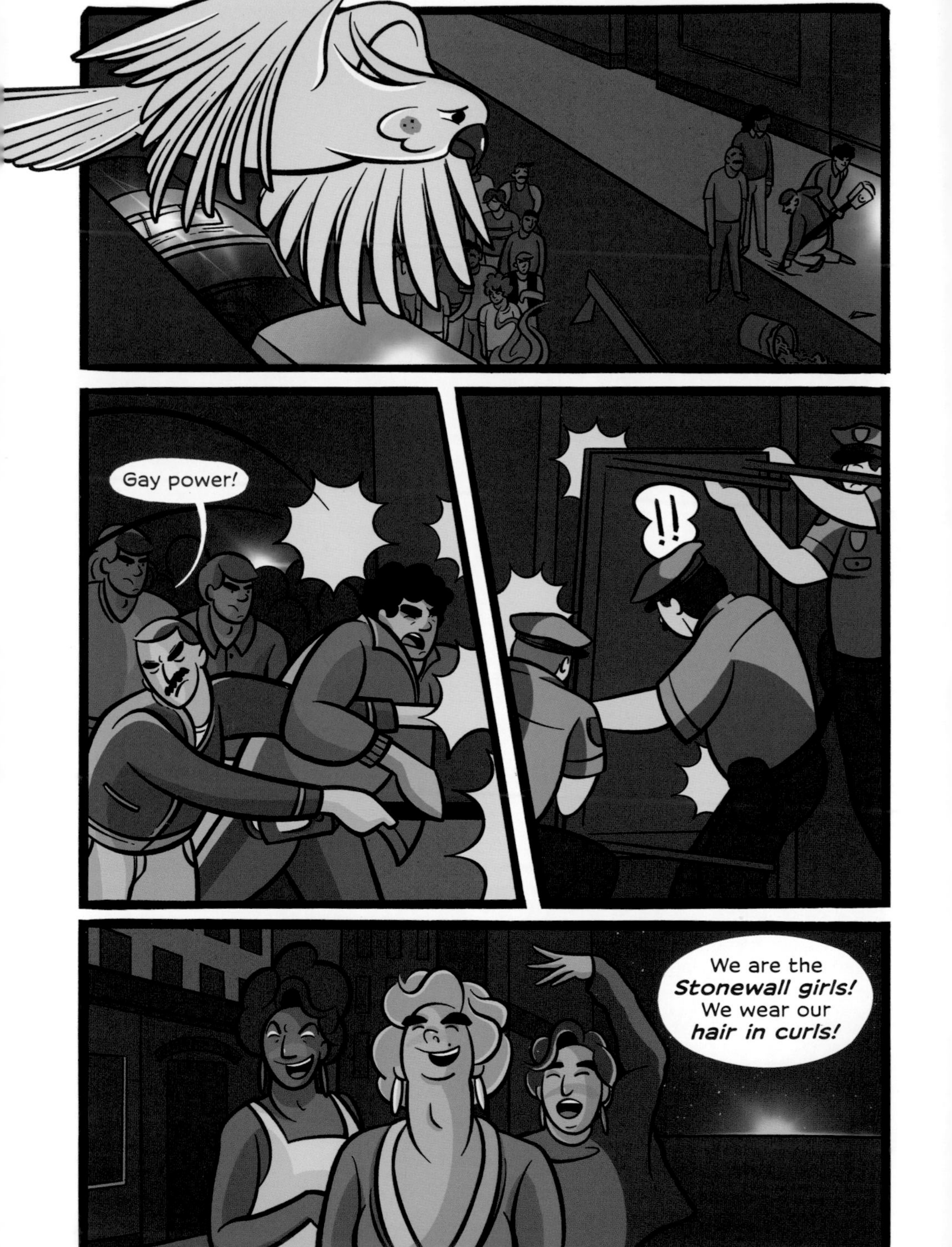
Gay power!
!!
We are the *Stonewall girls!* We wear our *hair in curls!*

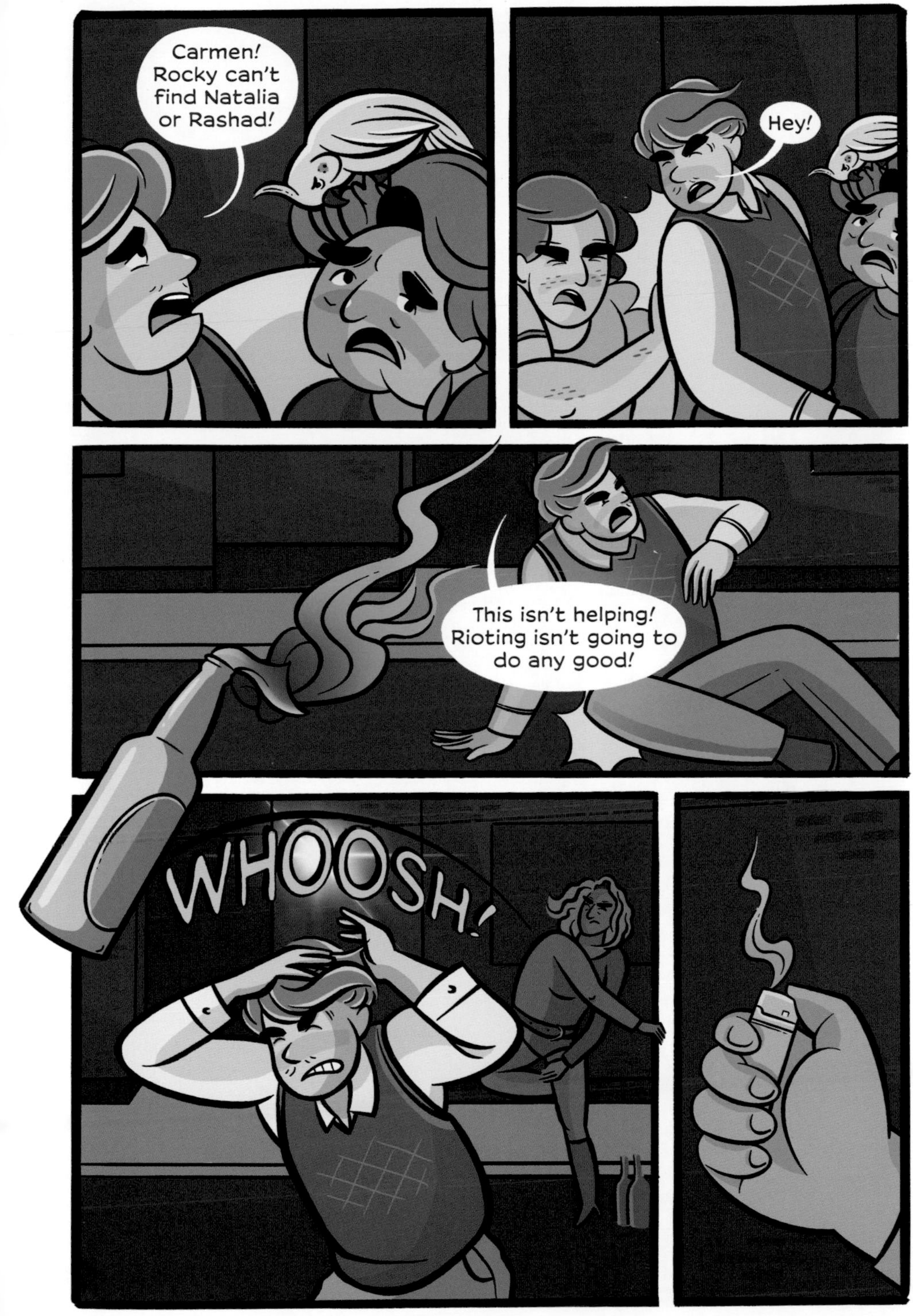
Carmen! Rocky can't find Natalia or Rashad!
Hey!
This isn't helping! Rioting isn't going to do any good!
WHOOSH!

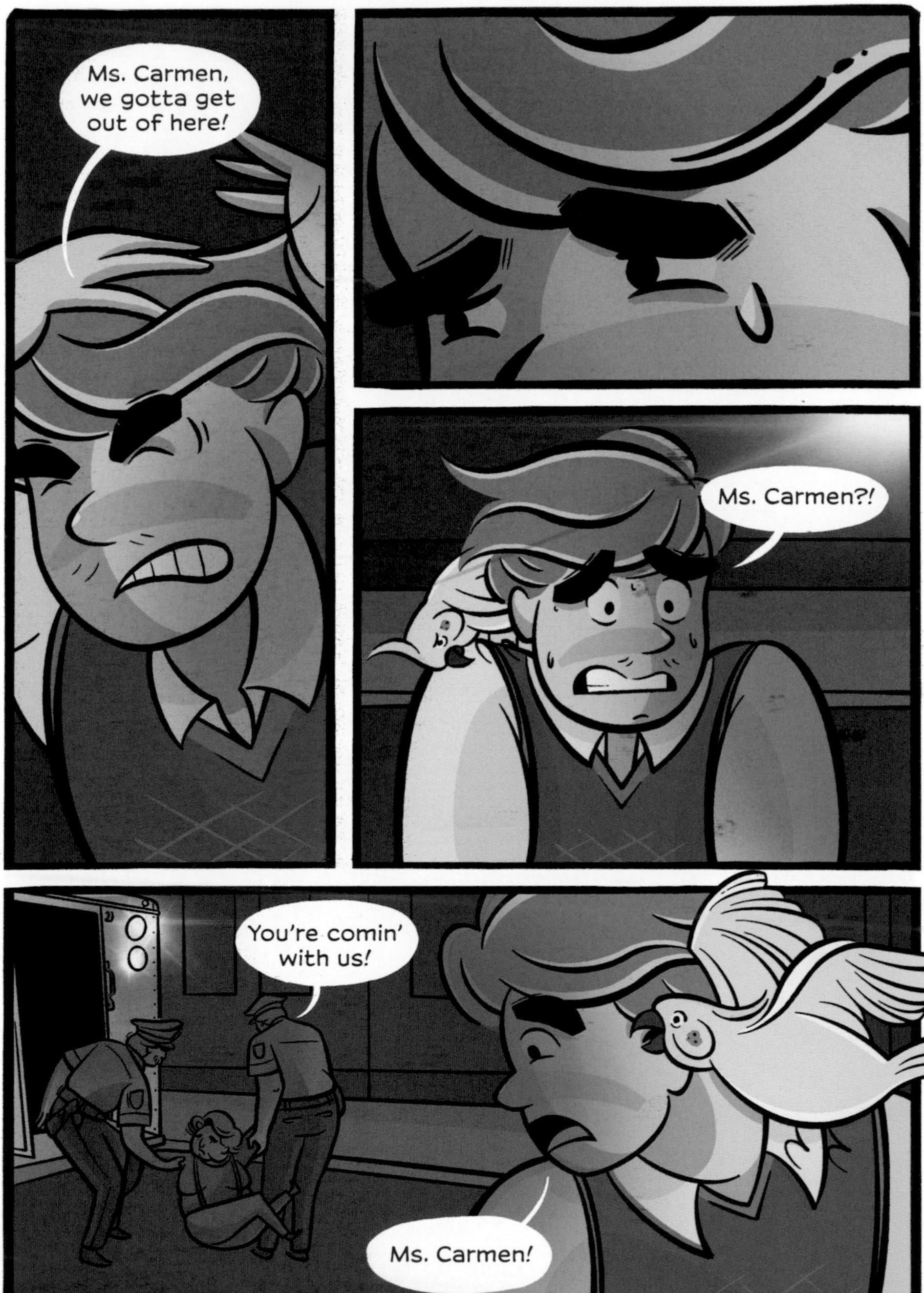

Ms. Carmen, we gotta get out of here!
Ms. Carmen?!
You're comin' with us!
Ms. Carmen!

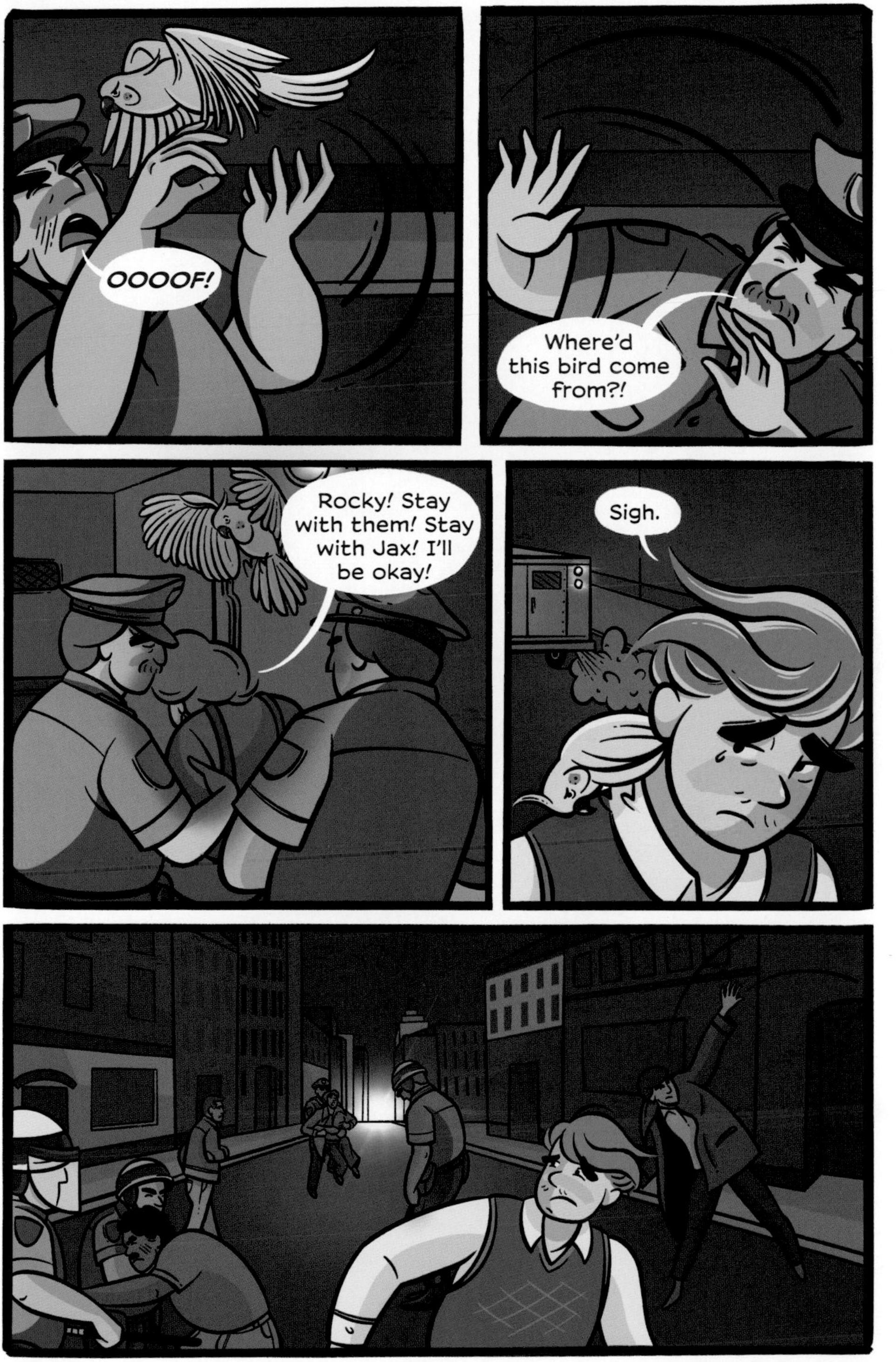
OOOOF!
Where'd this bird come from?!
Rocky! Stay with them! Stay with Jax! I'll be okay!
Sigh.

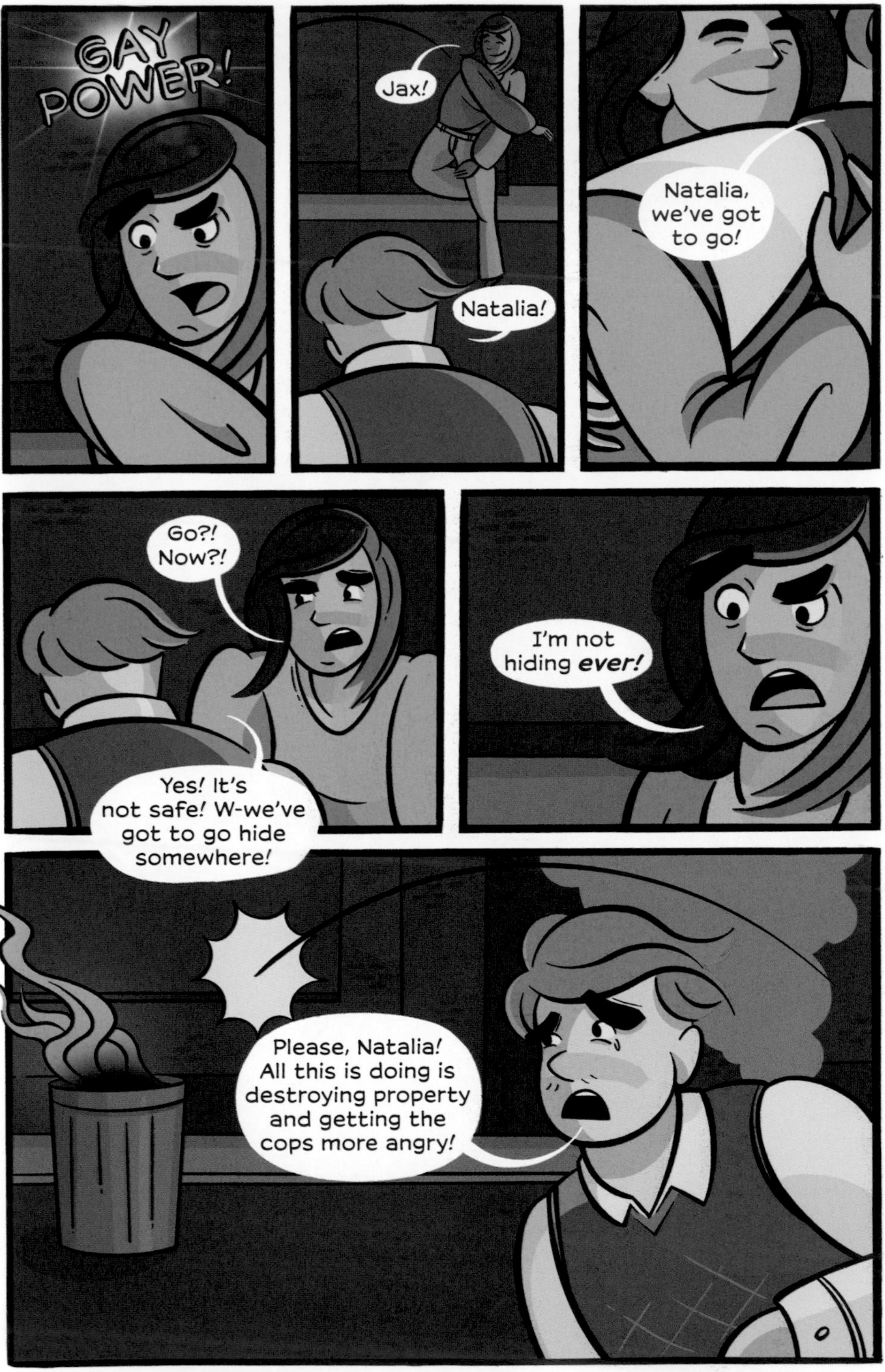
GAY POWER!
Jax!
Natalia!
Natalia, we've got to go!
Go?! Now?!
Yes! It's not safe! W-we've got to go hide somewhere!
I'm not hiding *ever!*
Please, Natalia! All this is doing is destroying property and getting the cops more angry!

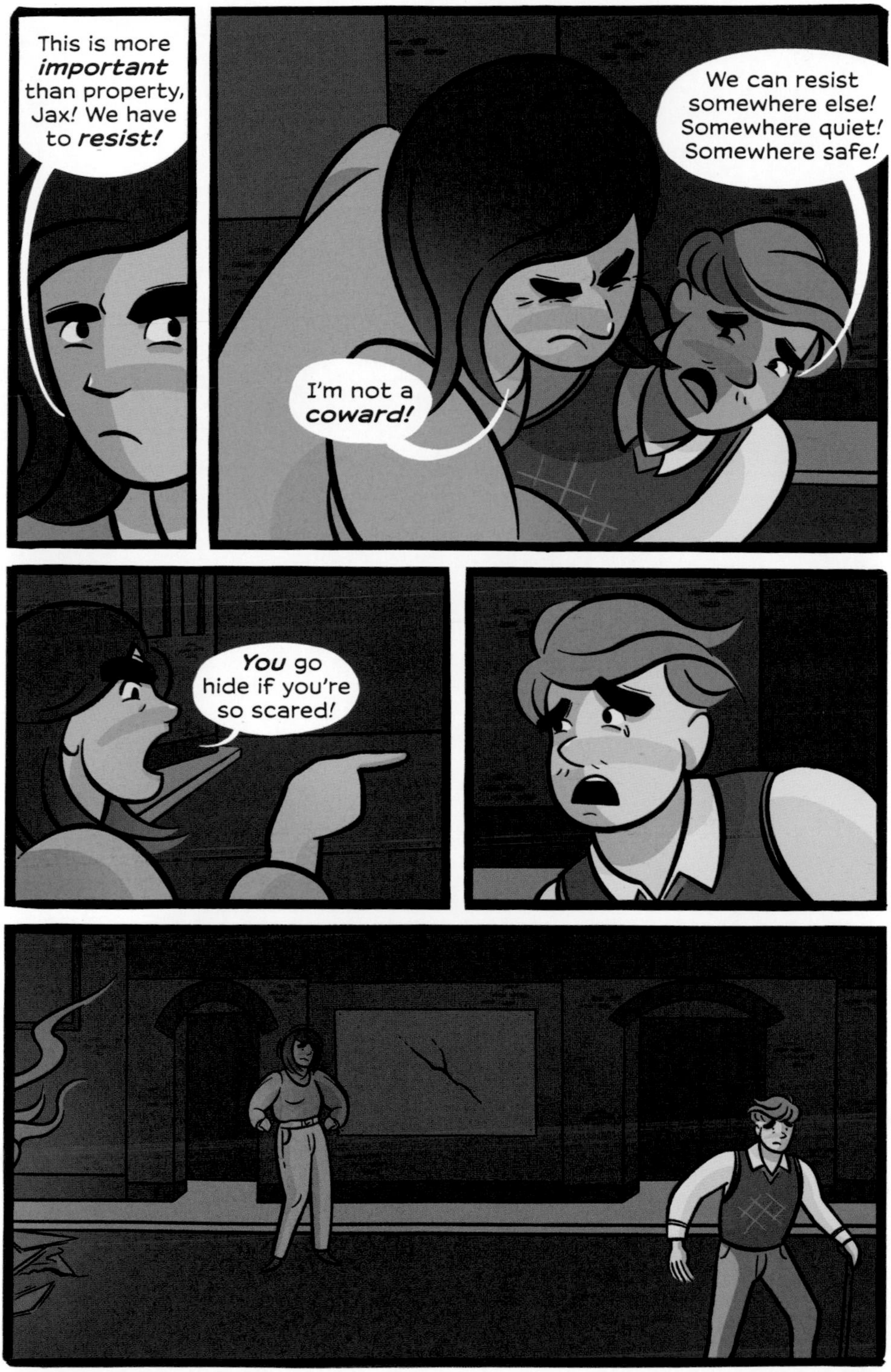
This is more *important* than property, Jax! We have to *resist!*
We can resist somewhere else! Somewhere quiet! Somewhere safe!
I'm not a *coward!*
You go hide if you're so scared!

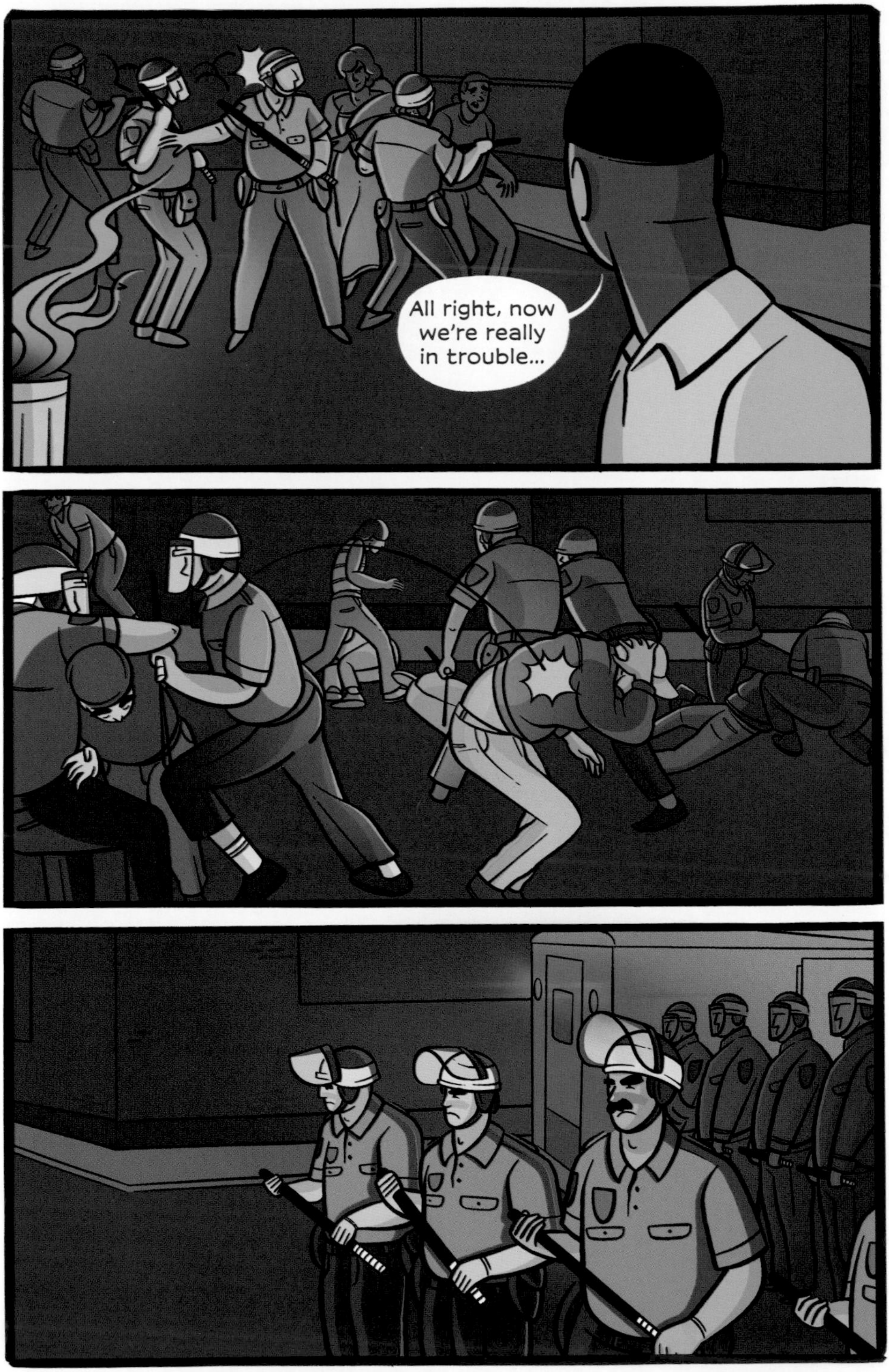
All right, now we're really in trouble...

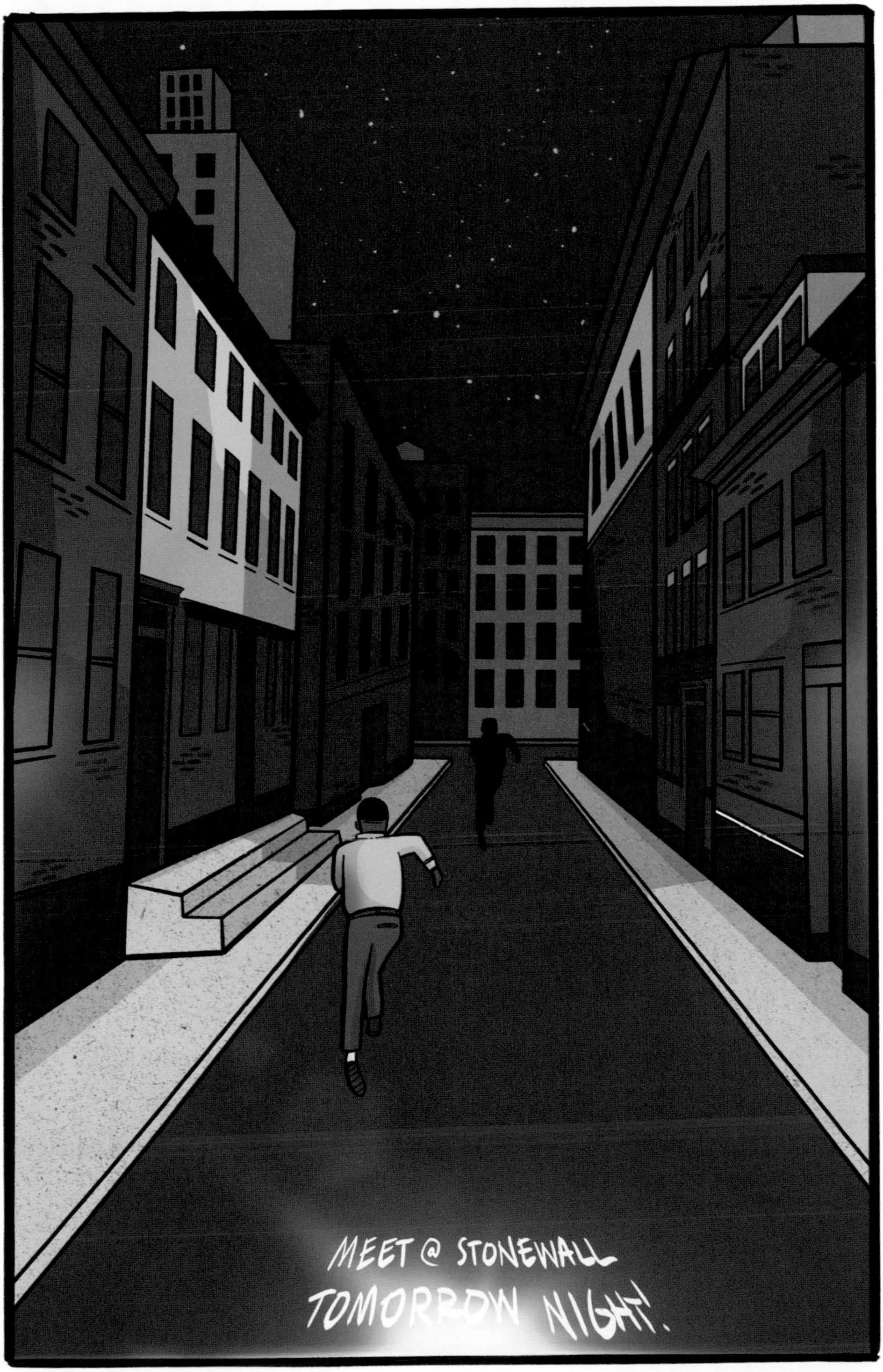
MEET @ STONEWALL
TOMORROW NIGHT.

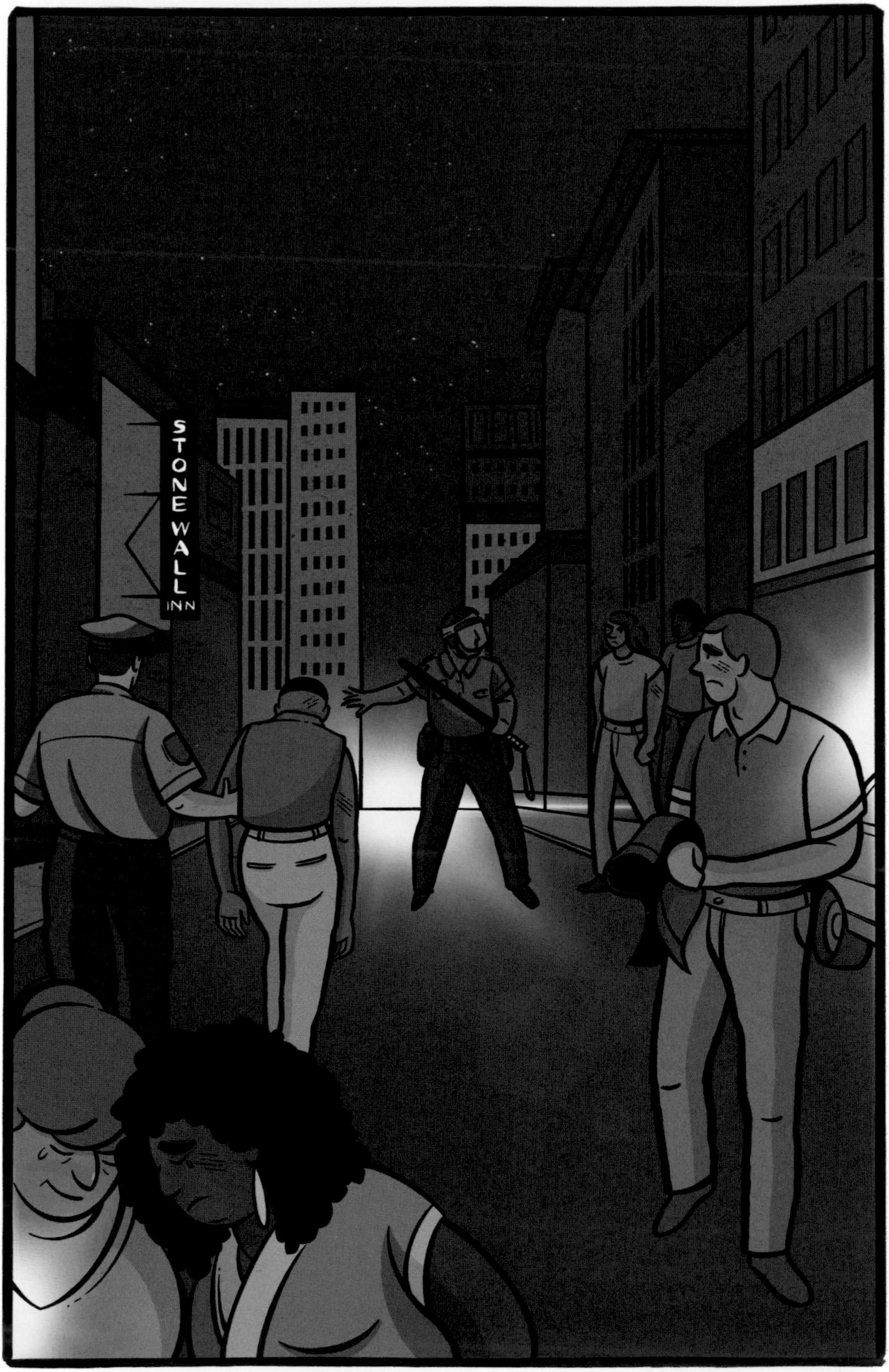
STONE WALL INN

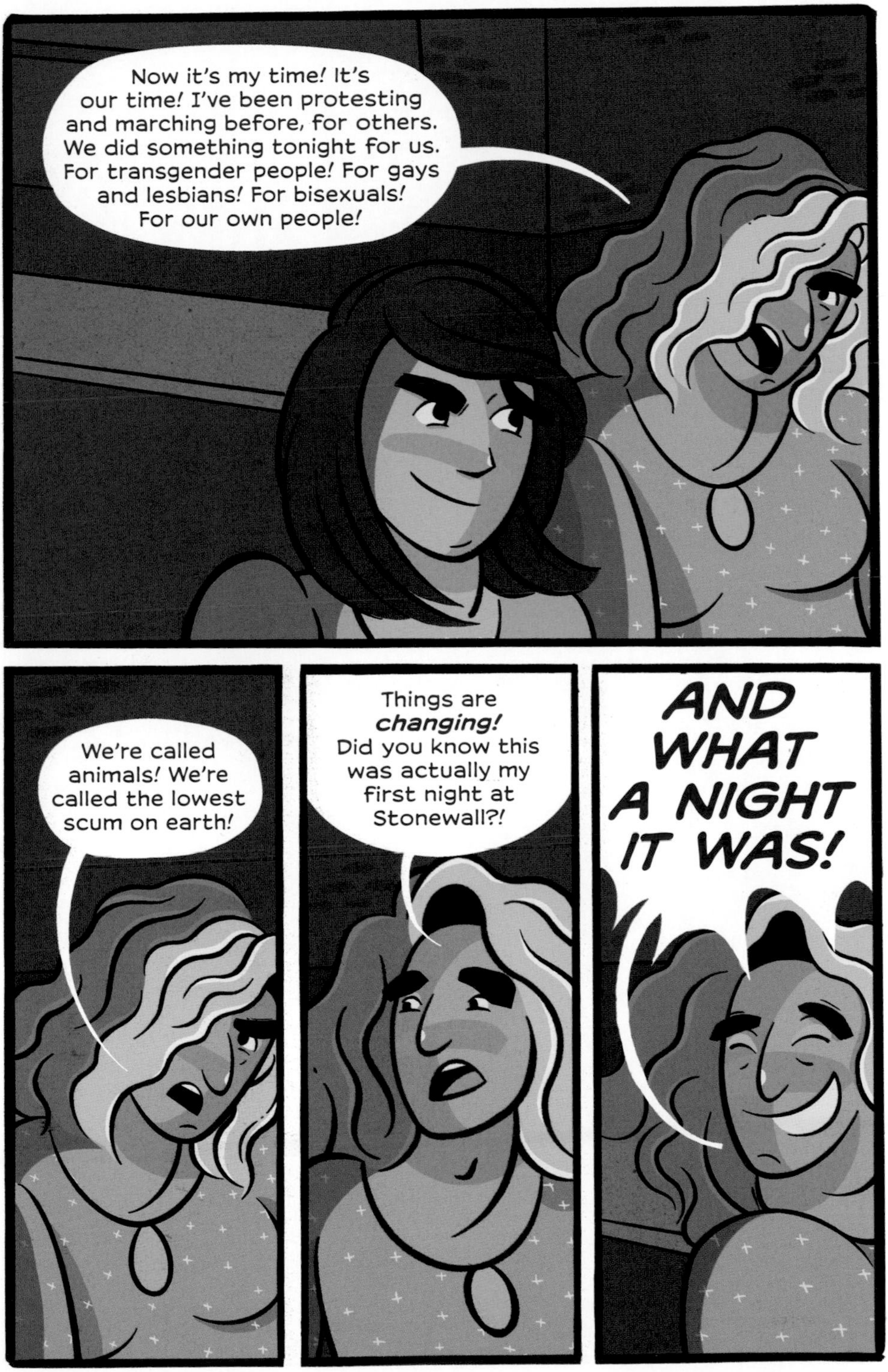
Now it's my time! It's our time! I've been protesting and marching before, for others. We did something tonight for us. For transgender people! For gays and lesbians! For bisexuals! For our own people!
We're called animals! We're called the lowest scum on earth!
Things are *changing!* Did you know this was actually my first night at Stonewall?!
AND WHAT A NIGHT IT WAS!

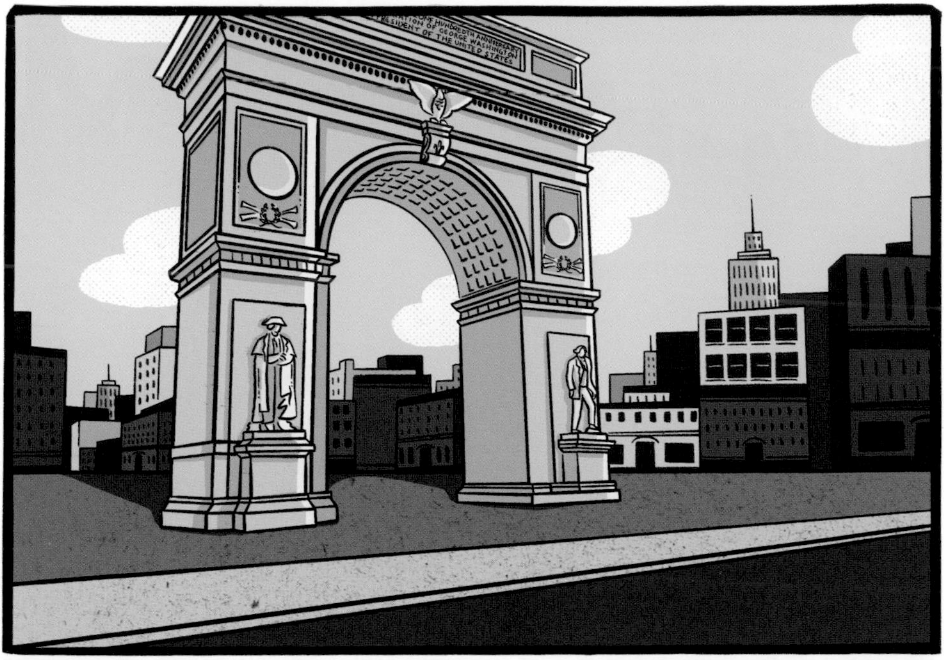
HUNDREDTH ANNIVERSARY
OF GEORGE WASHINGTON
OF THE UNITED STATES

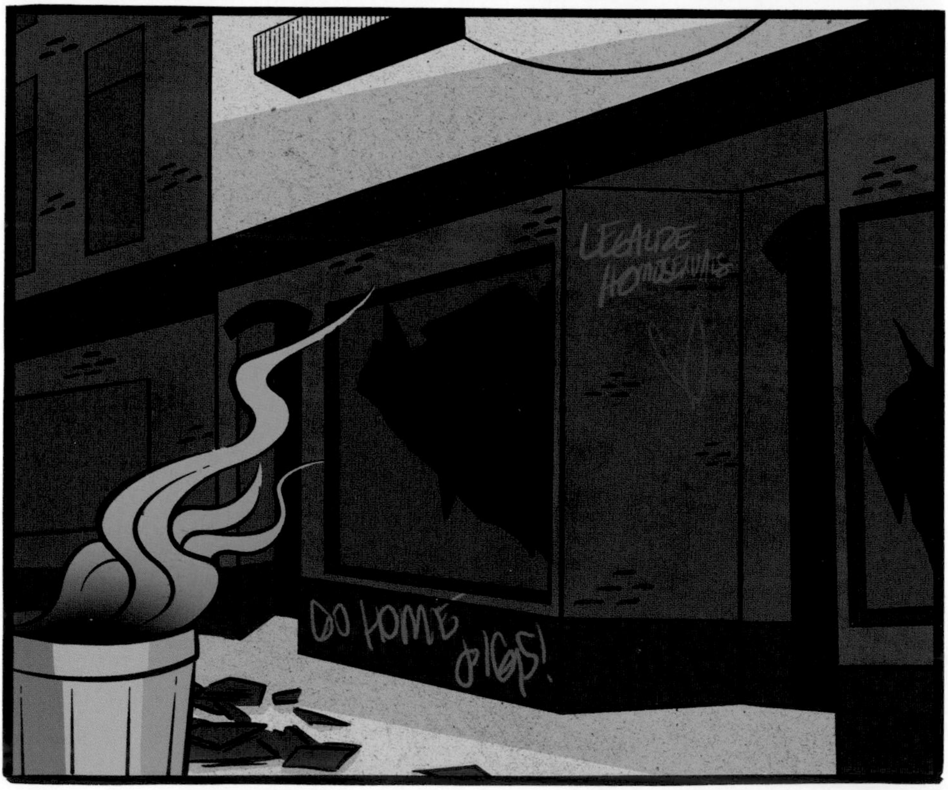
LEGALIZE HOMOSEXUALS
GO HOME PIGS!

NEW YORK POST

15¢ LATE CITY FINAL

SUNDAY, JUNE 29, 1969

Village Raid Stirs Melee

A police raid in the Stonewall Inn, a tavern frequented by homosexuals at 53 Christopher of Sheridan Square

Police reinforcements were rushed to the tavern to deal with the disturbances which continued for more than two hours. By the time calm returned to the 13 persons had been

DAILY ☐ NEWS

NEW YORK'S PICTURE NEWSPAPER ©

** SUNDAY NEWS, JUNE 29, 1969

3 Cops Hurt As Bar Raid Riles Crowd

BY DENNIS ESKOW

A predawn police raid on a reputed Greenwich Village homosexual hangout, the second raid within a week, touched off a two-hour melee yesterday as customers and villagers swarmed over the plainclothes cops.

Before order was restored, the cops were the targets of thrown coins, cobblestones and uprooted parking meters, windows were smashed, a police van was nearly overturned and the front of the raided bar, the Stonewall Inn, was fire-bombed.

Three cops suffered minor injuries and 13 persons were arrested. The fire was quickly doused by a hose from the bar.

Crowd attempts to impede police arrests outside the Stonewall Inn, Christopher St.

NEWS photo by Joseph Ambrosini

POLICEMEN HURT IN 'VILLAGE' RAID

Melee Near Sheridan Square Follows Action at Bar

Hundreds of young men went on a rampage in Greenwich Village shortly after 3 A.M. yesterday after a force of plain... raided a bar that ...llknown

Hostile Crowd Disperse Near Sheridan Squa

At least four persons we...
...ted and charged with har-
...t last night in the S...
...re area of...

63

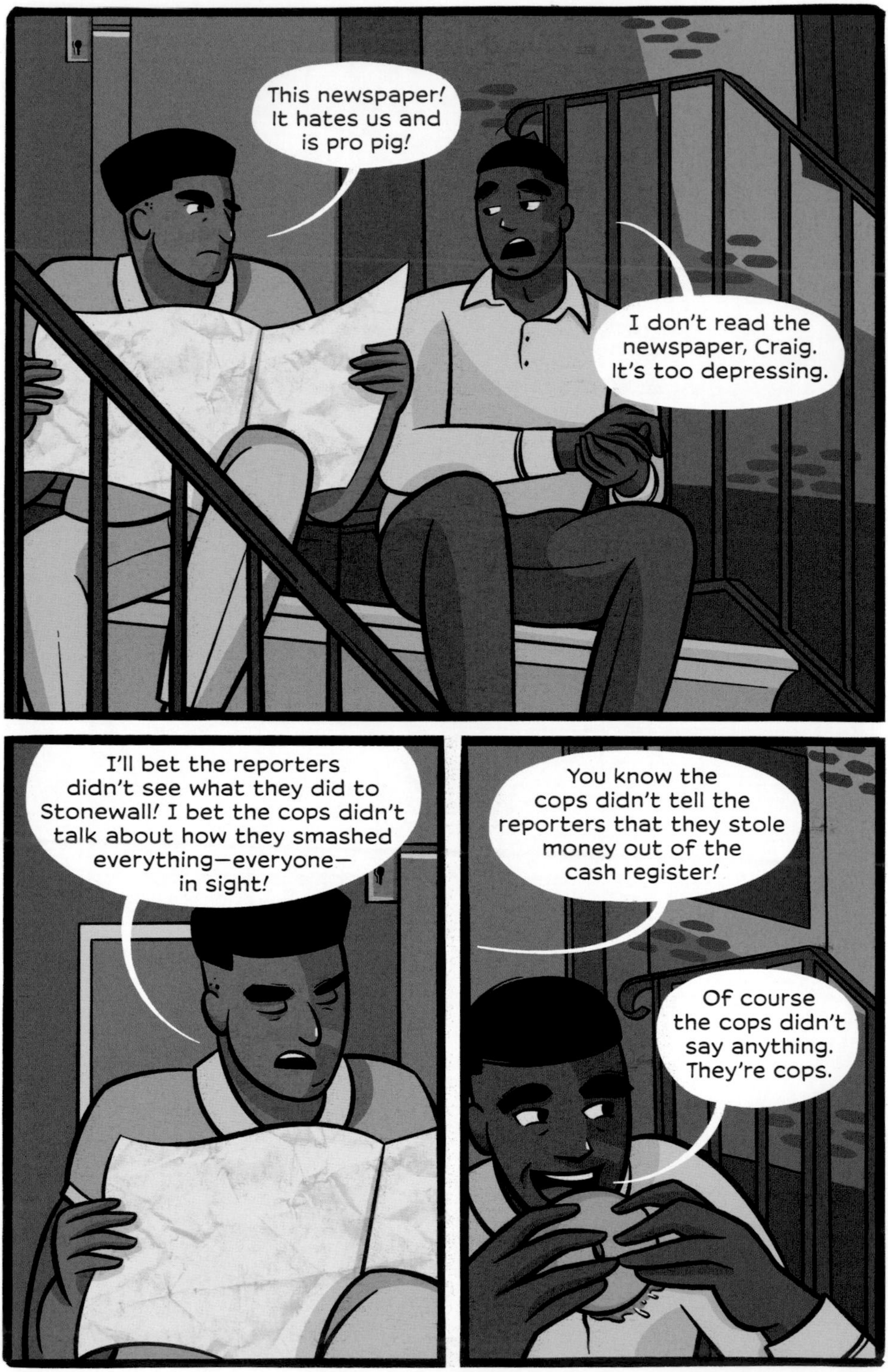
This newspaper! It hates us and is pro pig!
I don't read the newspaper, Craig. It's too depressing.
I'll bet the reporters didn't see what they did to Stonewall! I bet the cops didn't talk about how they smashed everything—everyone—in sight!
You know the cops didn't tell the reporters that they stole money out of the cash register!
Of course the cops didn't say anything. They're cops.

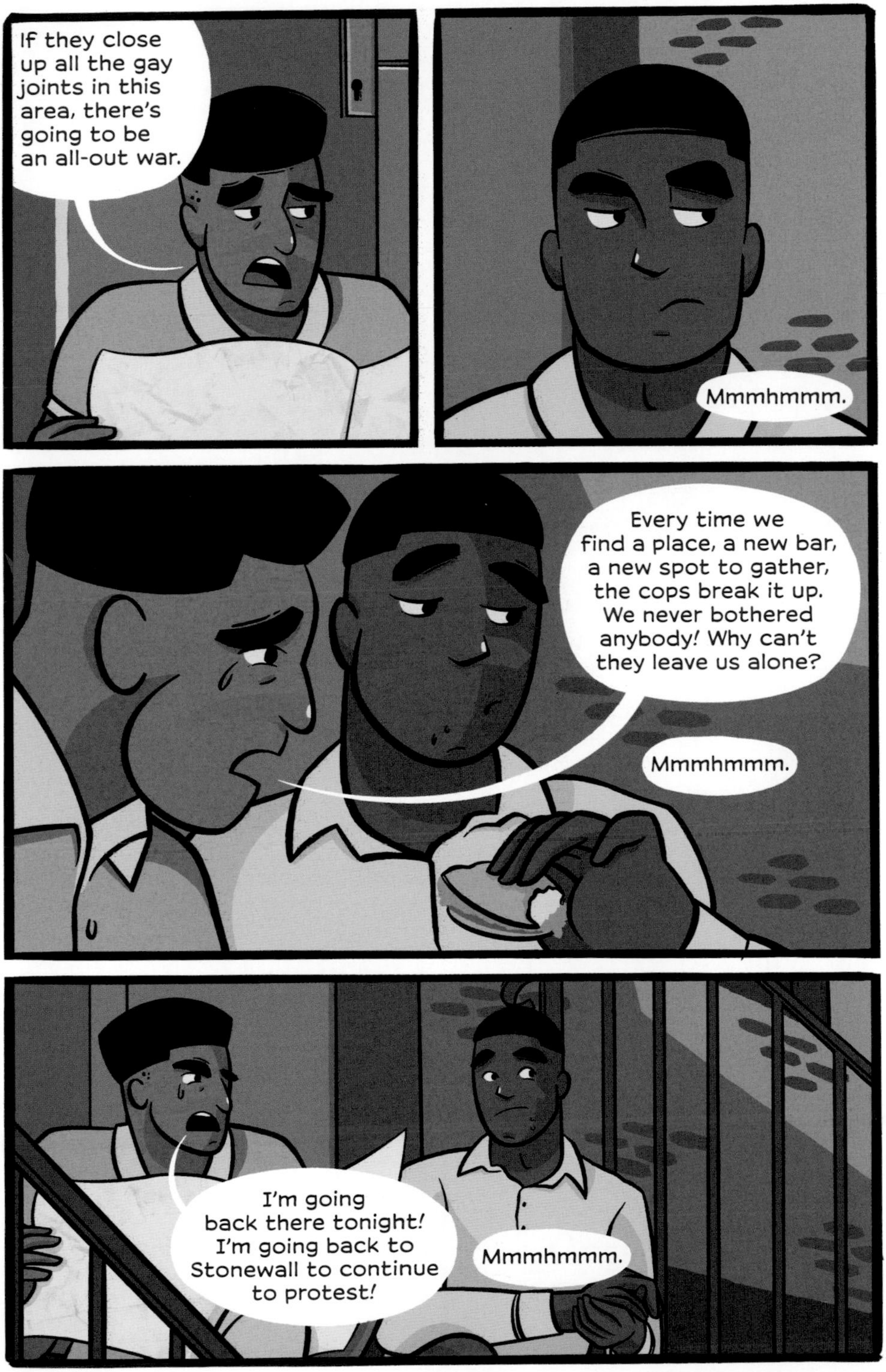
If they close up all the gay joints in this area, there's going to be an all-out war.
Mmmhmmm.
Every time we find a place, a new bar, a new spot to gather, the cops break it up. We never bothered anybody! Why can't they leave us alone?
Mmmhmmm.
I'm going back there tonight! I'm going back to Stonewall to continue to protest!
Mmmhmmm.

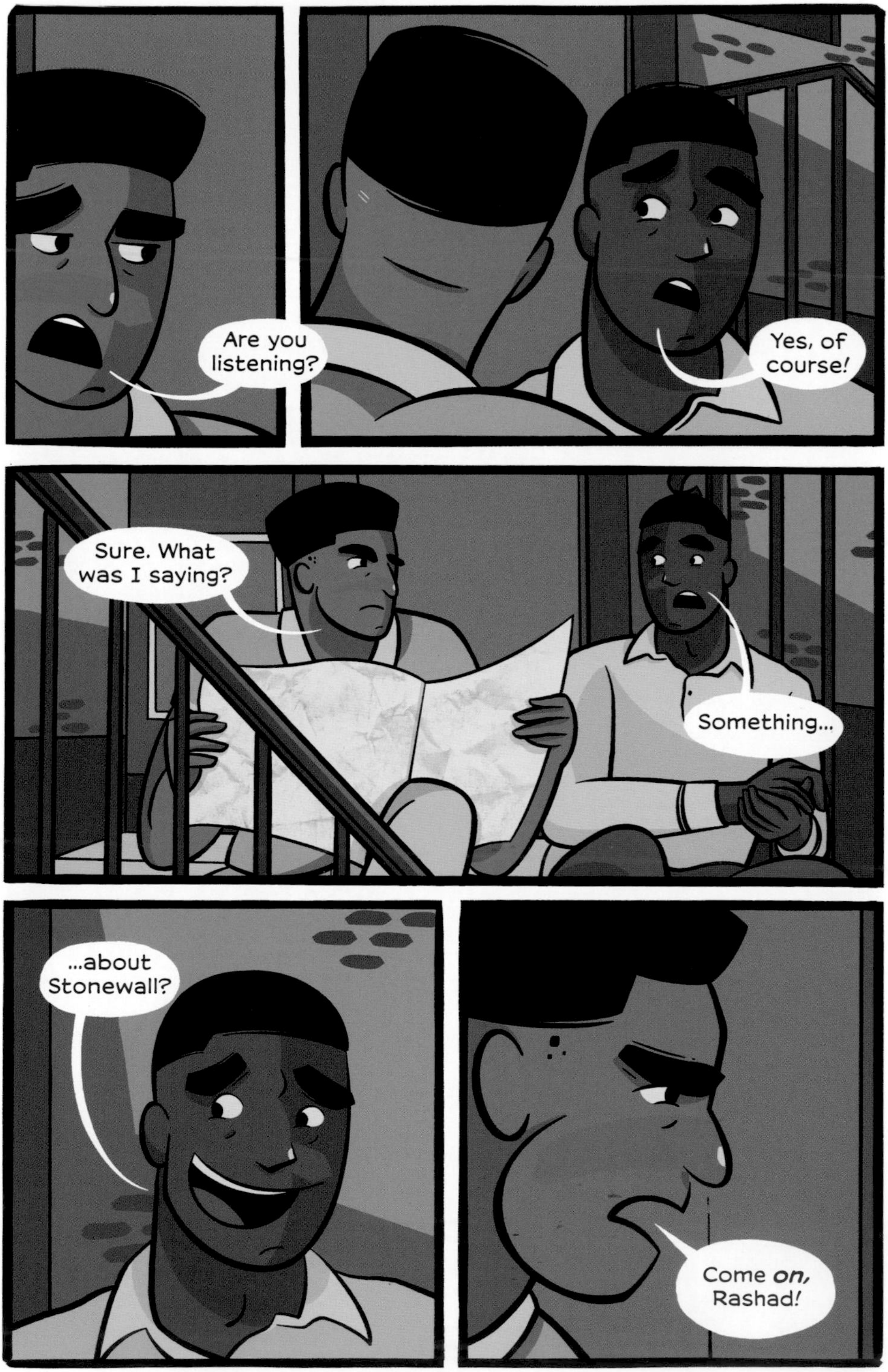
Are you listening?
Yes, of course!
Sure. What was I saying?
Something...
...about Stonewall?
Come *on*, Rashad!

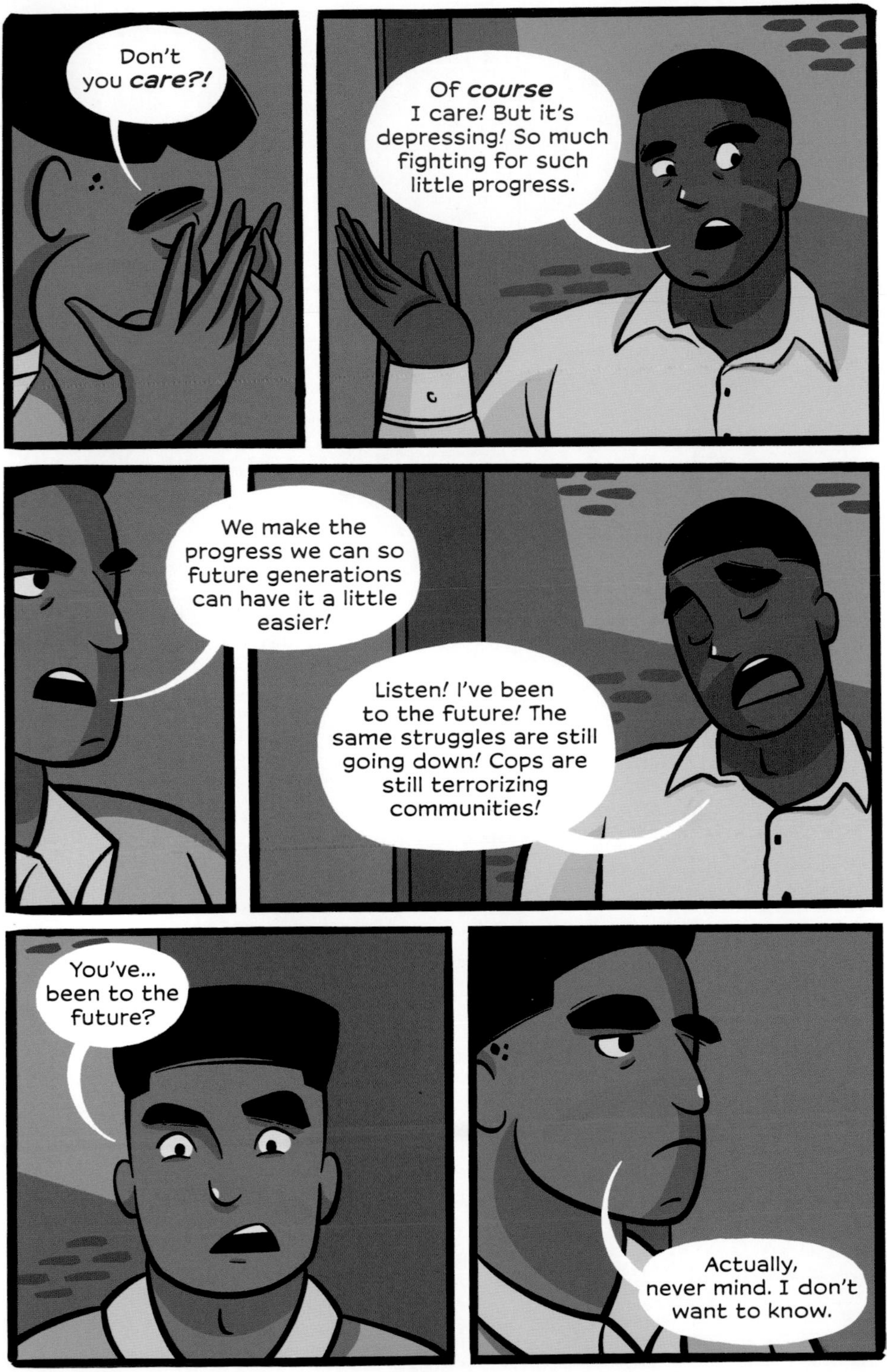
Don't you *care?!*
Of *course* I care! But it's depressing! So much fighting for such little progress.
We make the progress we can so future generations can have it a little easier!
Listen! I've been to the future! The same struggles are still going down! Cops are still terrorizing communities!
You've... been to the future?
Actually, never mind. I don't want to know.

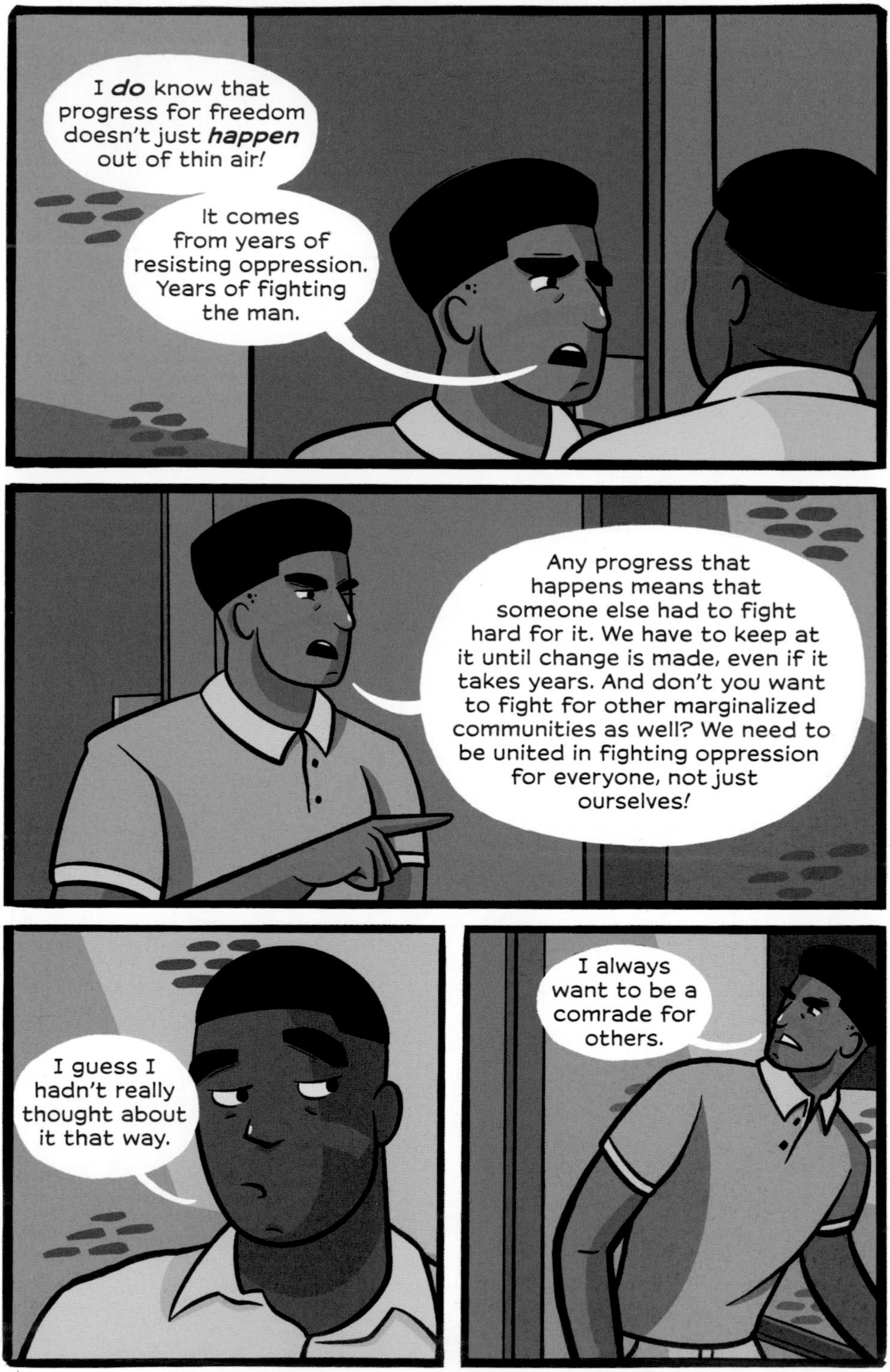
I *do* know that progress for freedom doesn't just ***happen*** out of thin air!
It comes from years of resisting oppression. Years of fighting the man.
Any progress that happens means that someone else had to fight hard for it. We have to keep at it until change is made, even if it takes years. And don't you want to fight for other marginalized communities as well? We need to be united in fighting oppression for everyone, not just ourselves!
I guess I hadn't really thought about it that way.
I always want to be a comrade for others.

Wait! Where are you going?

You're cute...

...but I need someone who can imagine a brighter future.

DAILY NEWS

NEW YORK'S PICTURE NEWSPAPER

3 Cops Hurt As Bar Raid Riles C...

SUNDAY NEWS, JUNE 29, 1969

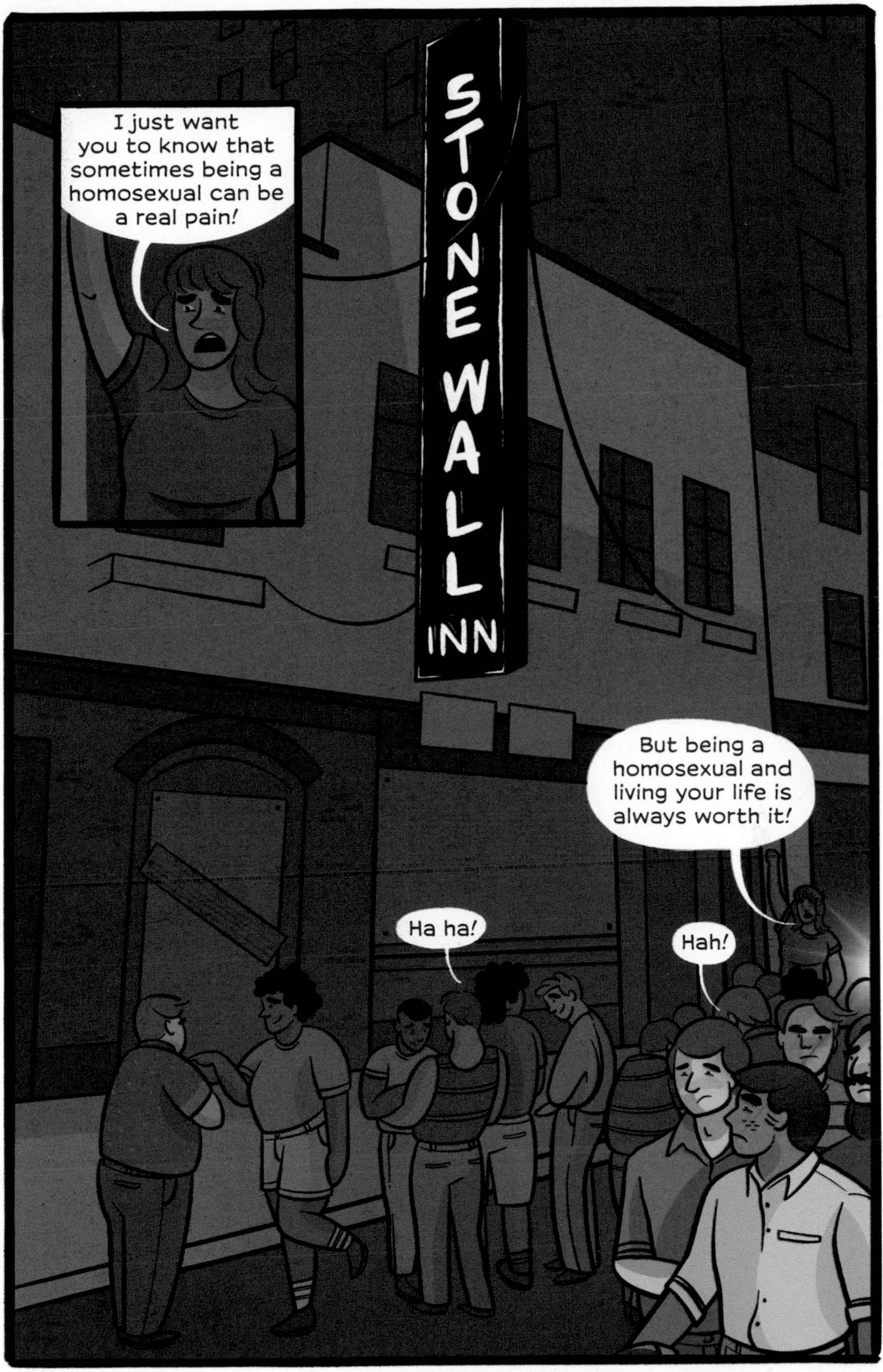
I just want you to know that sometimes being a homosexual can be a real pain!
STONEWALL INN
But being a homosexual and living your life is always worth it!
Ha ha!
Hah!

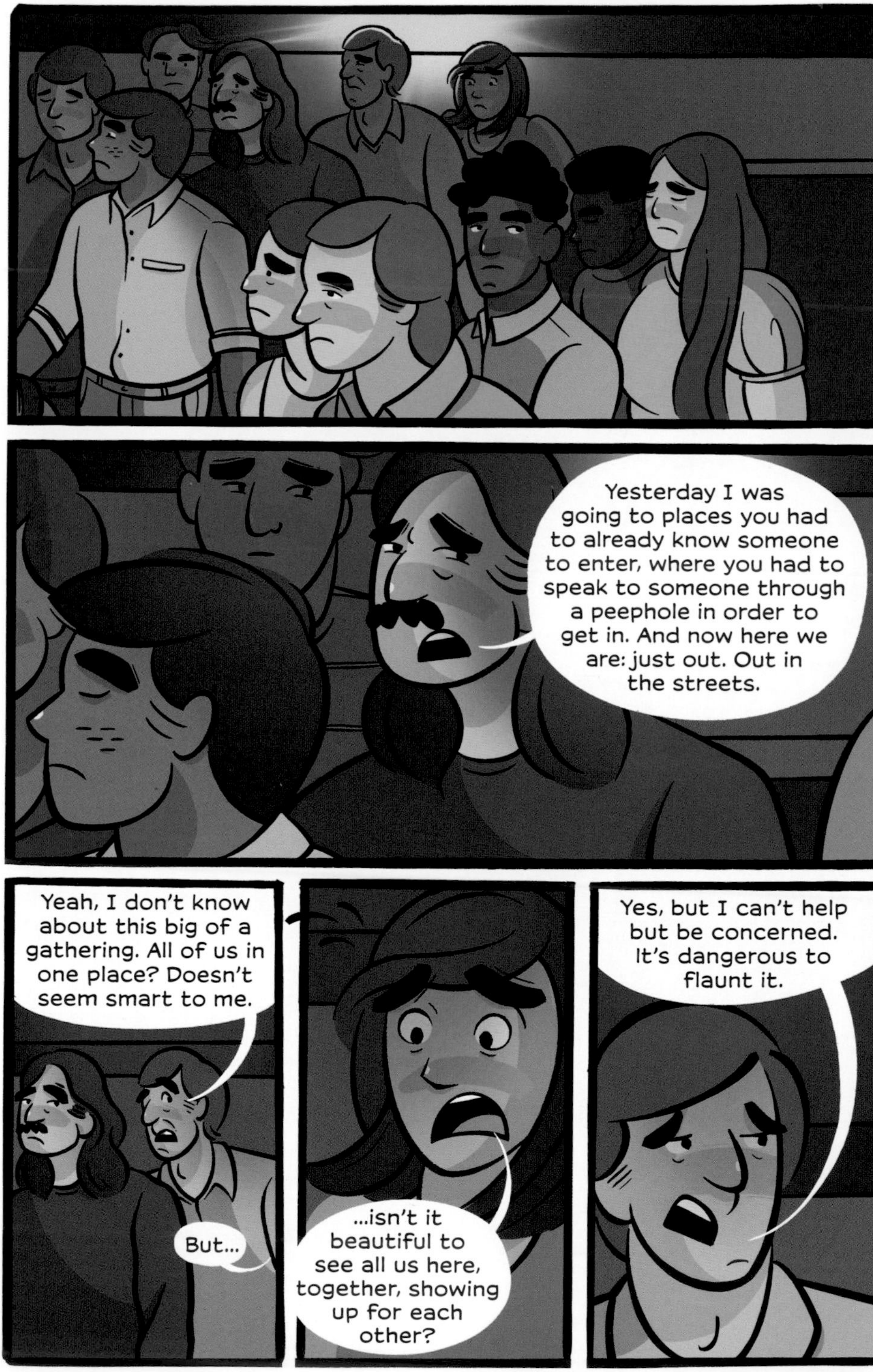
Yesterday I was going to places you had to already know someone to enter, where you had to speak to someone through a peephole in order to get in. And now here we are: just out. Out in the streets.
Yeah, I don't know about this big of a gathering. All of us in one place? Doesn't seem smart to me.
But...
...isn't it beautiful to see all us here, together, showing up for each other?
Yes, but I can't help but be concerned. It's dangerous to flaunt it.

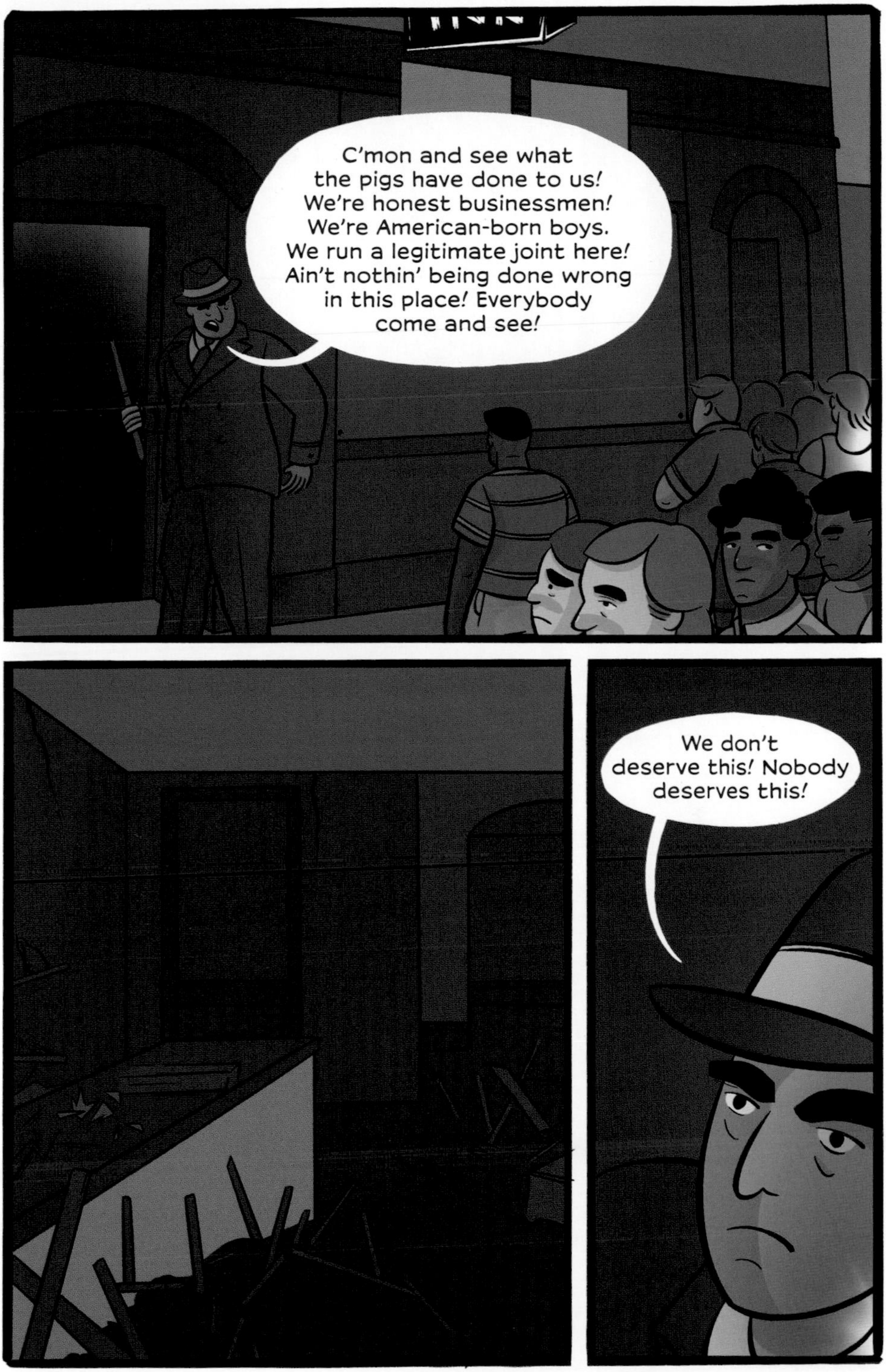
C'mon and see what the pigs have done to us! We're honest businessmen! We're American-born boys. We run a legitimate joint here! Ain't nothin' being done wrong in this place! Everybody come and see!
We don't deserve this! Nobody deserves this!

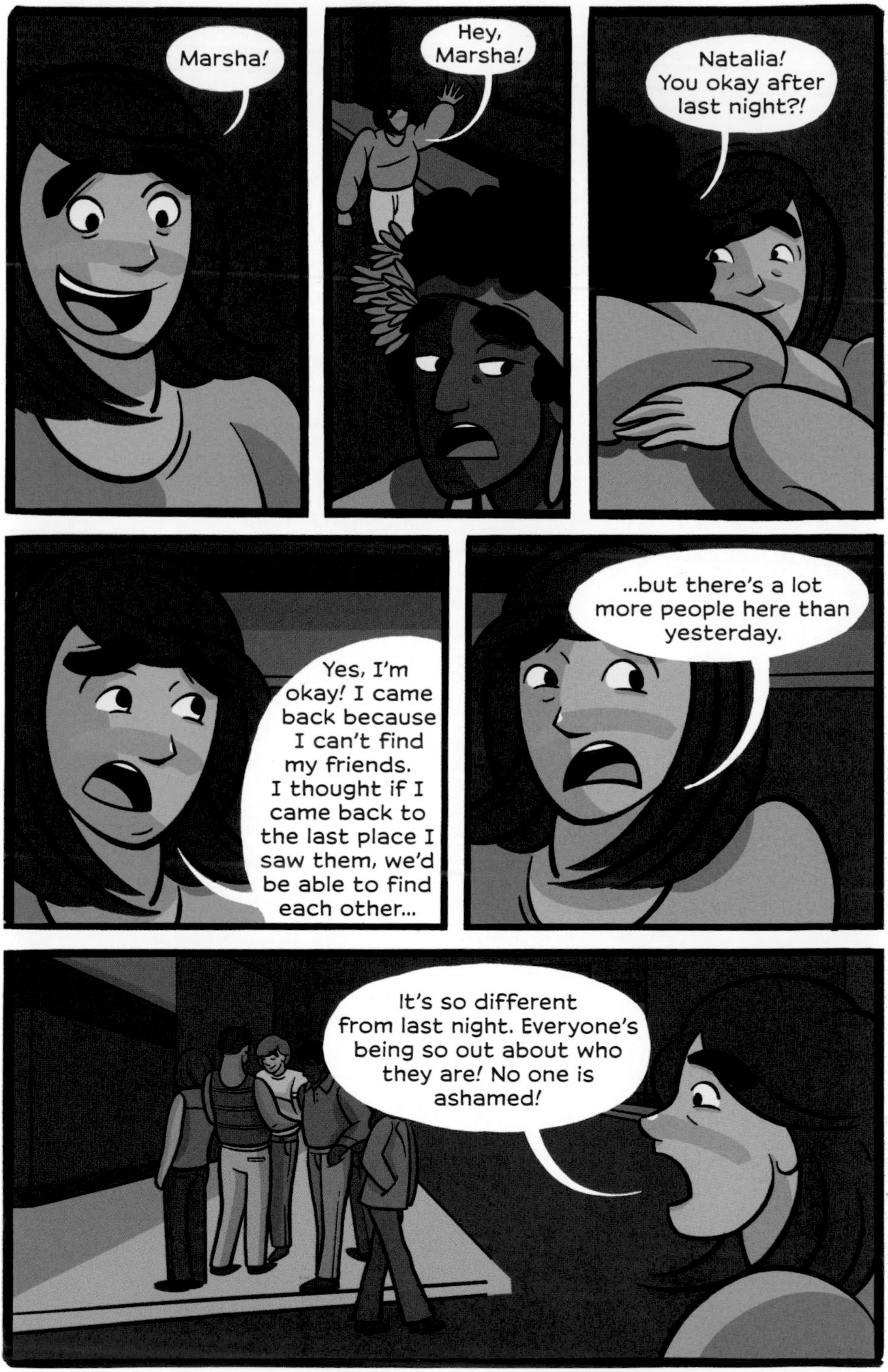
Marsha!
Hey, Marsha!
Natalia! You okay after last night?!
Yes, I'm okay! I came back because I can't find my friends. I thought if I came back to the last place I saw them, we'd be able to find each other...
...but there's a lot more people here than yesterday.
It's so different from last night. Everyone's being so out about who they are! No one is ashamed!

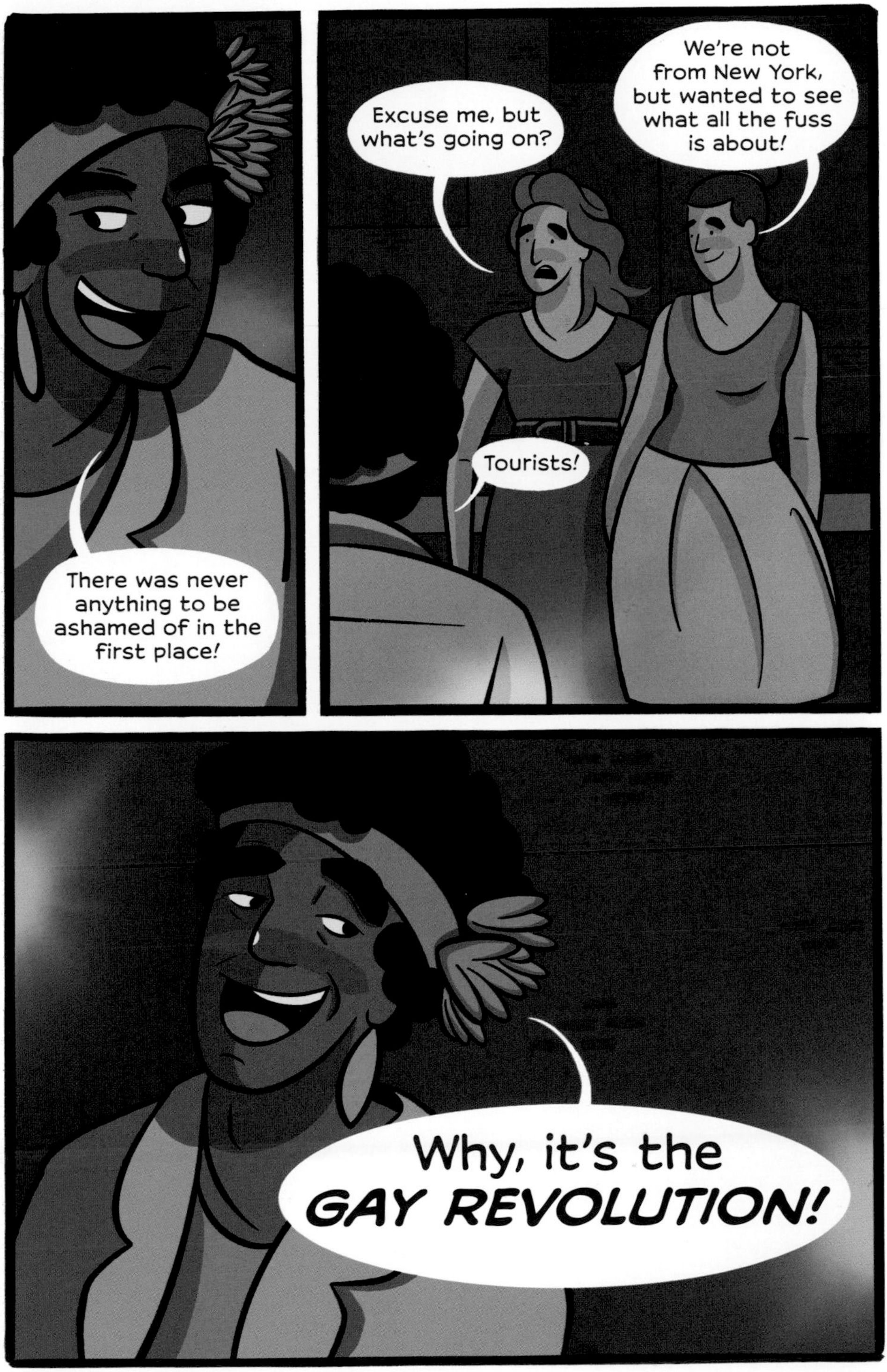
There was never anything to be ashamed of in the first place!
Excuse me, but what's going on?
We're not from New York, but wanted to see what all the fuss is about!
Tourists!
Why, it's the *GAY REVOLUTION!*

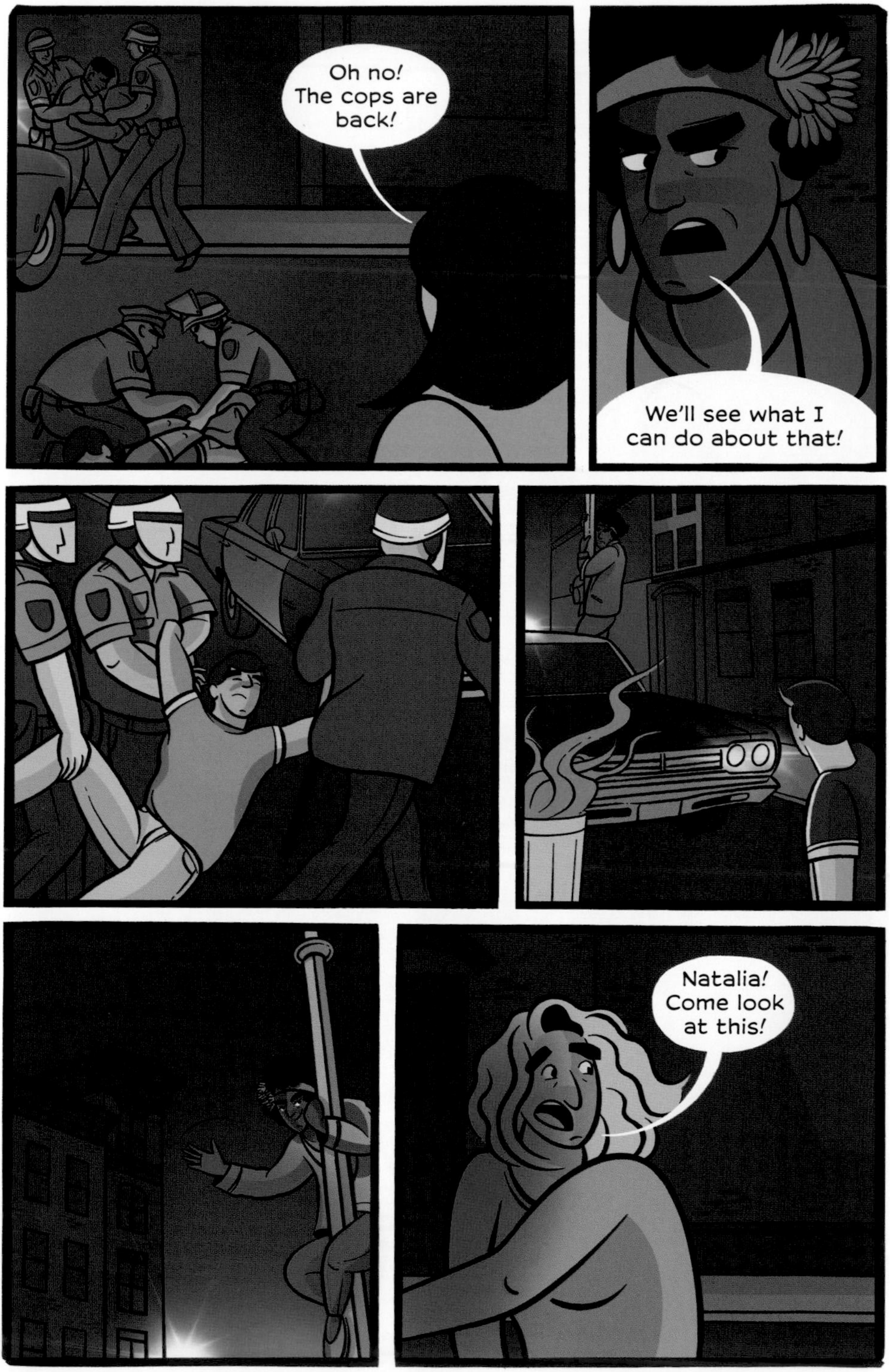
Oh no! The cops are back!
We'll see what I can do about that!
Natalia! Come look at this!

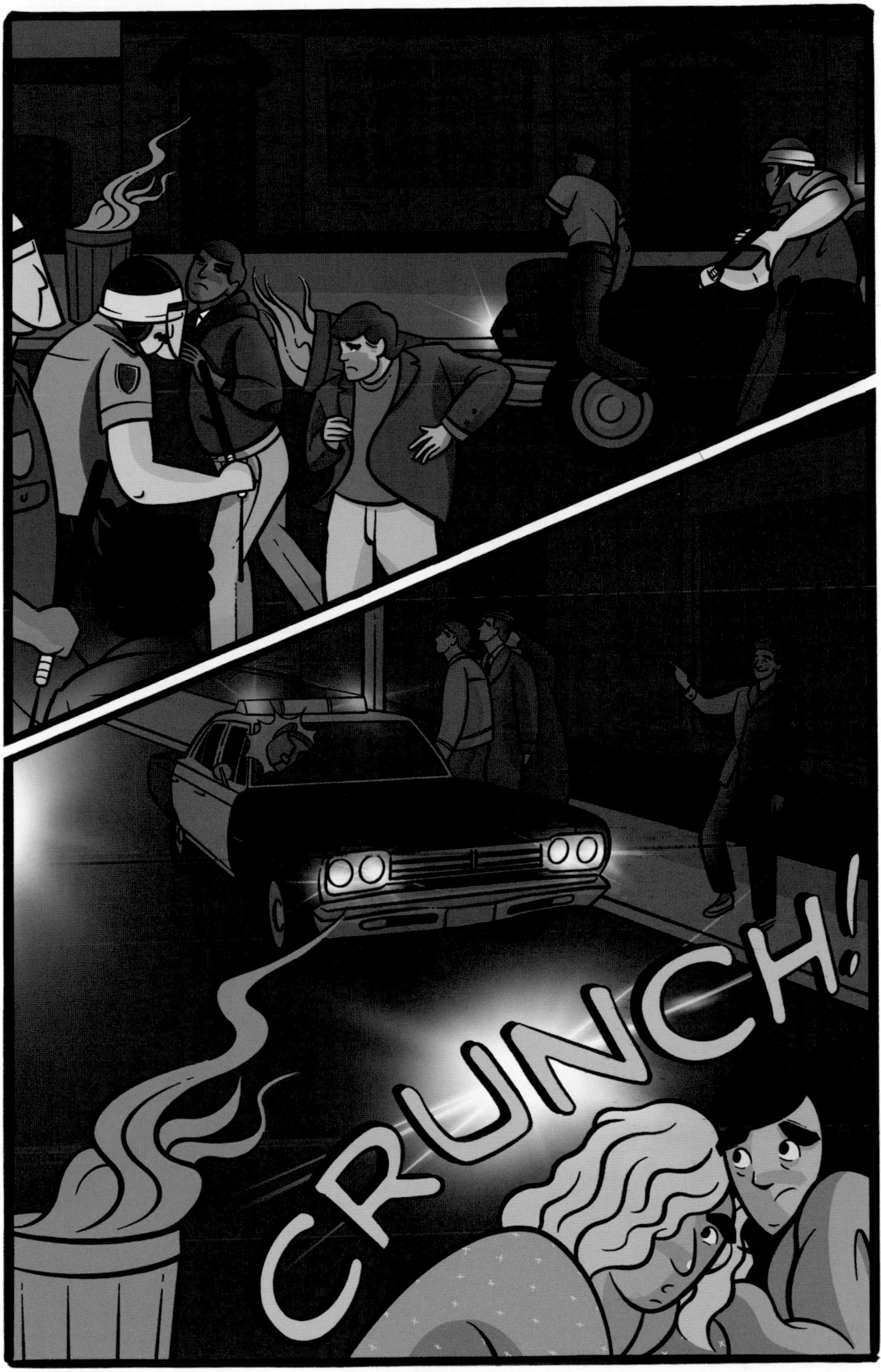
CRUNCH!

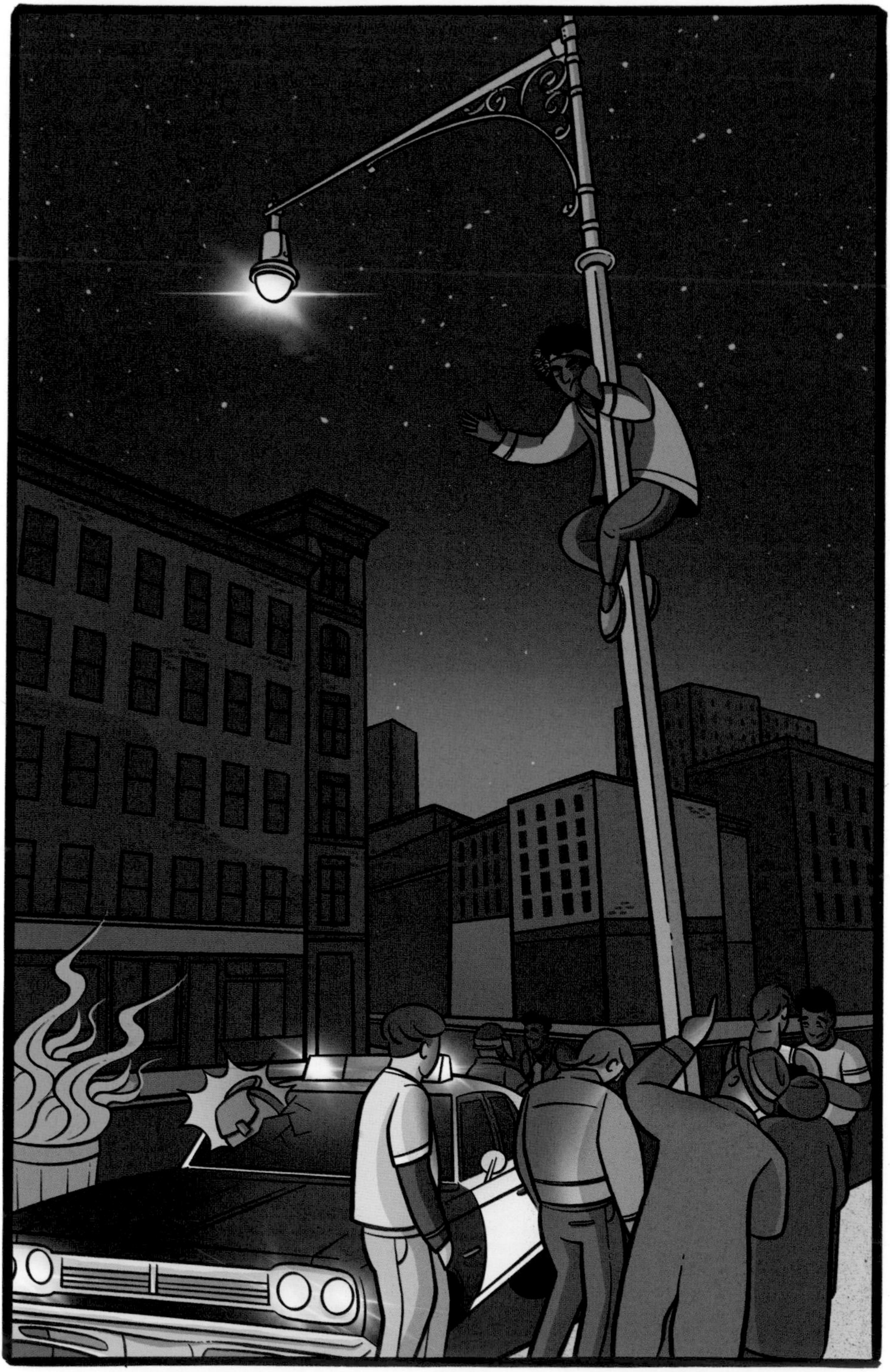

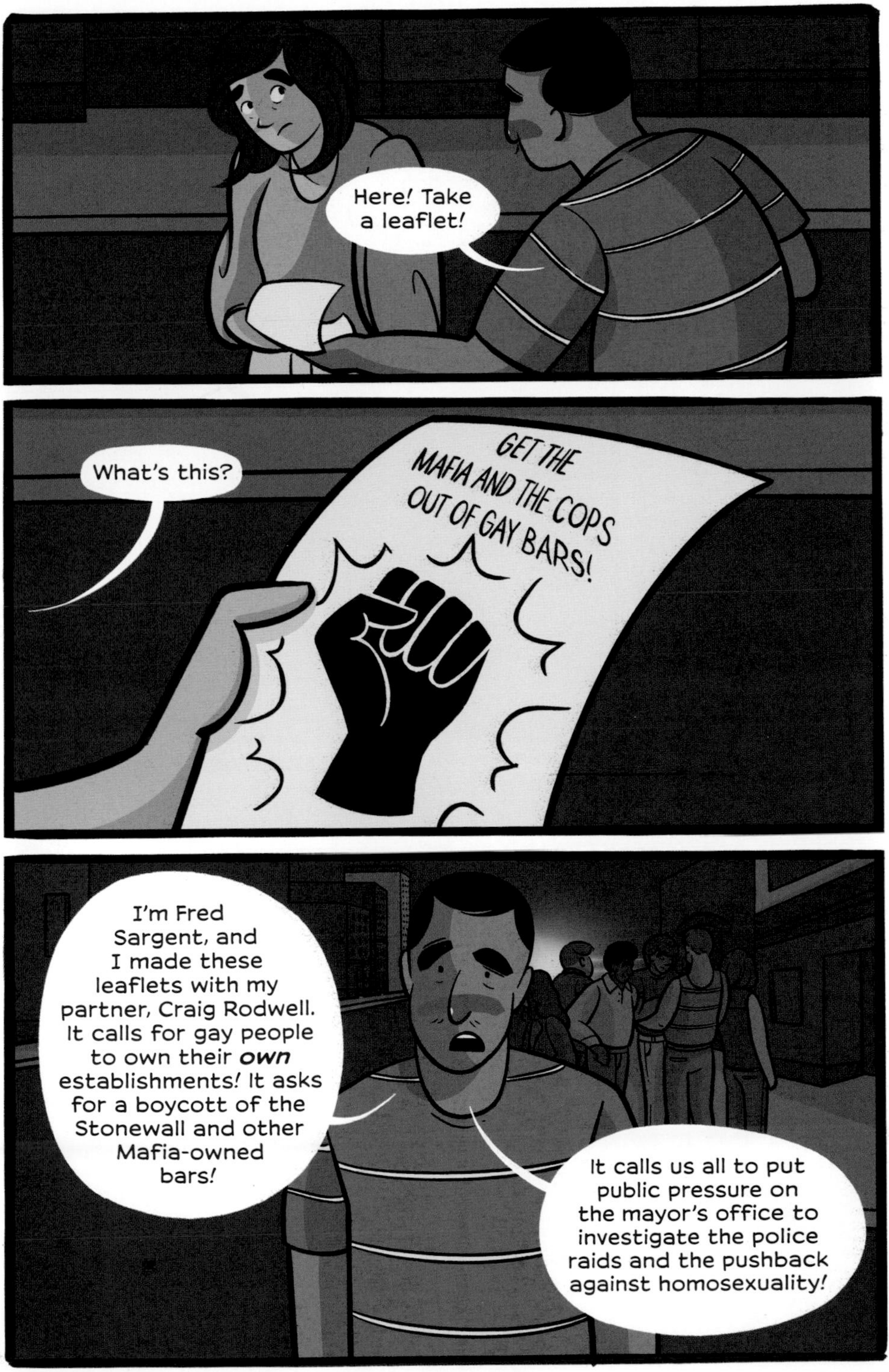
Here! Take a leaflet!
What's this?
GET THE MAFIA AND THE COPS OUT OF GAY BARS!
I'm Fred Sargent, and I made these leaflets with my partner, Craig Rodwell. It calls for gay people to own their ***own*** establishments! It asks for a boycott of the Stonewall and other Mafia-owned bars!
It calls us all to put public pressure on the mayor's office to investigate the police raids and the pushback against homosexuality!

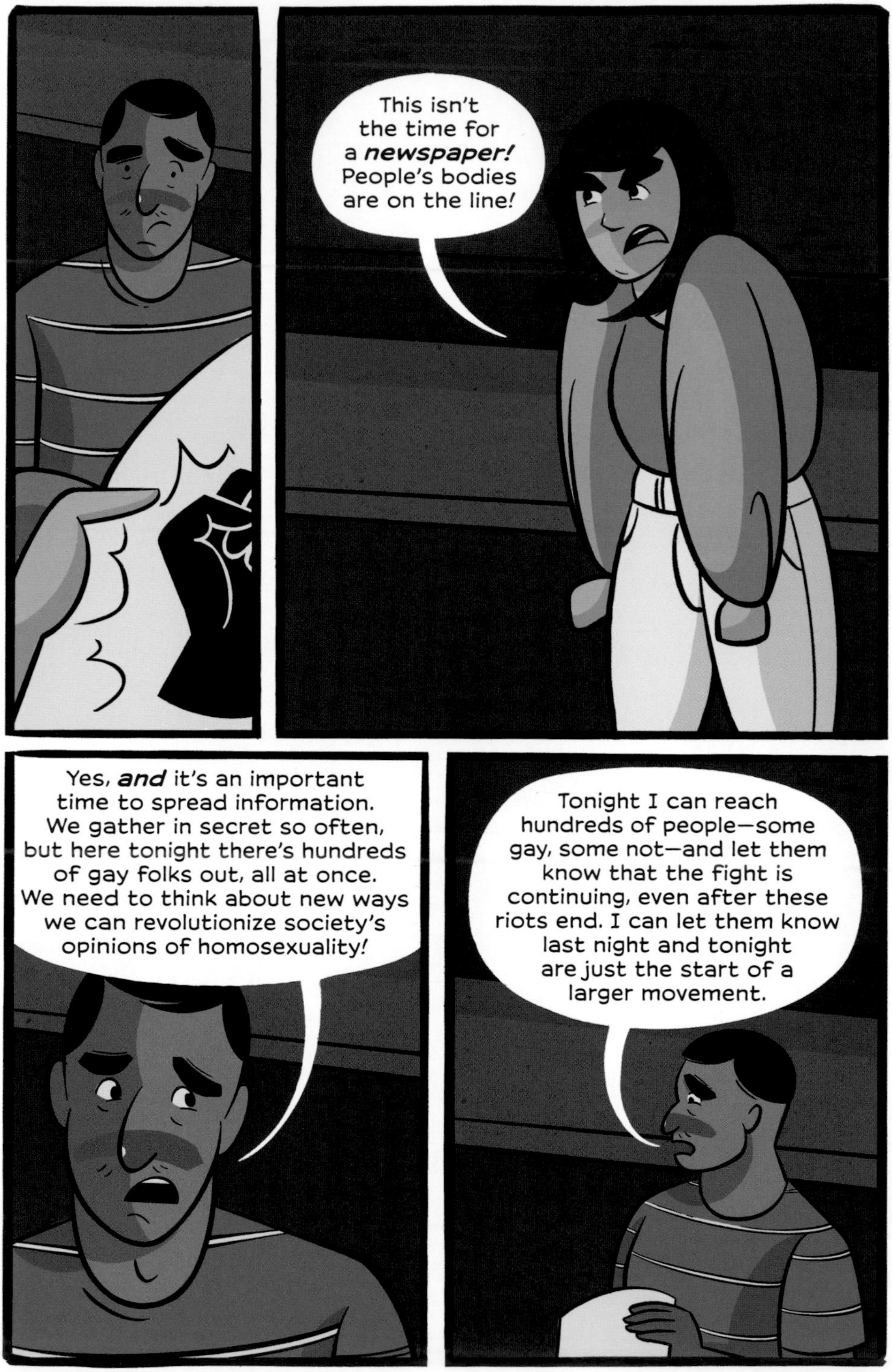
This isn't the time for a ***newspaper!*** People's bodies are on the line!
Yes, ***and*** it's an important time to spread information. We gather in secret so often, but here tonight there's hundreds of gay folks out, all at once. We need to think about new ways we can revolutionize society's opinions of homosexuality!
Tonight I can reach hundreds of people—some gay, some not—and let them know that the fight is continuing, even after these riots end. I can let them know last night and tonight are just the start of a larger movement.

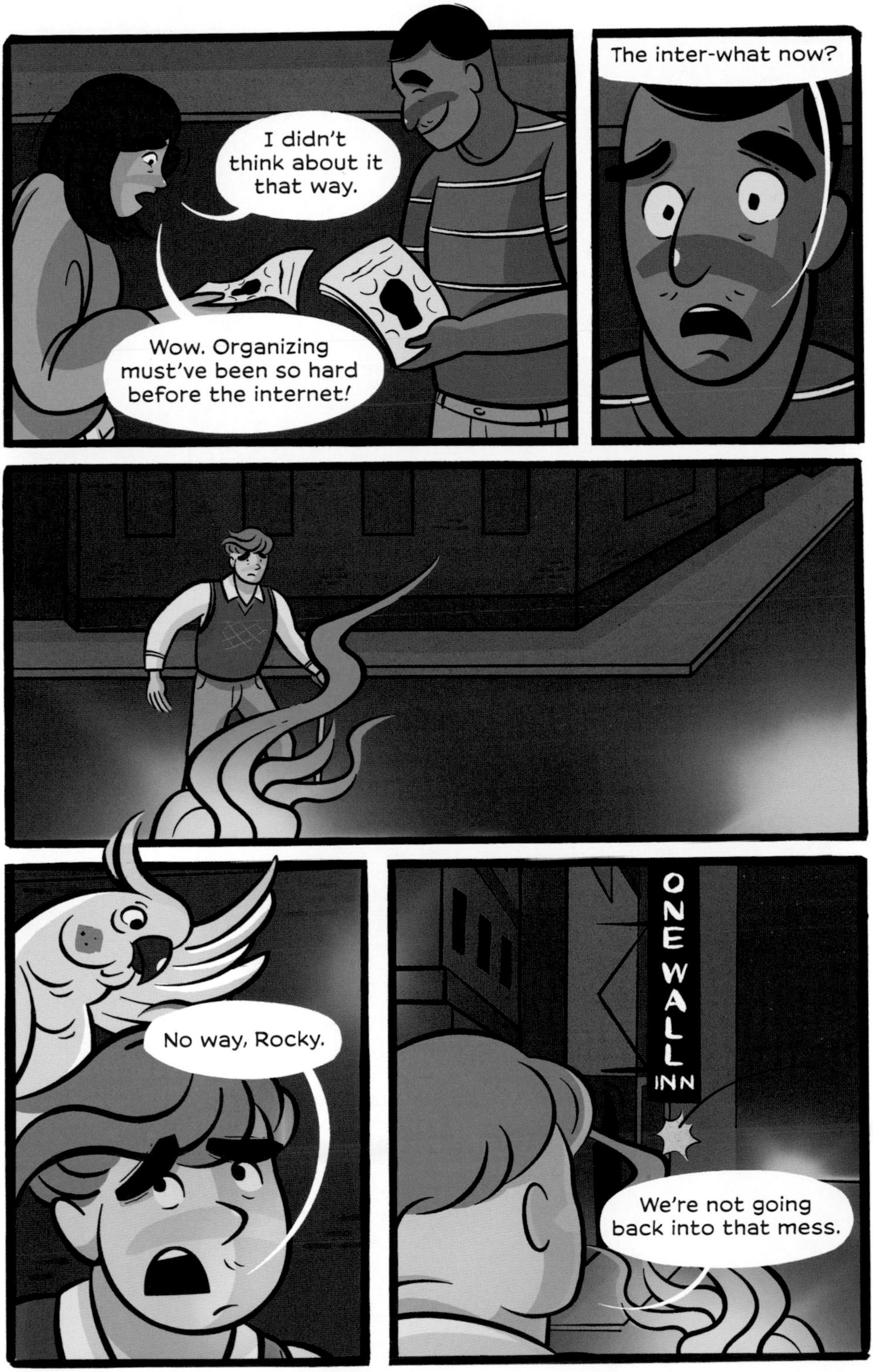
I didn't think about it that way.
Wow. Organizing must've been so hard before the internet!
The inter-what now?
No way, Rocky.
ONE WALL INN
We're not going back into that mess.

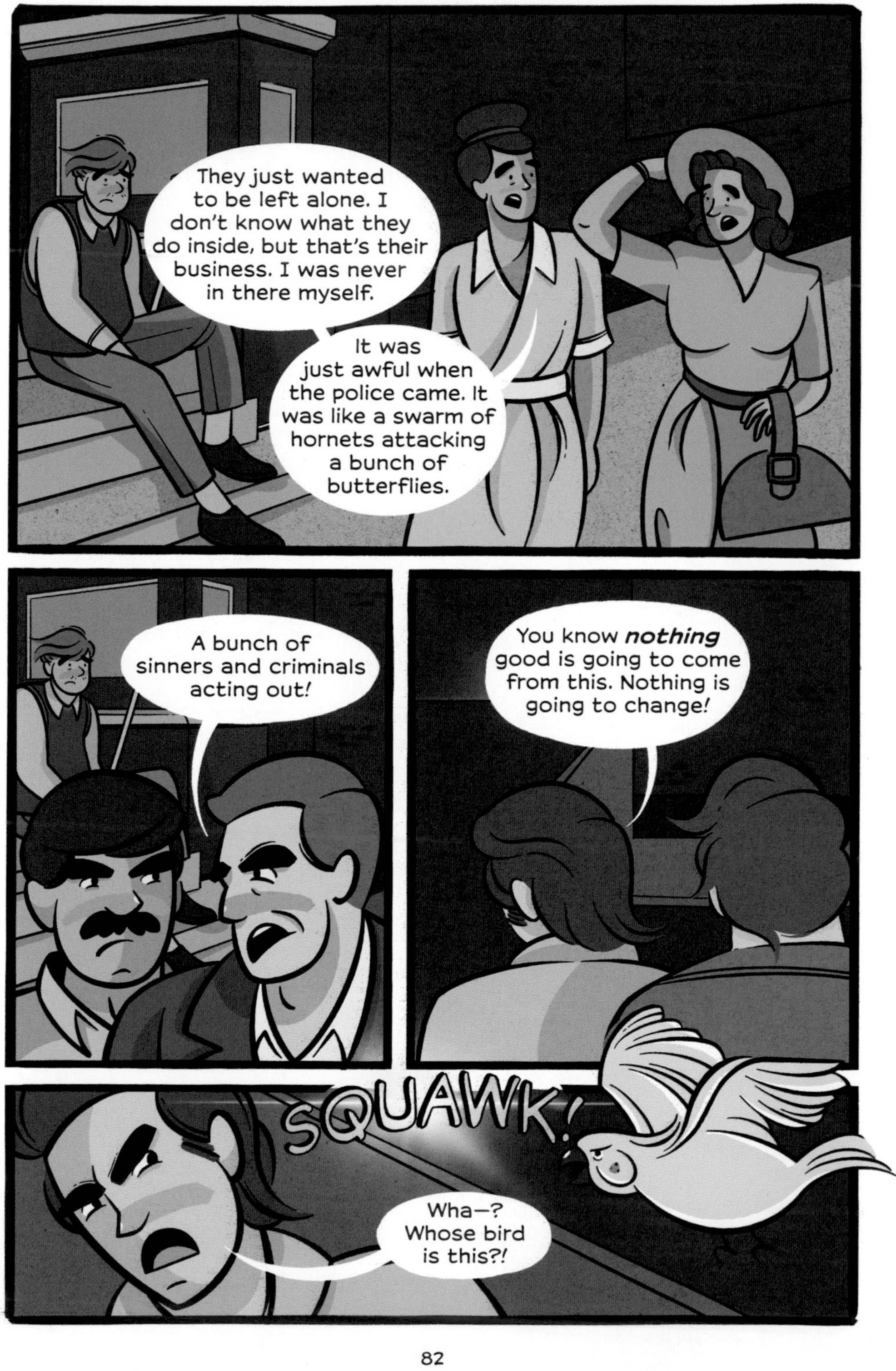
They just wanted to be left alone. I don't know what they do inside, but that's their business. I was never in there myself.
It was just awful when the police came. It was like a swarm of hornets attacking a bunch of butterflies.
A bunch of sinners and criminals acting out!
You know **nothing** good is going to come from this. Nothing is going to change!
SQUAWK!
Wha—? Whose bird is this?!

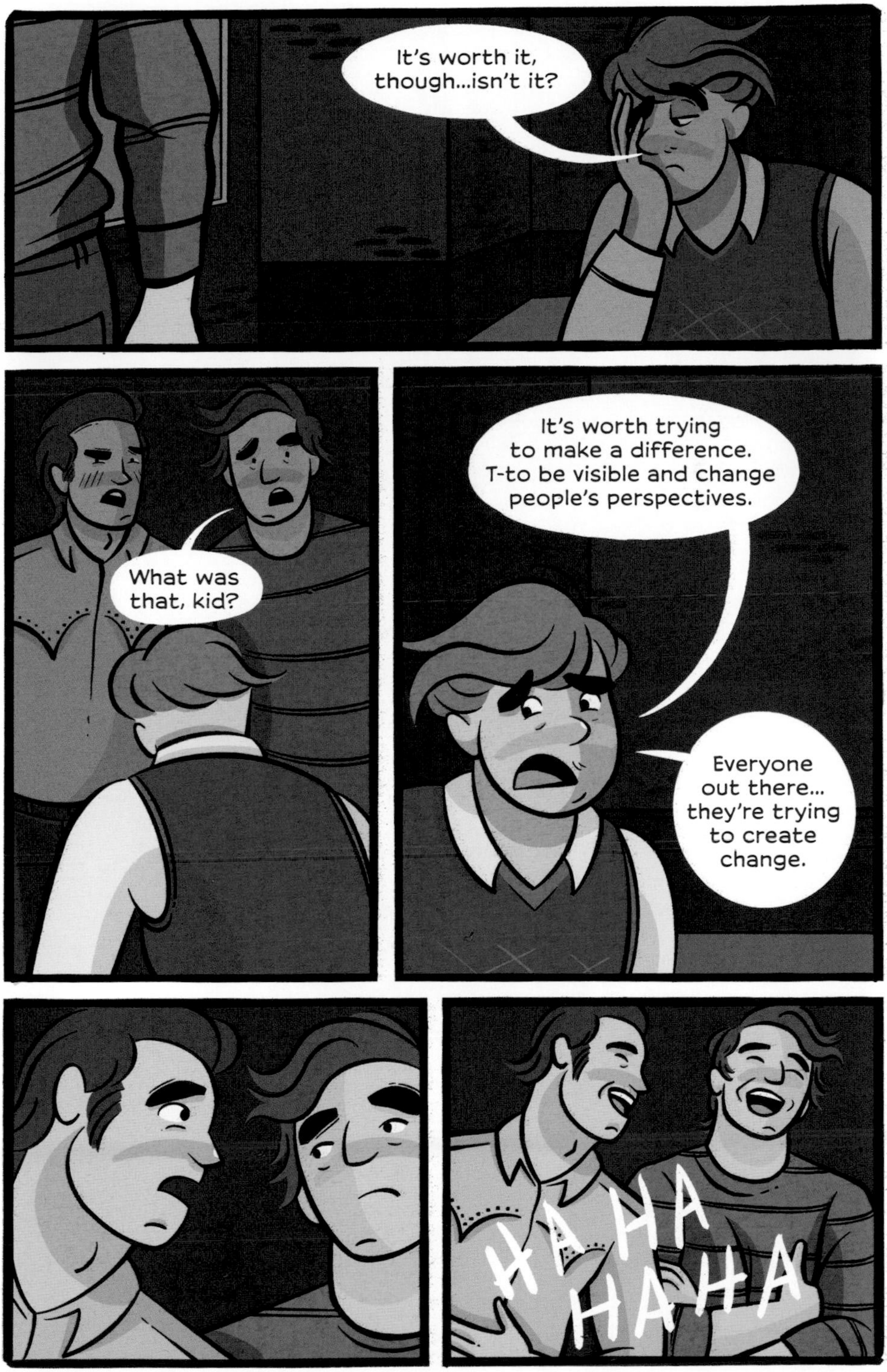
It's worth it, though...isn't it?
What was that, kid?
It's worth trying to make a difference. T-to be visible and change people's perspectives.
Everyone out there... they're trying to create change.
HA HA HA HA

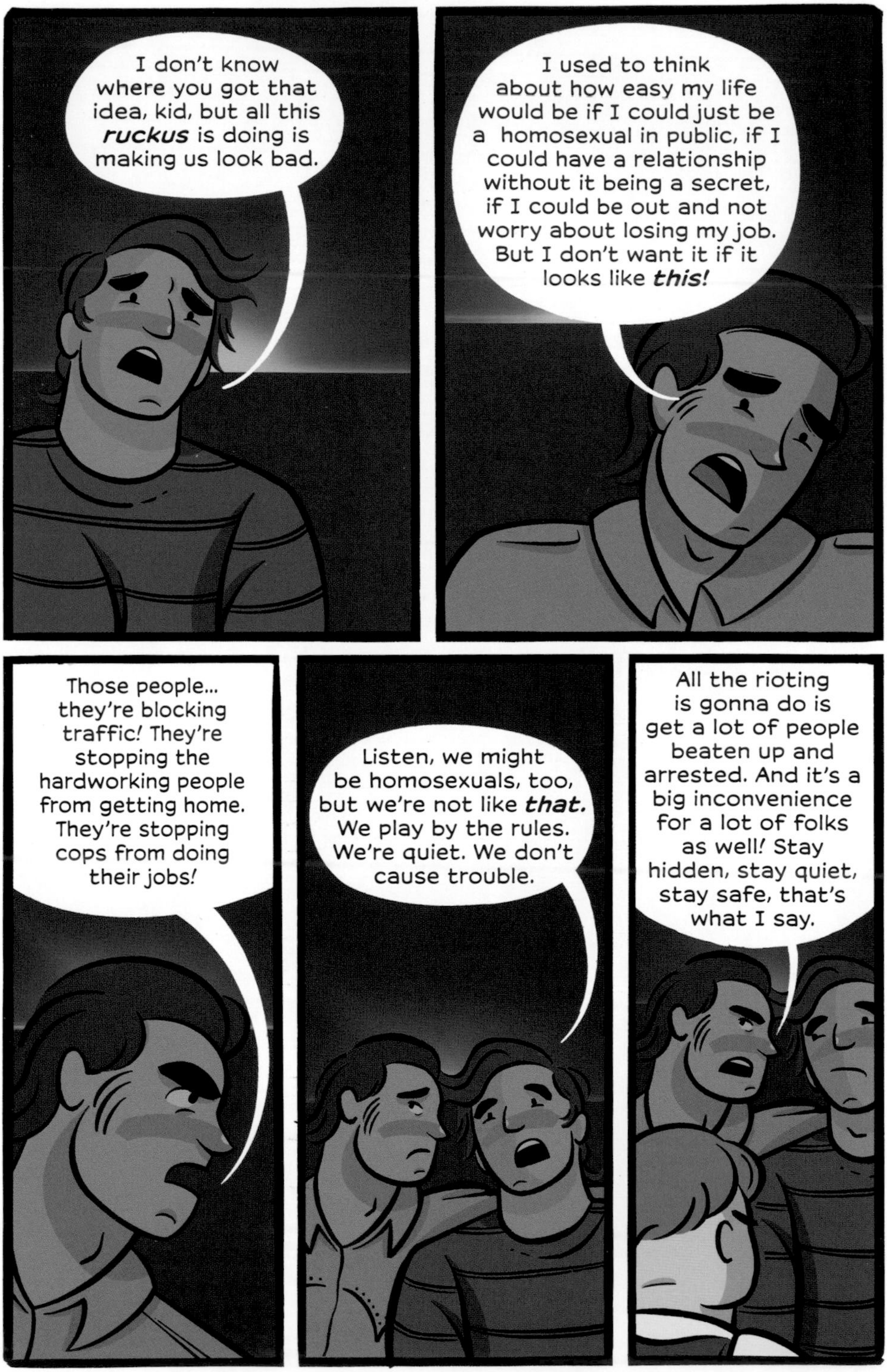
I don't know where you got that idea, kid, but all this *ruckus* is doing is making us look bad.
I used to think about how easy my life would be if I could just be a homosexual in public, if I could have a relationship without it being a secret, if I could be out and not worry about losing my job. But I don't want it if it looks like *this!*
Those people... they're blocking traffic! They're stopping the hardworking people from getting home. They're stopping cops from doing their jobs!
Listen, we might be homosexuals, too, but we're not like *that.* We play by the rules. We're quiet. We don't cause trouble.
All the rioting is gonna do is get a lot of people beaten up and arrested. And it's a big inconvenience for a lot of folks as well! Stay hidden, stay quiet, stay safe, that's what I say.

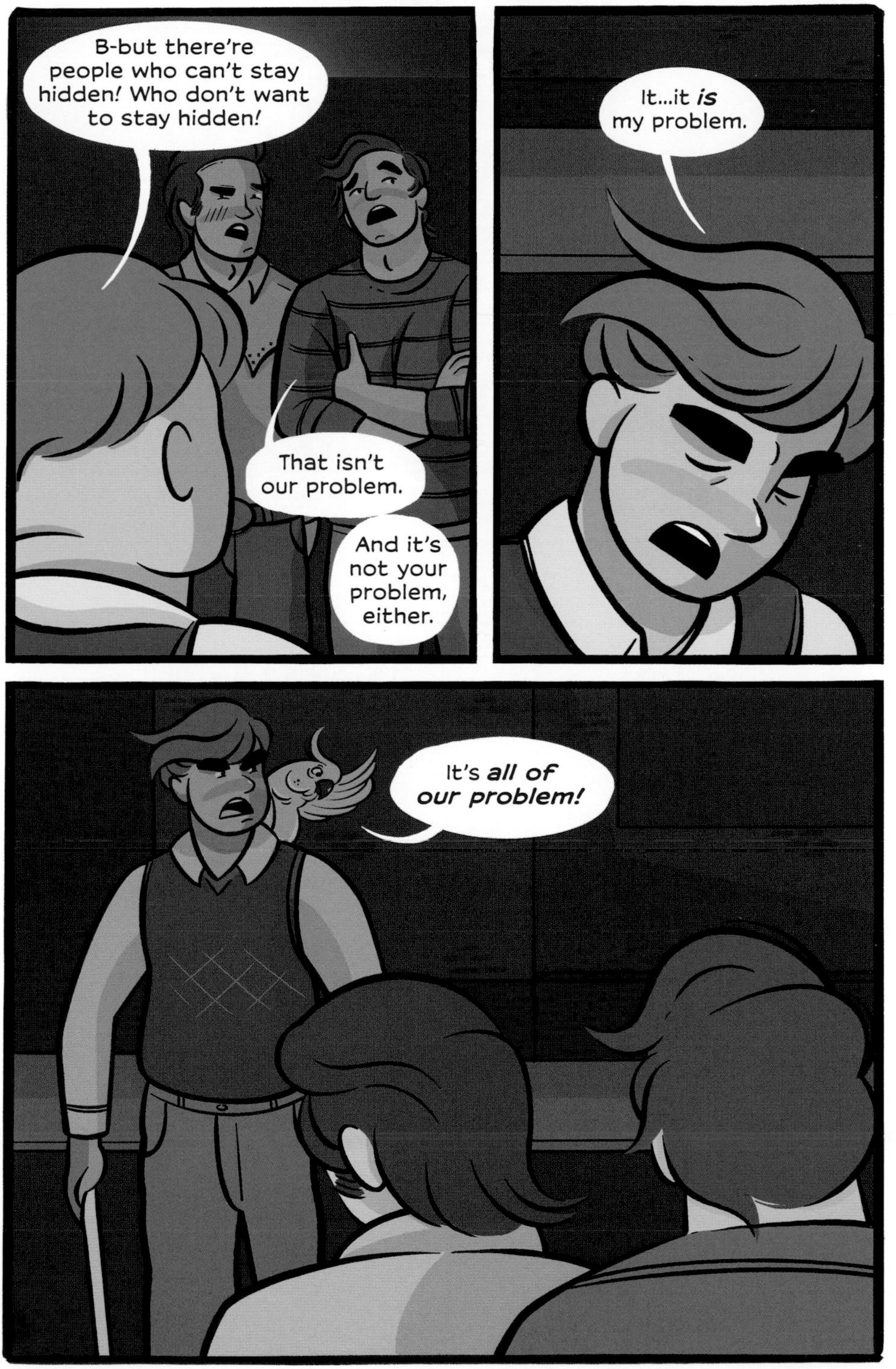
B-but there're people who can't stay hidden! Who don't want to stay hidden!
That isn't our problem.
And it's not your problem, either.
It...it *is* my problem.
It's ***all of our problem!***

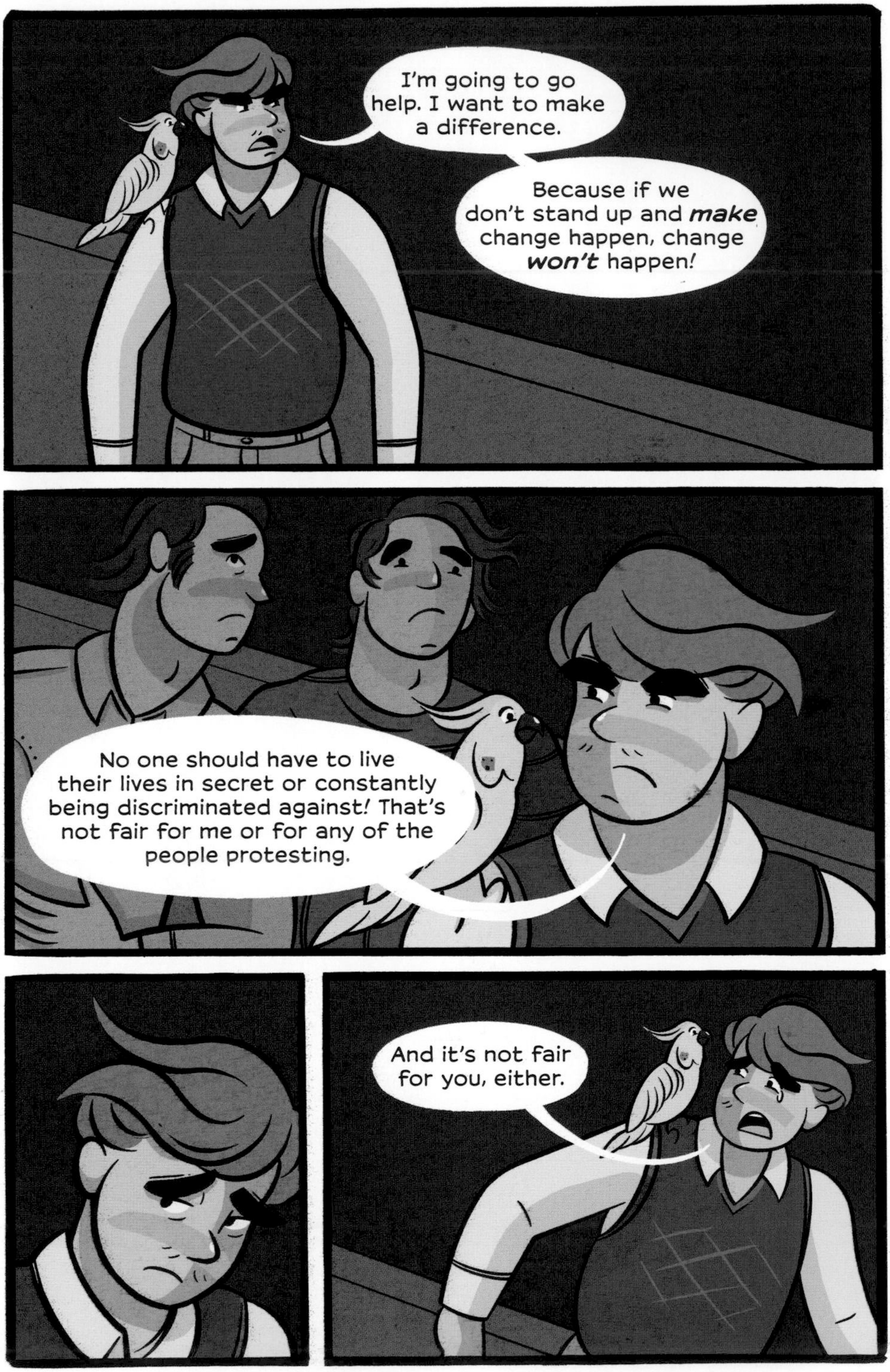
I'm going to go help. I want to make a difference.
Because if we don't stand up and ***make*** change happen, change ***won't*** happen!
No one should have to live their lives in secret or constantly being discriminated against! That's not fair for me or for any of the people protesting.
And it's not fair for you, either.

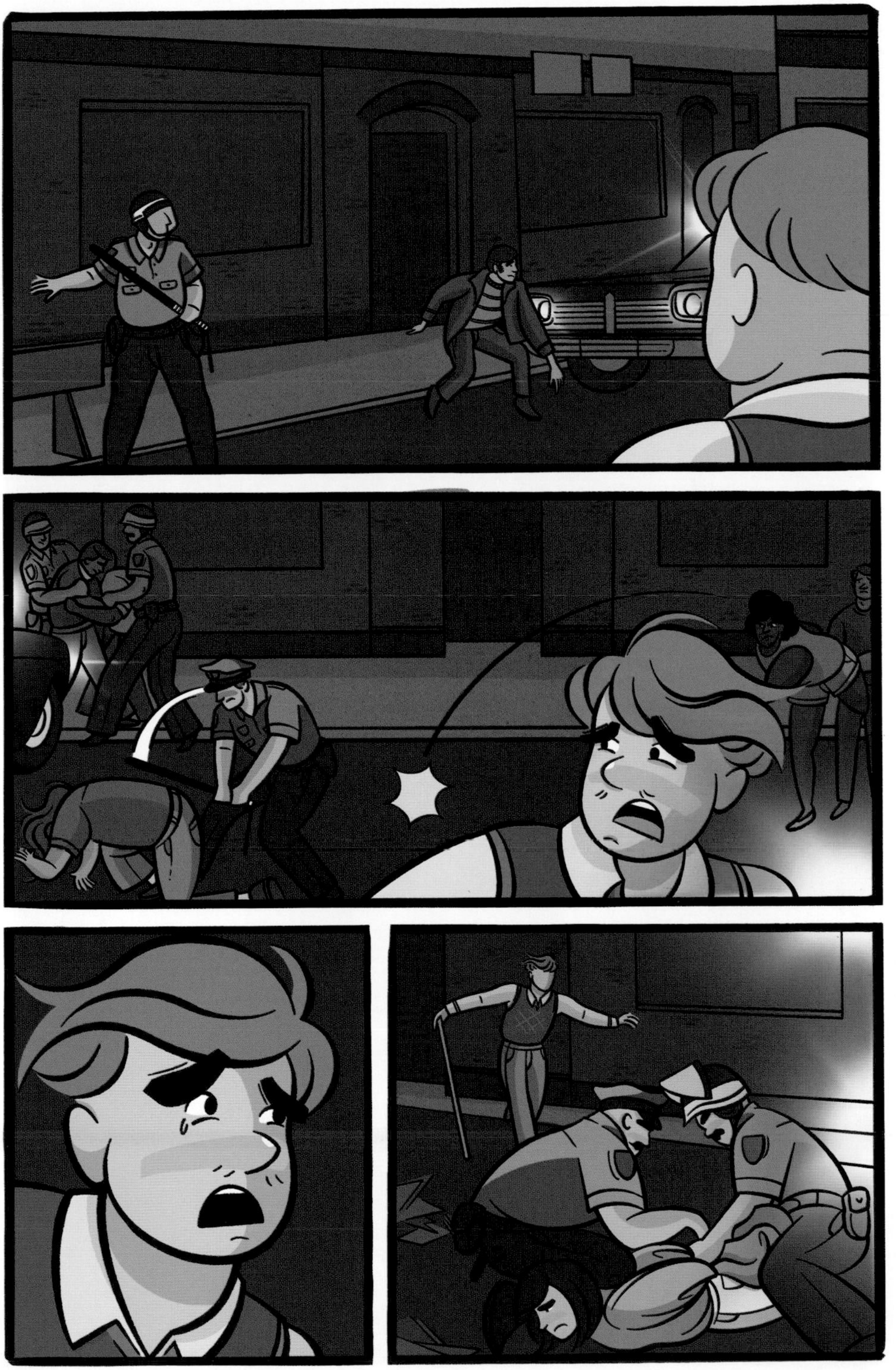

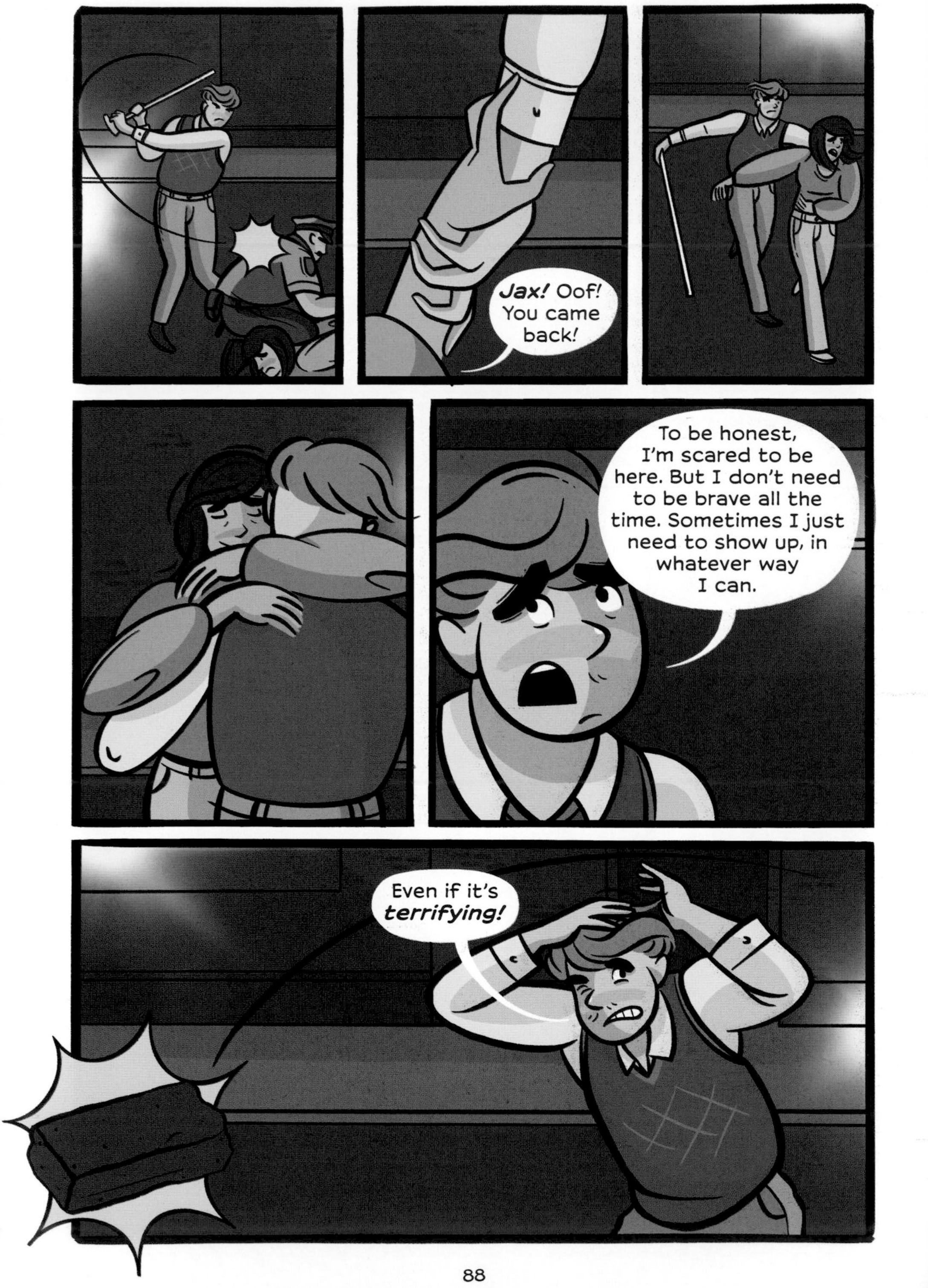
Jax! Oof! You came back!
To be honest, I'm scared to be here. But I don't need to be brave all the time. Sometimes I just need to show up, in whatever way I can.
Even if it's ***terrifying!***

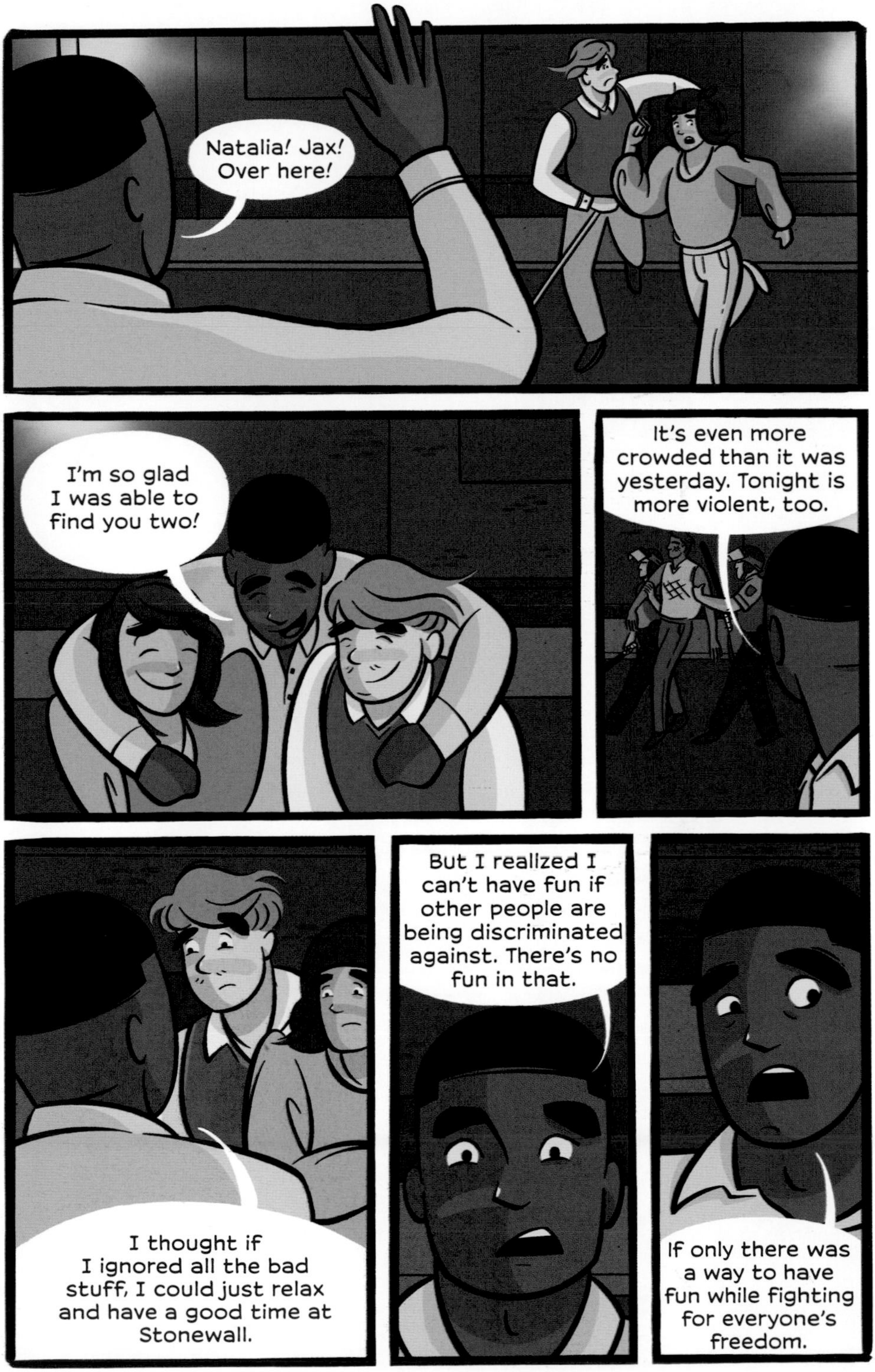
Natalia! Jax! Over here!
I'm so glad I was able to find you two!
It's even more crowded than it was yesterday. Tonight is more violent, too.
I thought if I ignored all the bad stuff, I could just relax and have a good time at Stonewall.
But I realized I can't have fun if other people are being discriminated against. There's no fun in that.
If only there was a way to have fun while fighting for everyone's freedom.

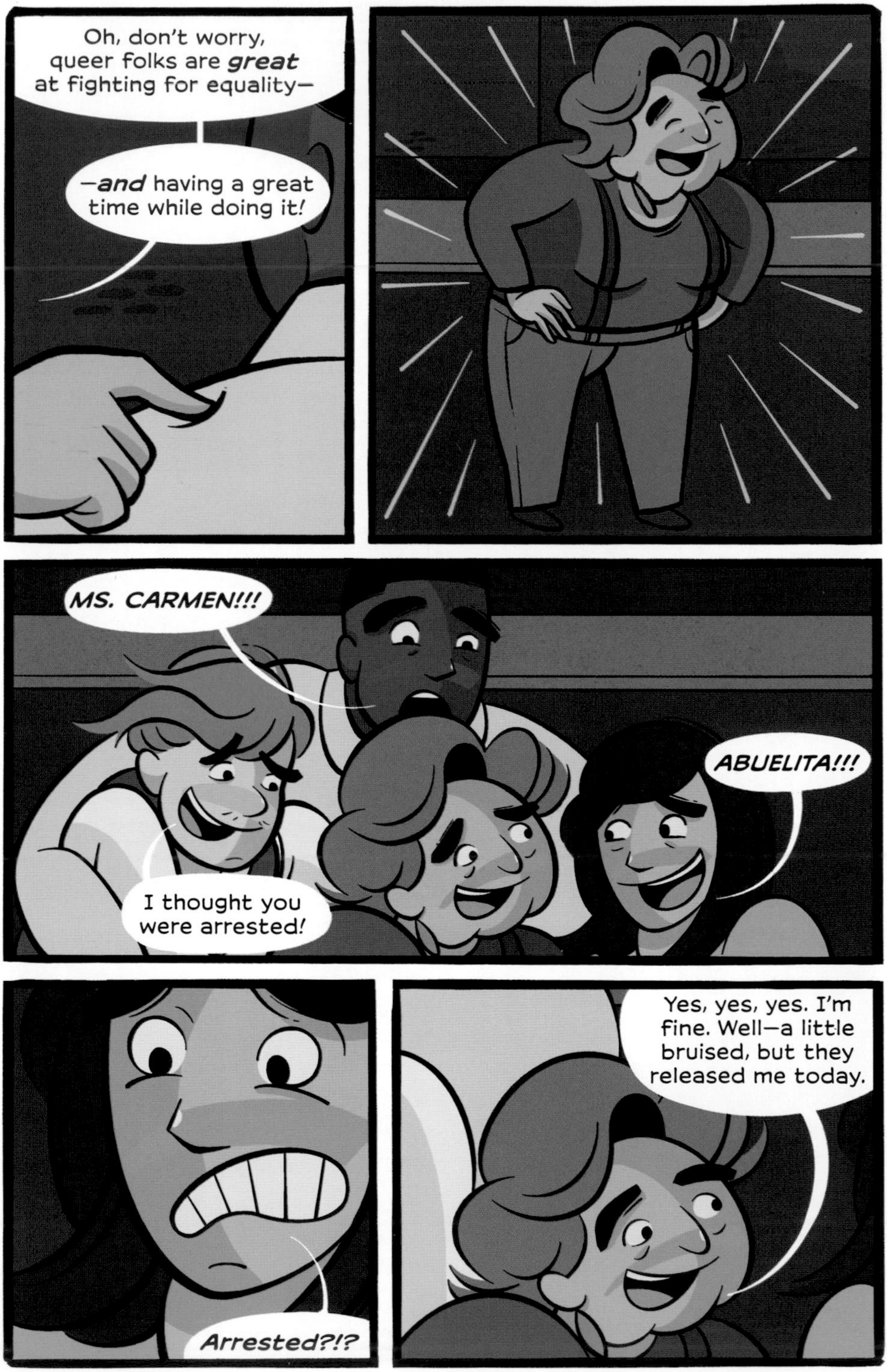
Oh, don't worry, queer folks are ***great*** at fighting for equality—
—***and*** having a great time while doing it!
MS. CARMEN!!!
I thought you were arrested!
ABUELITA!!!
Arrested?!?
Yes, yes, yes. I'm fine. Well—a little bruised, but they released me today.

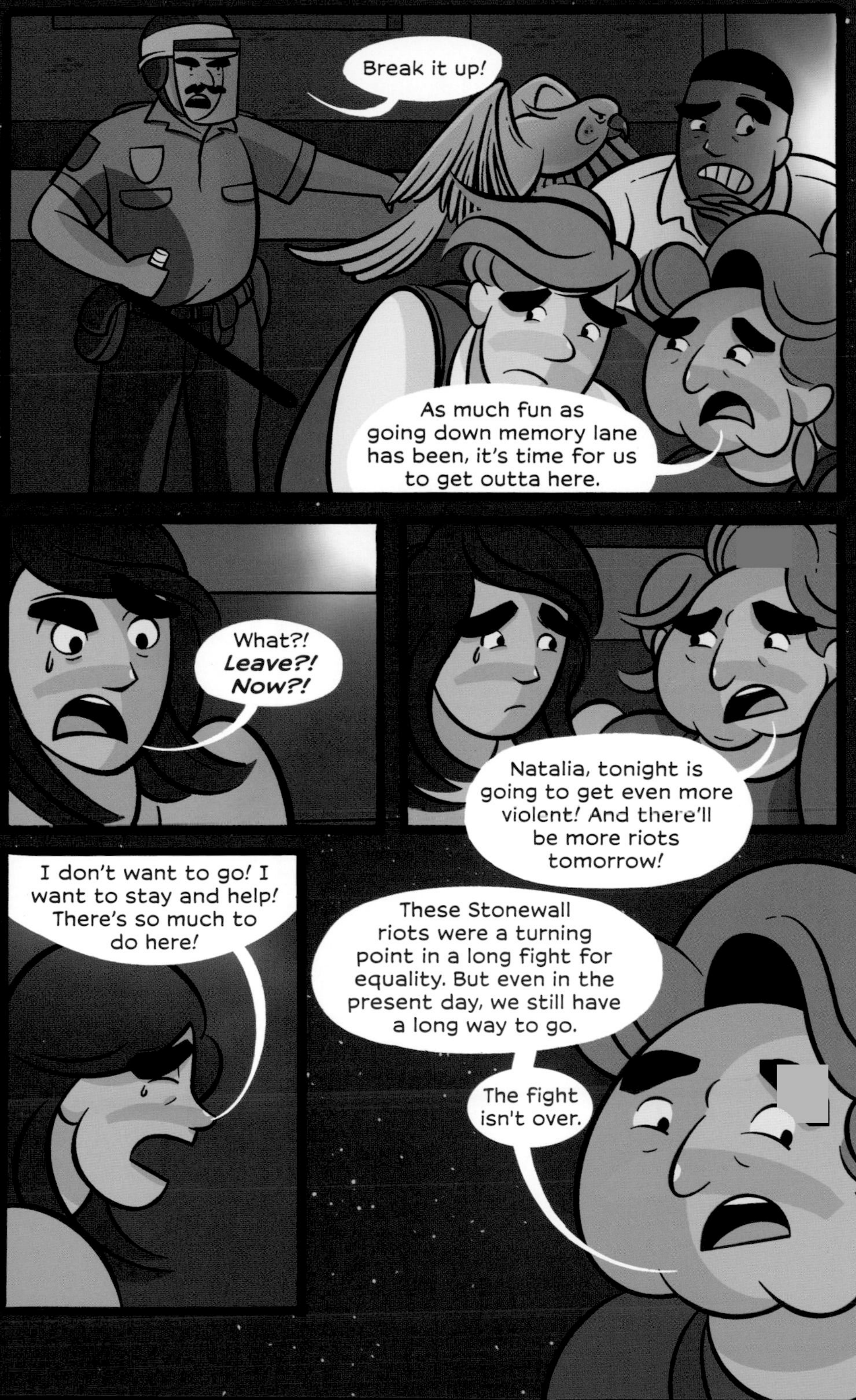
Break it up!
As much fun as going down memory lane has been, it's time for us to get outta here.
What?! Leave?! Now?!
Natalia, tonight is going to get even more violent! And there'll be more riots tomorrow!
I don't want to go! I want to stay and help! There's so much to do here!
These Stonewall riots were a turning point in a long fight for equality. But even in the present day, we still have a long way to go.
The fight isn't over.

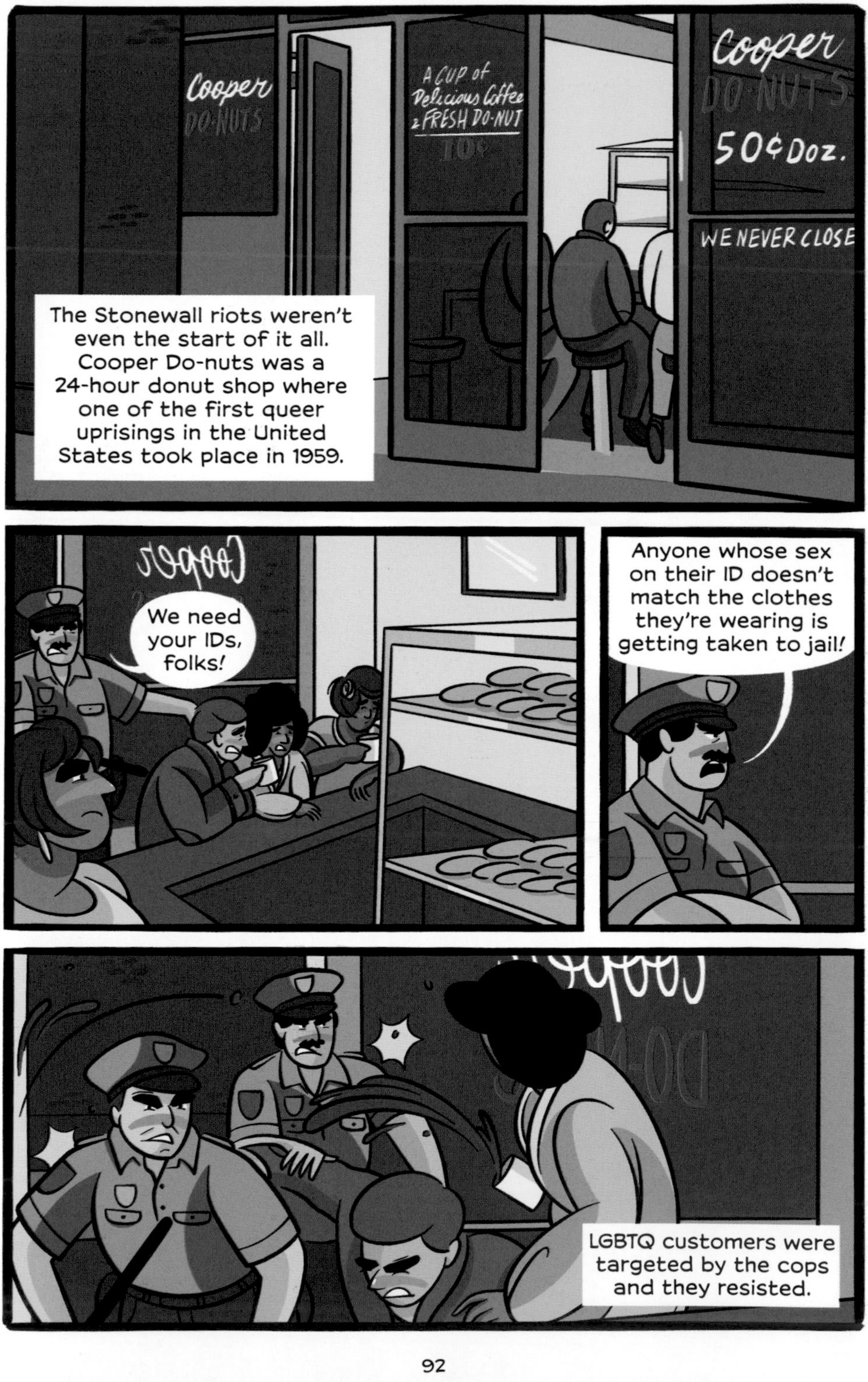
Cooper
DO-NUTS
A CUP of Delicious Coffee & FRESH DO-NUT 10¢
Cooper
DO-NUTS
50¢ Doz.
WE NEVER CLOSE
The Stonewall riots weren't even the start of it all. Cooper Do-nuts was a 24-hour donut shop where one of the first queer uprisings in the United States took place in 1959.
We need your IDs, folks!
Anyone whose sex on their ID doesn't match the clothes they're wearing is getting taken to jail!
LGBTQ customers were targeted by the cops and they resisted.

In 1965, a hamburger joint called Dewey's refused service to anyone they perceived as gay, transgender, or gender-nonconforming.

Three teenagers staged a sit-in, where they refused to leave until they were arrested.

The next week they partnered with activist Clark Polak and the Janus Society and handed out more than 1,500 leaflets about the incident and staged another sit-in.

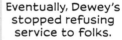

Eventually, Dewey's stopped refusing service to folks.

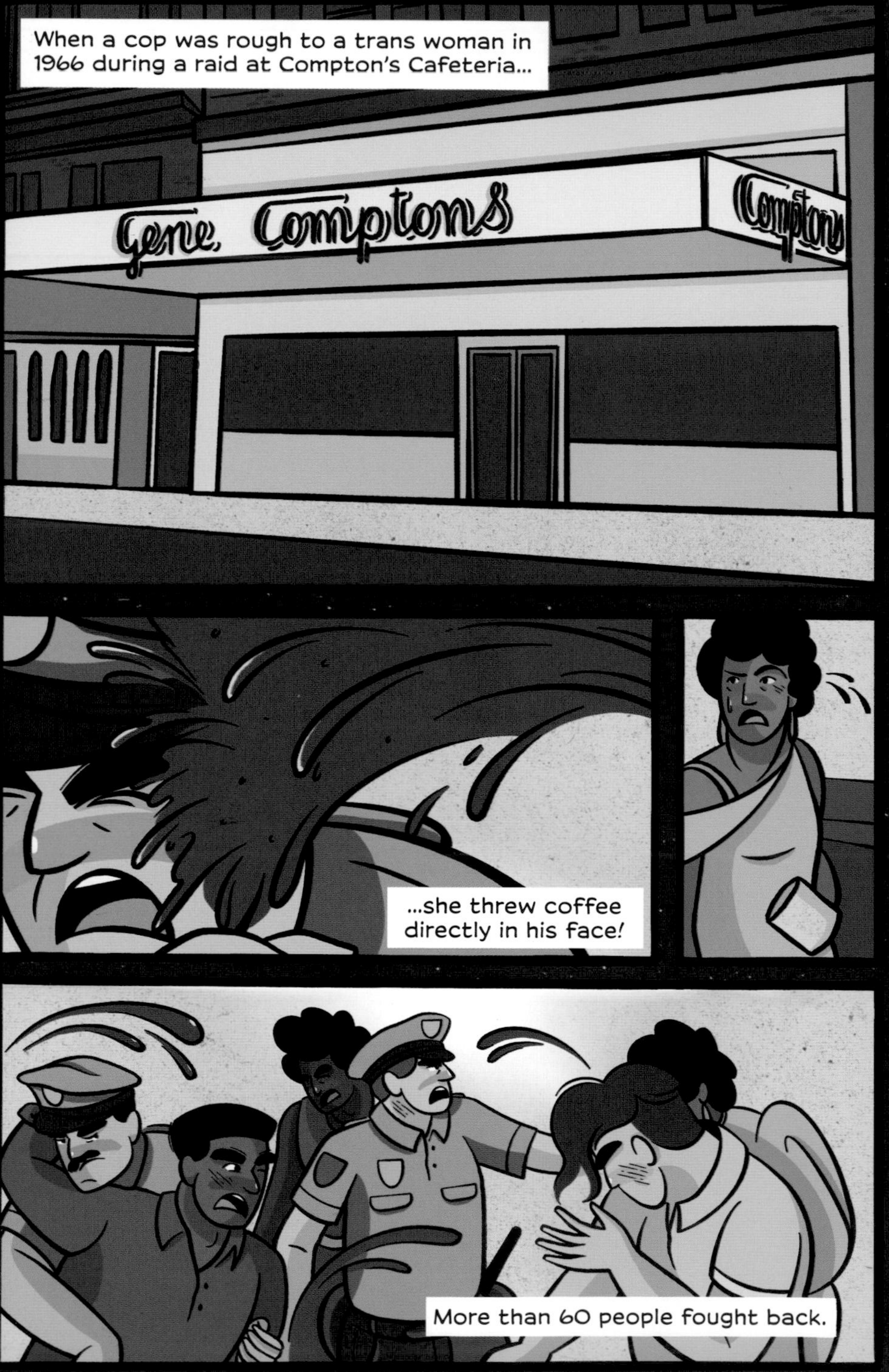
When a cop was rough to a trans woman in 1966 during a raid at Compton's Cafeteria...
Gene Comptons
Comptons
...she threw coffee directly in his face!
More than 60 people fought back.

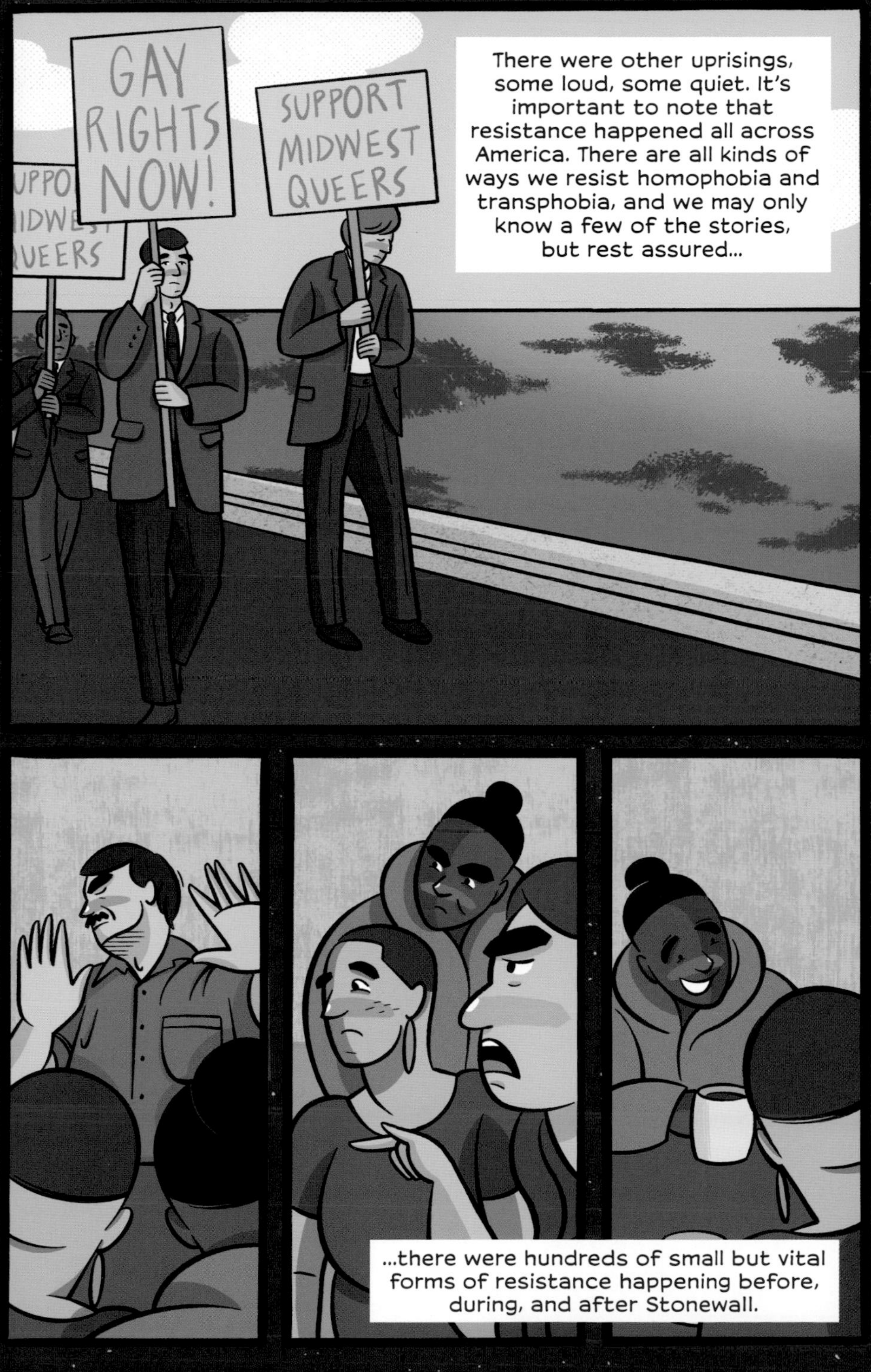
GAY RIGHTS NOW!
SUPPORT MIDWEST QUEERS
UPPO IDWE QUEERS
There were other uprisings, some loud, some quiet. It's important to note that resistance happened all across America. There are all kinds of ways we resist homophobia and transphobia, and we may only know a few of the stories, but rest assured...
...there were hundreds of small but vital forms of resistance happening before, during, and after Stonewall.

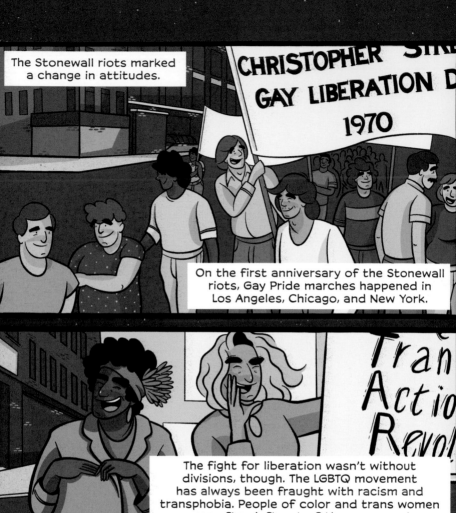

The Stonewall riots marked a change in attitudes.
CHRISTOPHER
GAY LIBERATION
1970
On the first anniversary of the Stonewall riots, Gay Pride marches happened in Los Angeles, Chicago, and New York.
Tran
Actio
Revol
The fight for liberation wasn't without divisions, though. The LGBTQ movement has always been fraught with racism and transphobia. People of color and trans women were often left out of the movement, including our friends Sylvia and Marsha.
Street
Transve
Action
The two of them cofounded STAR, which helped homeless and trans youth. They were often at demonstrations, marches, and political actions.

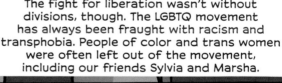

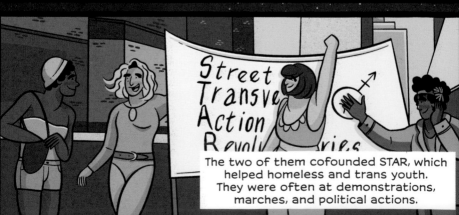

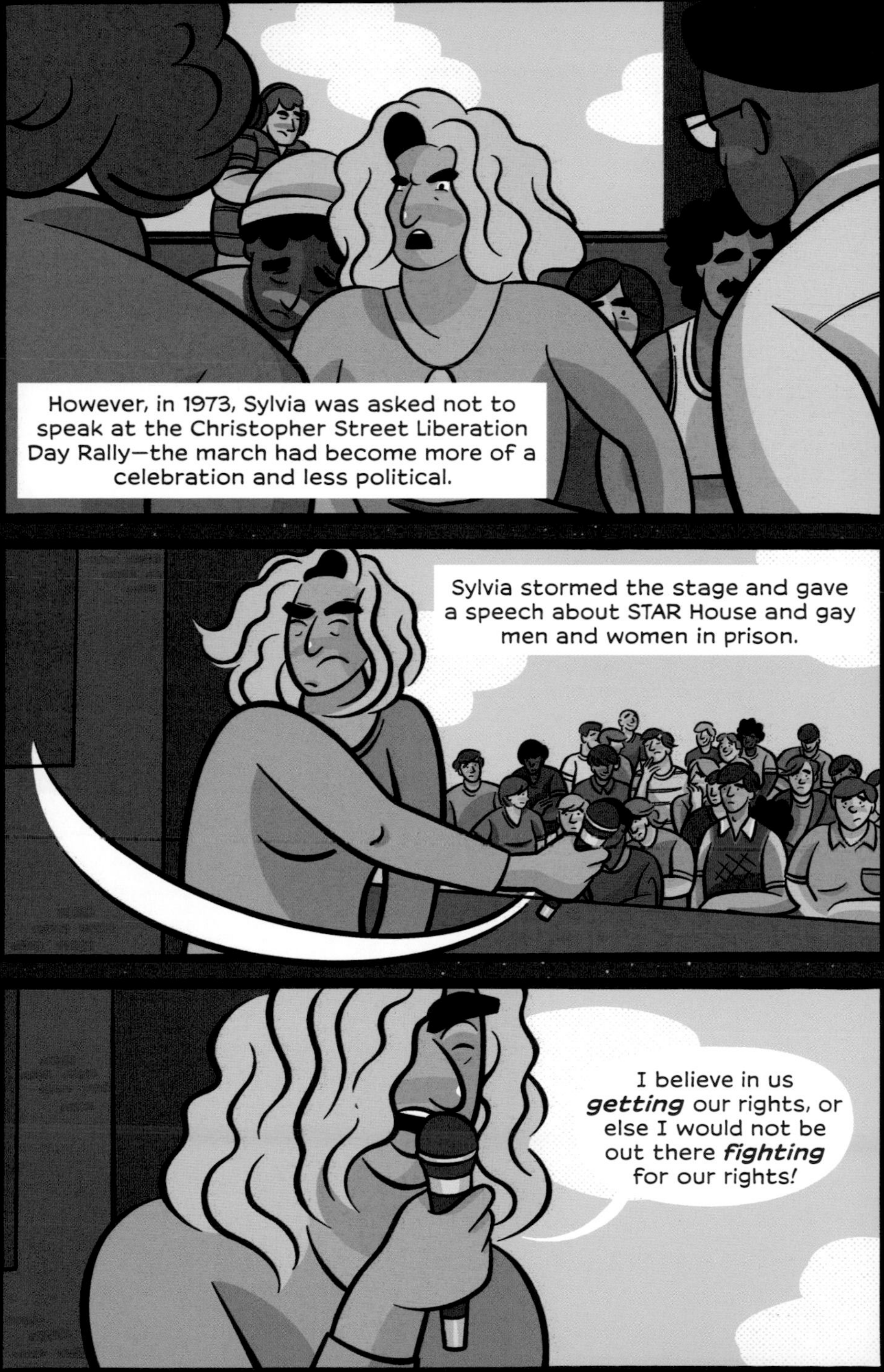
However, in 1973, Sylvia was asked not to speak at the Christopher Street Liberation Day Rally—the march had become more of a celebration and less political.
Sylvia stormed the stage and gave a speech about STAR House and gay men and women in prison.
I believe in us *getting* our rights, or else I would not be out there *fighting* for our rights!

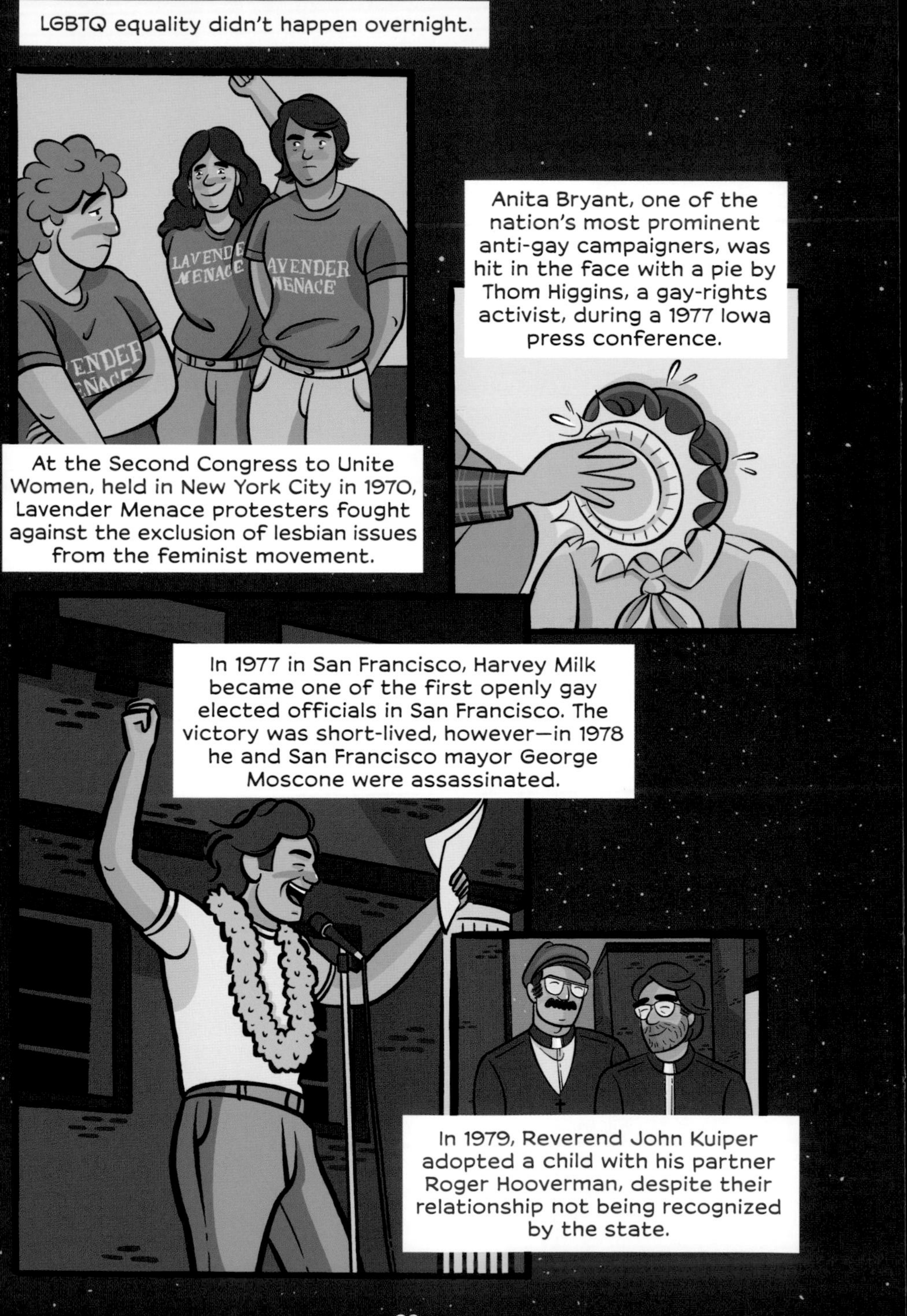
LGBTQ equality didn't happen overnight.
At the Second Congress to Unite Women, held in New York City in 1970, Lavender Menace protesters fought against the exclusion of lesbian issues from the feminist movement.
Anita Bryant, one of the nation's most prominent anti-gay campaigners, was hit in the face with a pie by Thom Higgins, a gay-rights activist, during a 1977 Iowa press conference.
In 1977 in San Francisco, Harvey Milk became one of the first openly gay elected officials in San Francisco. The victory was short-lived, however—in 1978 he and San Francisco mayor George Moscone were assassinated.
In 1979, Reverend John Kuiper adopted a child with his partner Roger Hooverman, despite their relationship not being recognized by the state.

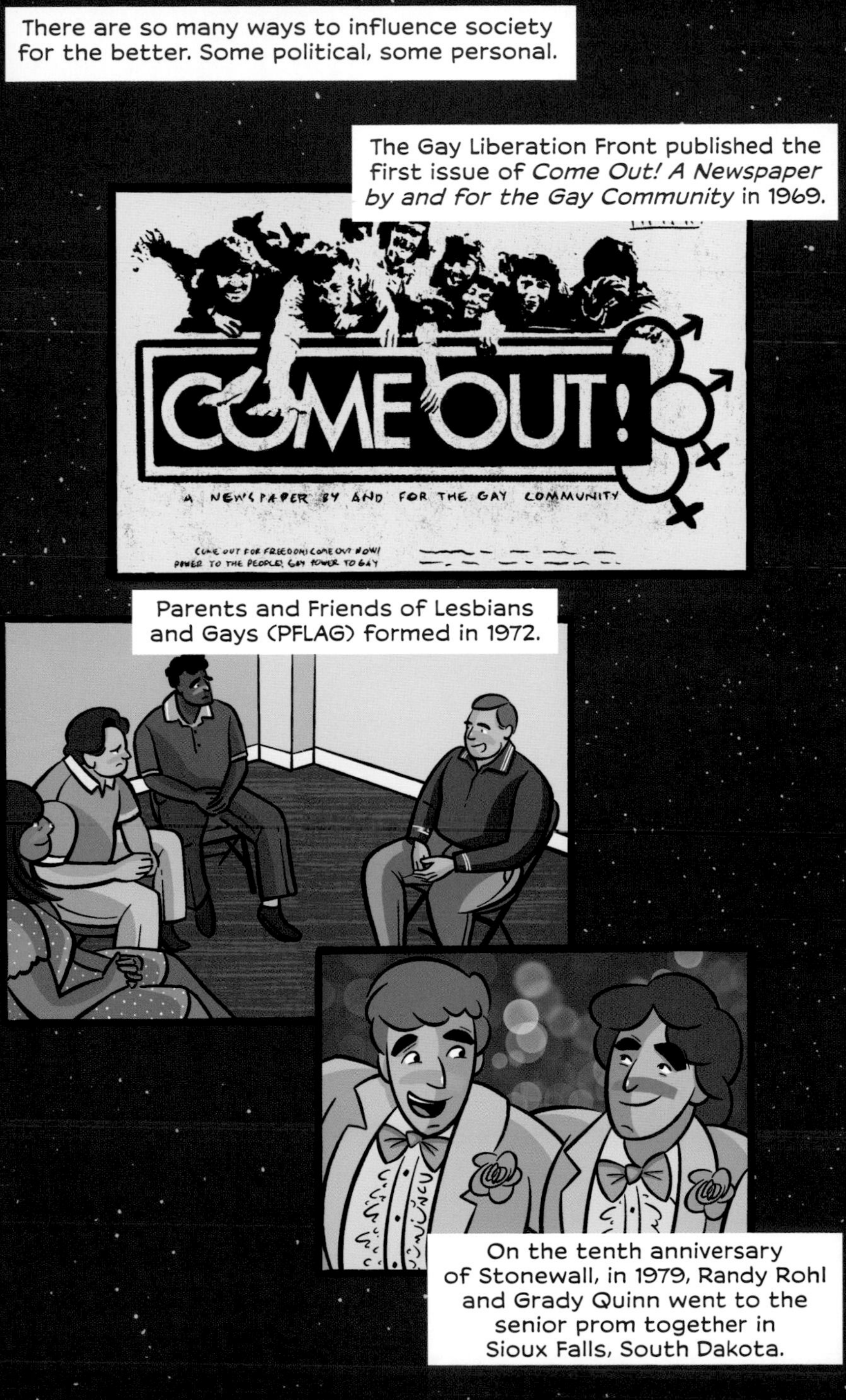
There are so many ways to influence society for the better. Some political, some personal.
The Gay Liberation Front published the first issue of *Come Out! A Newspaper by and for the Gay Community* in 1969.
COME OUT!
A NEWSPAPER BY AND FOR THE GAY COMMUNITY
COME OUT FOR FREEDOM! COME OUT NOW!
POWER TO THE PEOPLE! GAY POWER TO GAY
Parents and Friends of Lesbians and Gays (PFLAG) formed in 1972.
On the tenth anniversary of Stonewall, in 1979, Randy Rohl and Grady Quinn went to the senior prom together in Sioux Falls, South Dakota.

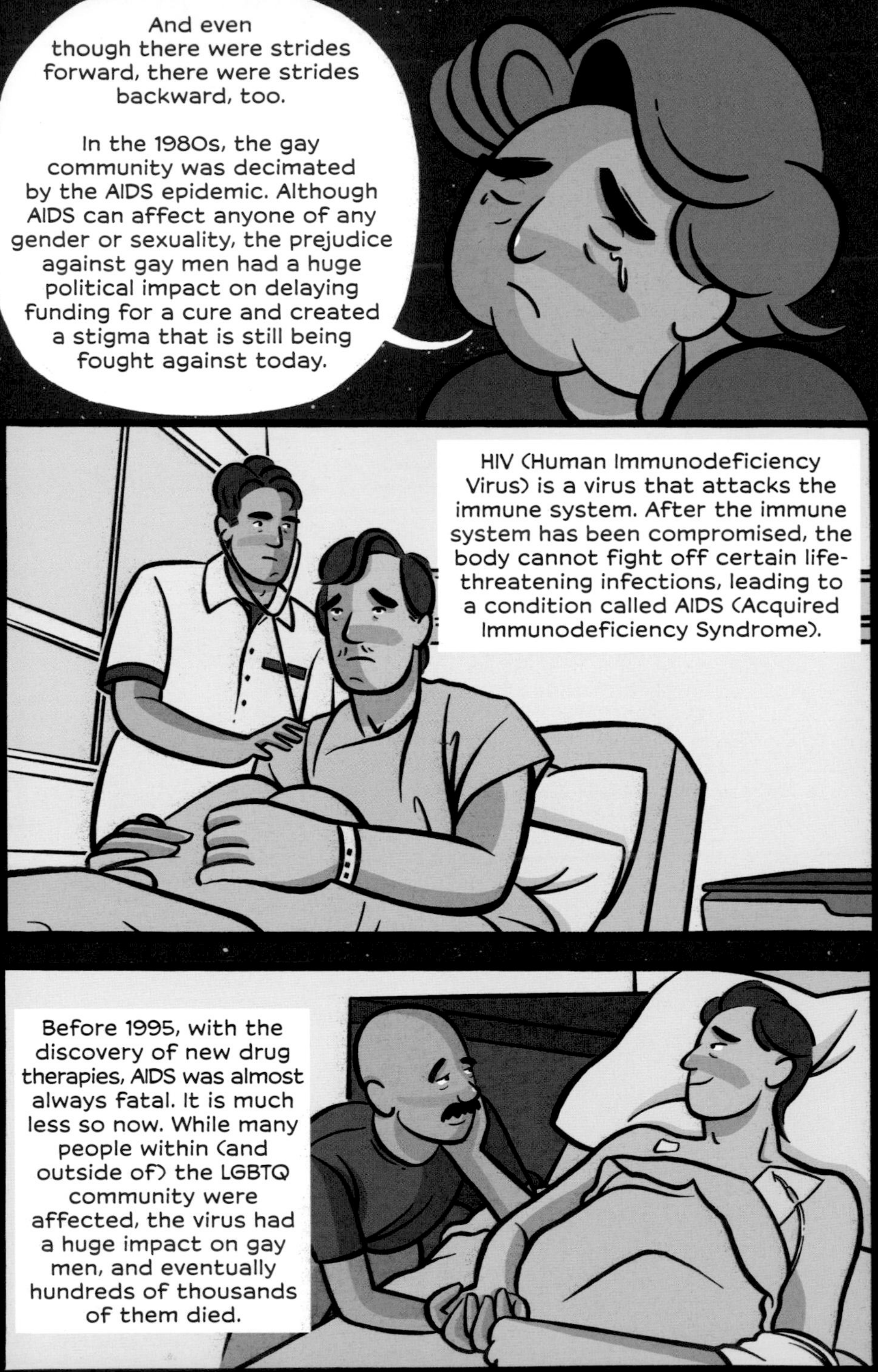
And even though there were strides forward, there were strides backward, too.
In the 1980s, the gay community was decimated by the AIDS epidemic. Although AIDS can affect anyone of any gender or sexuality, the prejudice against gay men had a huge political impact on delaying funding for a cure and created a stigma that is still being fought against today.
HIV (Human Immunodeficiency Virus) is a virus that attacks the immune system. After the immune system has been compromised, the body cannot fight off certain life-threatening infections, leading to a condition called AIDS (Acquired Immunodeficiency Syndrome).
Before 1995, with the discovery of new drug therapies, AIDS was almost always fatal. It is much less so now. While many people within (and outside of) the LGBTQ community were affected, the virus had a huge impact on gay men, and eventually hundreds of thousands of them died.

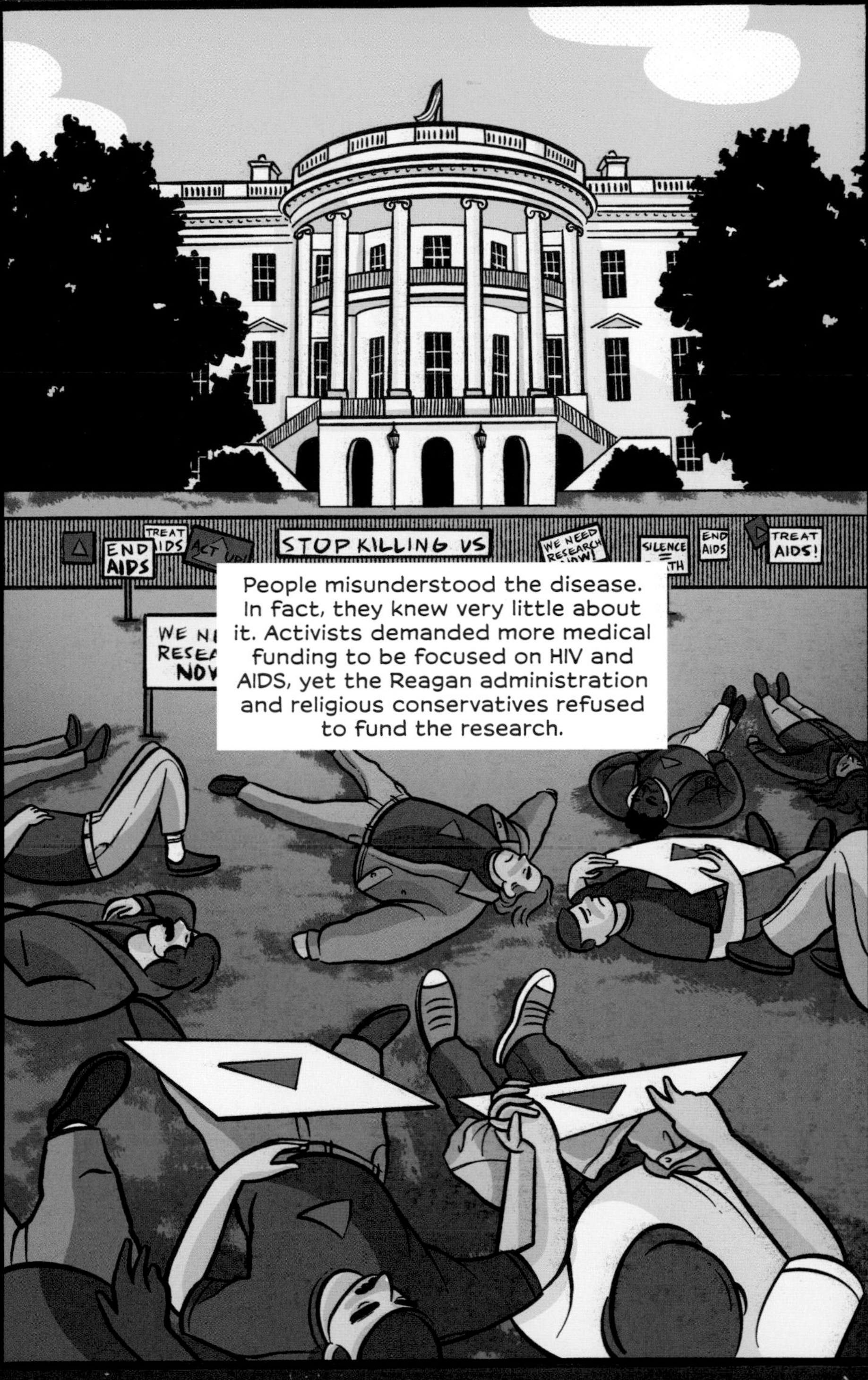
END AIDS
STOP KILLING US
END AIDS
TREAT AIDS!
People misunderstood the disease. In fact, they knew very little about it. Activists demanded more medical funding to be focused on HIV and AIDS, yet the Reagan administration and religious conservatives refused to fund the research.

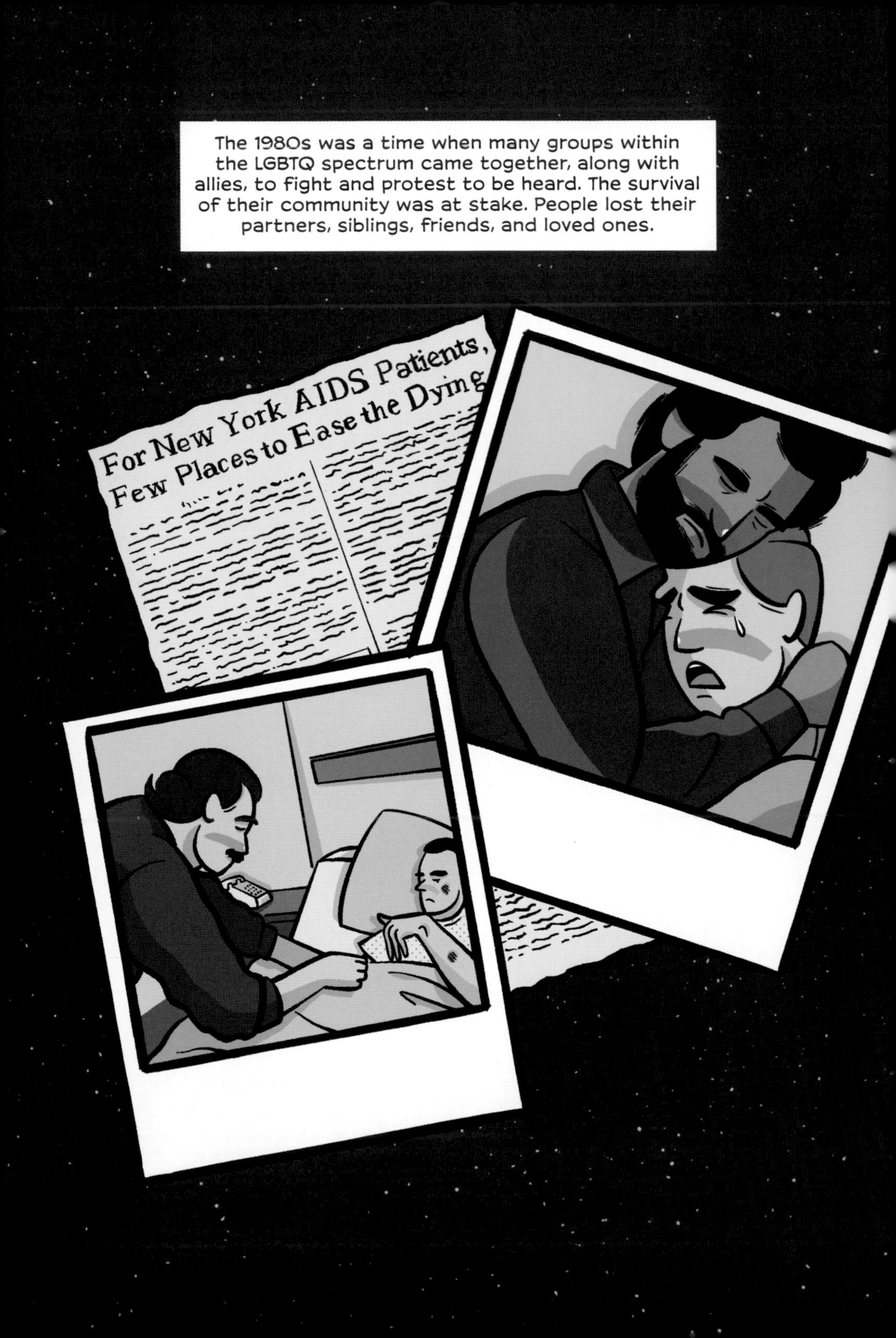
The 1980s was a time when many groups within the LGBTQ spectrum came together, along with allies, to fight and protest to be heard. The survival of their community was at stake. People lost their partners, siblings, friends, and loved ones.
For New York AIDS Patients, Few Places to Ease the Dying

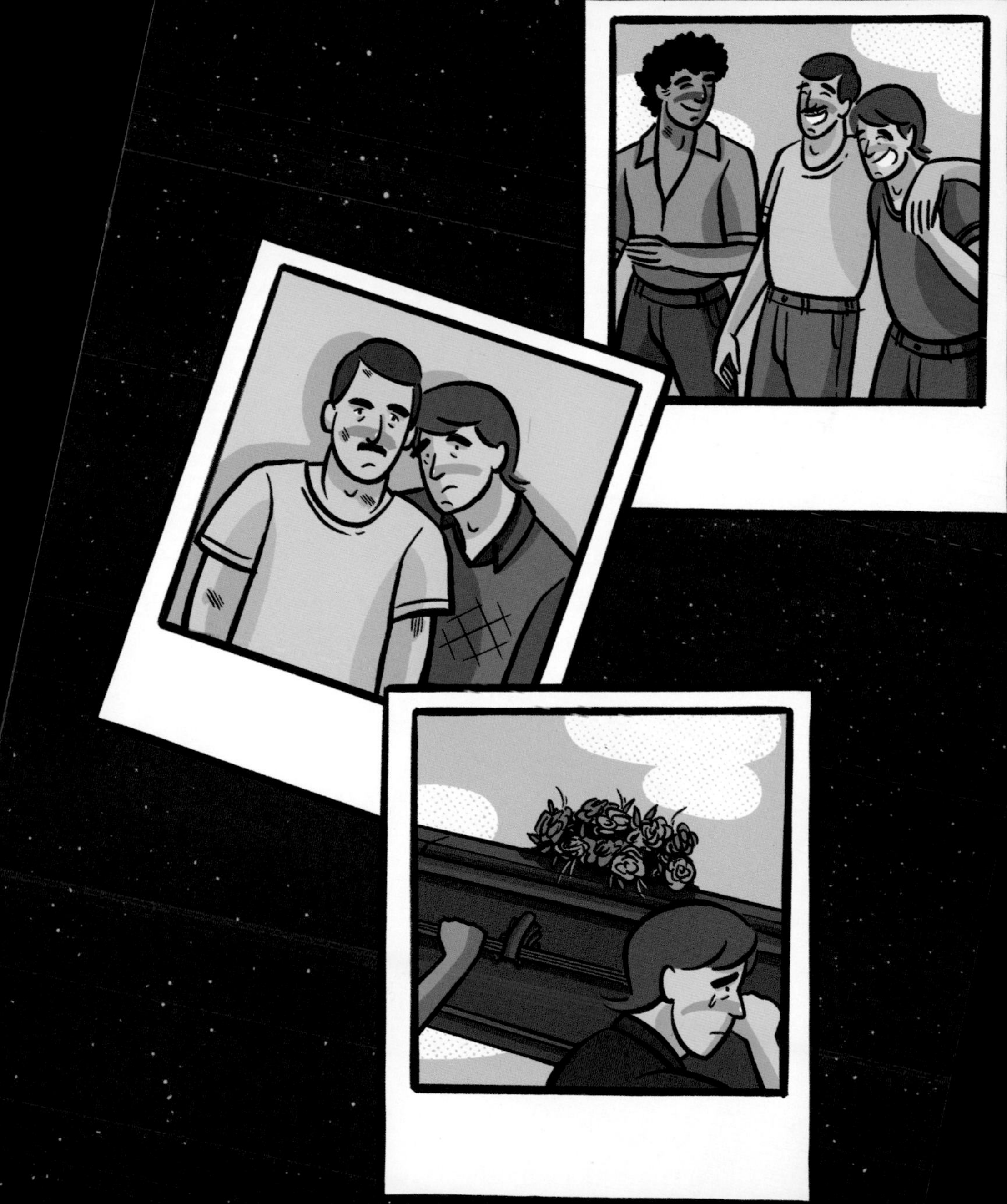

In 1987, AIDS Coalition to Unleash Power (ACT UP) was a collection of people working to end the AIDS epidemic through direct action, whose demands included medical research and treatment.

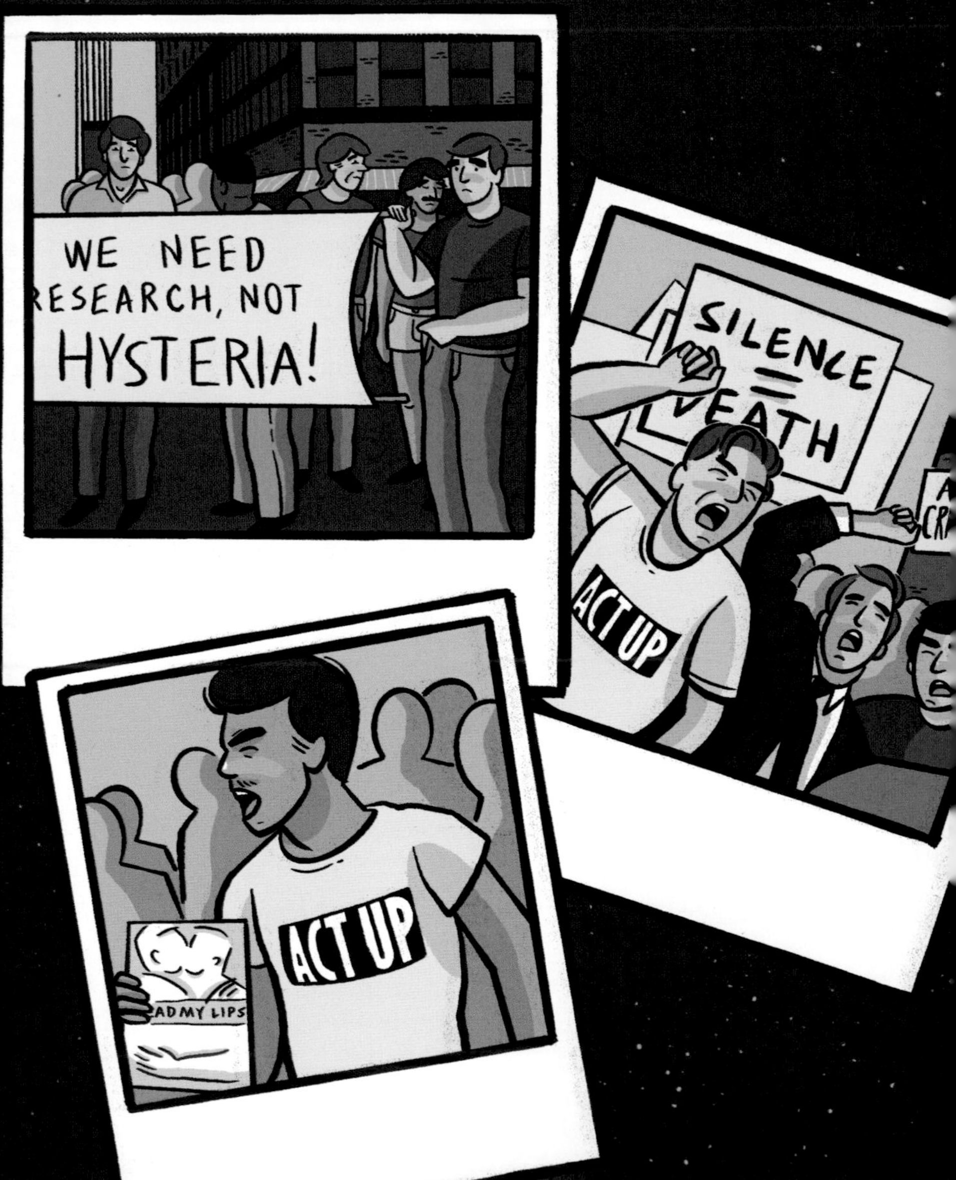
WE NEED
ESEARCH, NOT
HYSTERIA!
SILENCE
=
EATH
ACT UP
ACT UP
ADMY LIPS

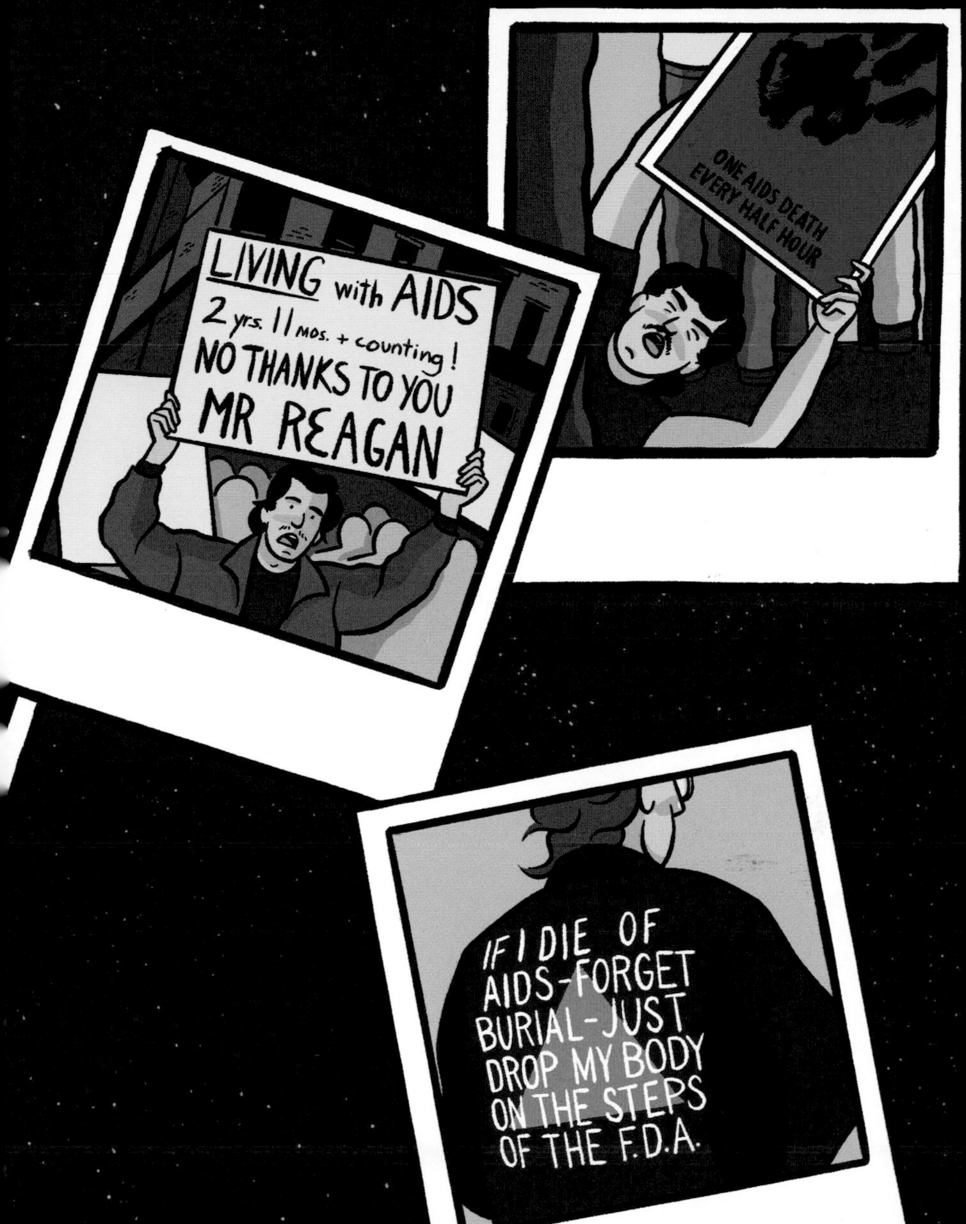

ONE AIDS DEATH EVERY HALF HOUR
LIVING with AIDS
2 yrs. 11 mos. + counting!
NO THANKS TO YOU
MR REAGAN
IF I DIE OF AIDS-FORGET BURIAL-JUST DROP MY BODY ON THE STEPS OF THE F.D.A.

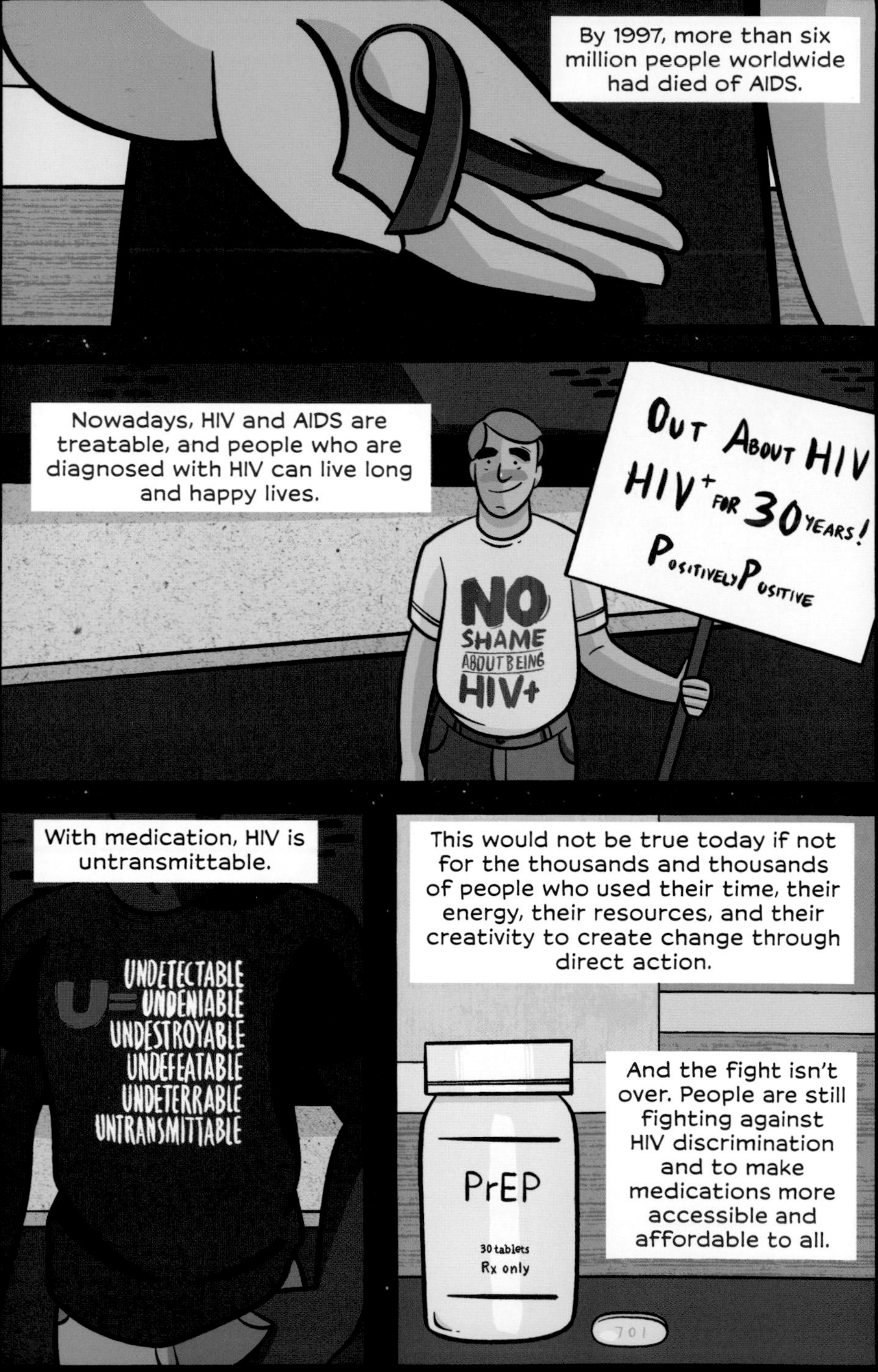
By 1997, more than six million people worldwide had died of AIDS.
Nowadays, HIV and AIDS are treatable, and people who are diagnosed with HIV can live long and happy lives.
OUT ABOUT HIV
HIV+ FOR 30 YEARS!
POSITIVELY POSITIVE
NO SHAME ABOUT BEING HIV+
With medication, HIV is untransmittable.
U=
UNDETECTABLE
UNDENIABLE
UNDESTROYABLE
UNDEFEATABLE
UNDETERRABLE
UNTRANSMITTABLE
This would not be true today if not for the thousands and thousands of people who used their time, their energy, their resources, and their creativity to create change through direct action.
PrEP
30 tablets
Rx only
701
And the fight isn't over. People are still fighting against HIV discrimination and to make medications more accessible and affordable to all.

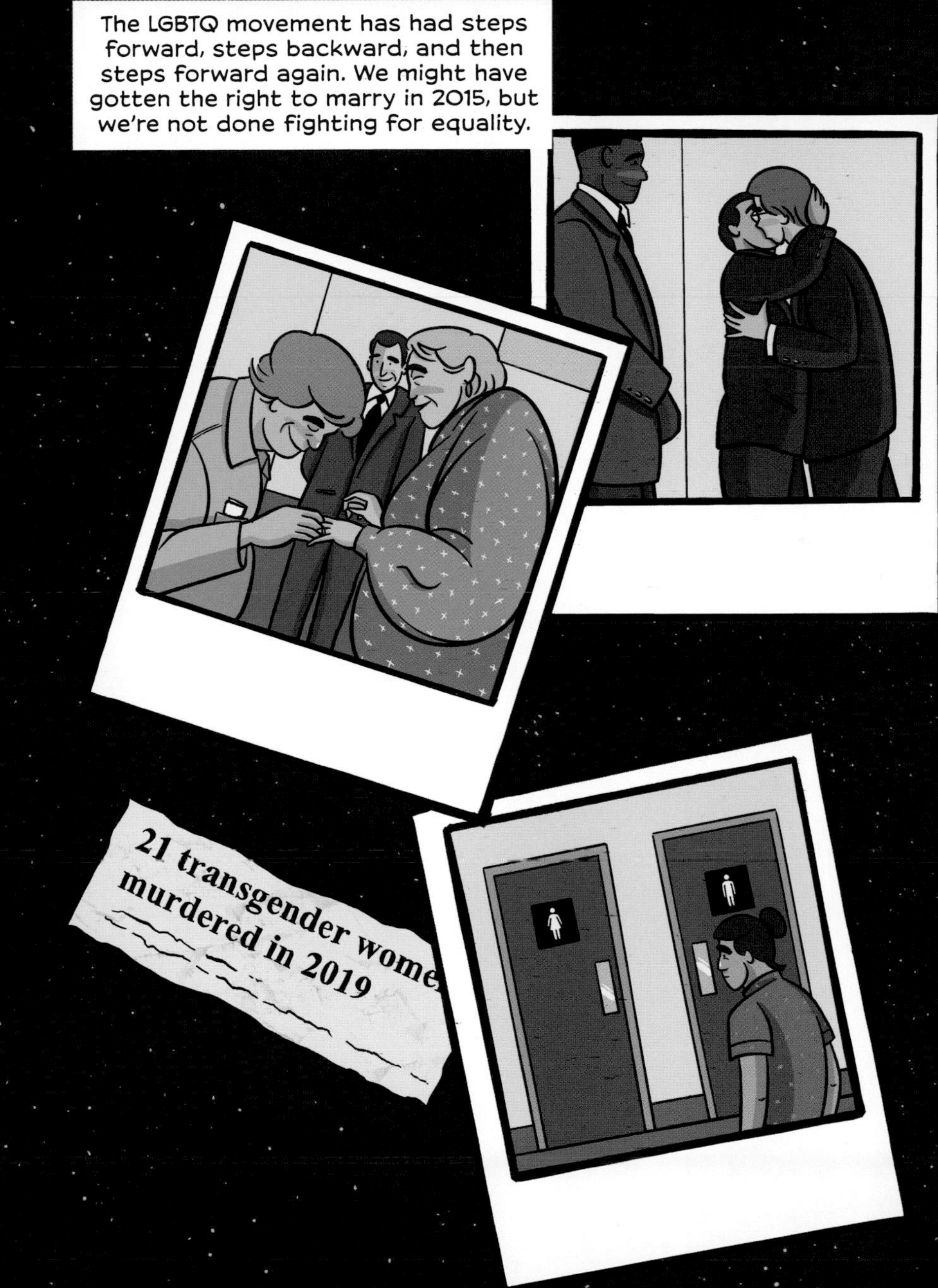
The LGBTQ movement has had steps forward, steps backward, and then steps forward again. We might have gotten the right to marry in 2015, but we're not done fighting for equality.
21 transgender wome
murdered in 2019

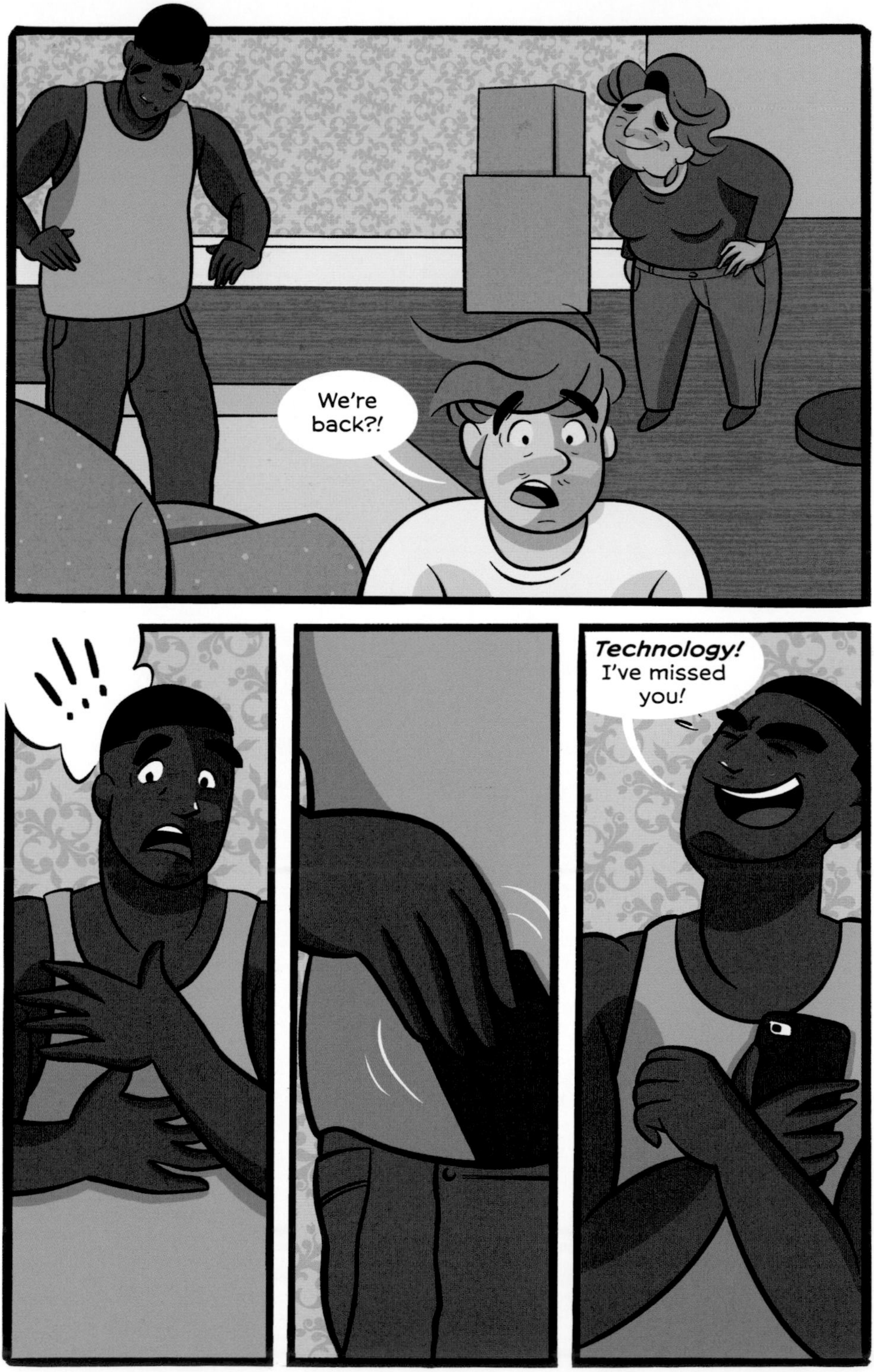
We're back?!
!!!
Technology! I've missed you!

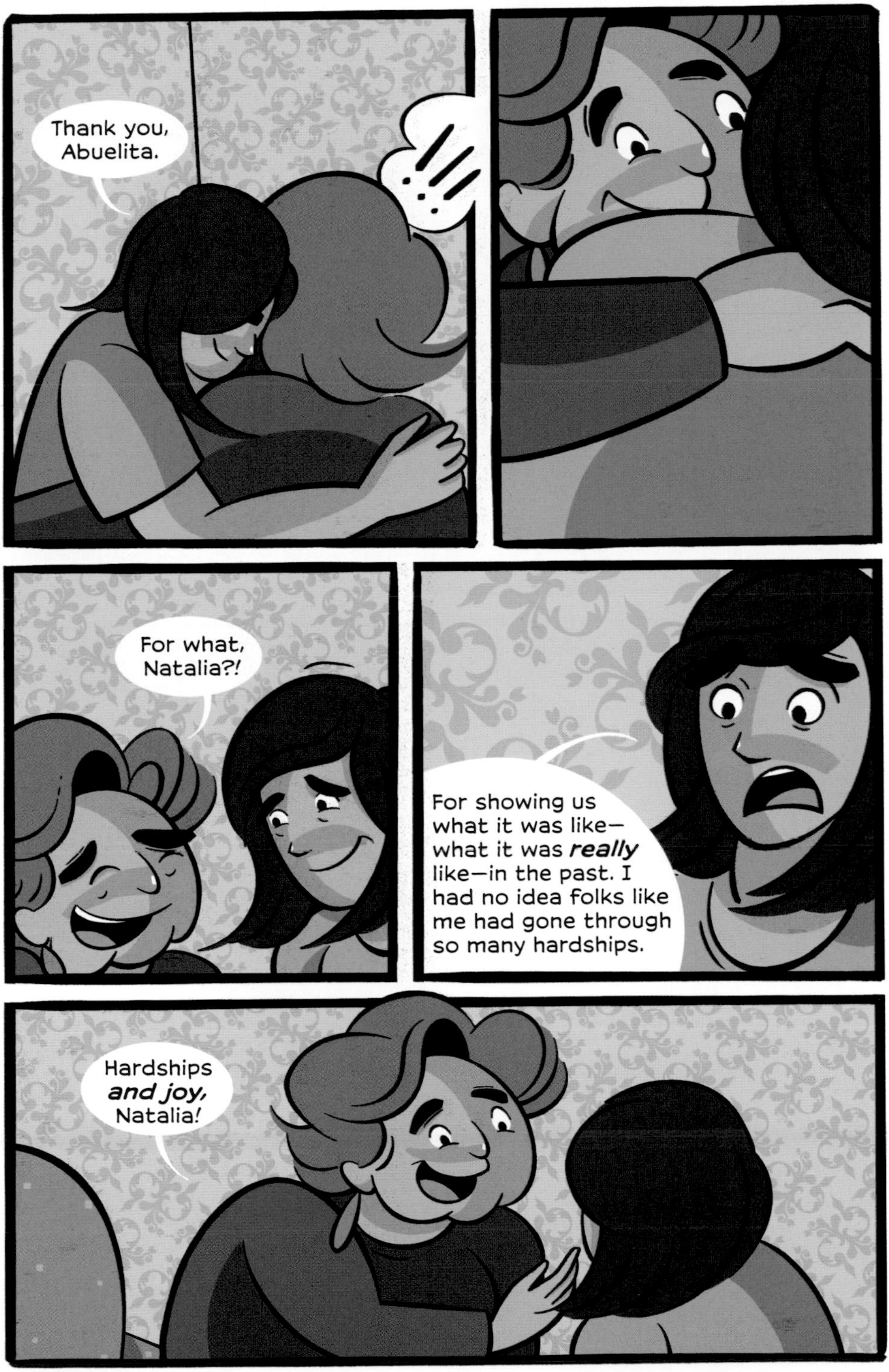
Thank you, Abuelita.
!
For what, Natalia?!
For showing us what it was like—what it was *really* like—in the past. I had no idea folks like me had gone through so many hardships.
Hardships *and joy,* Natalia!

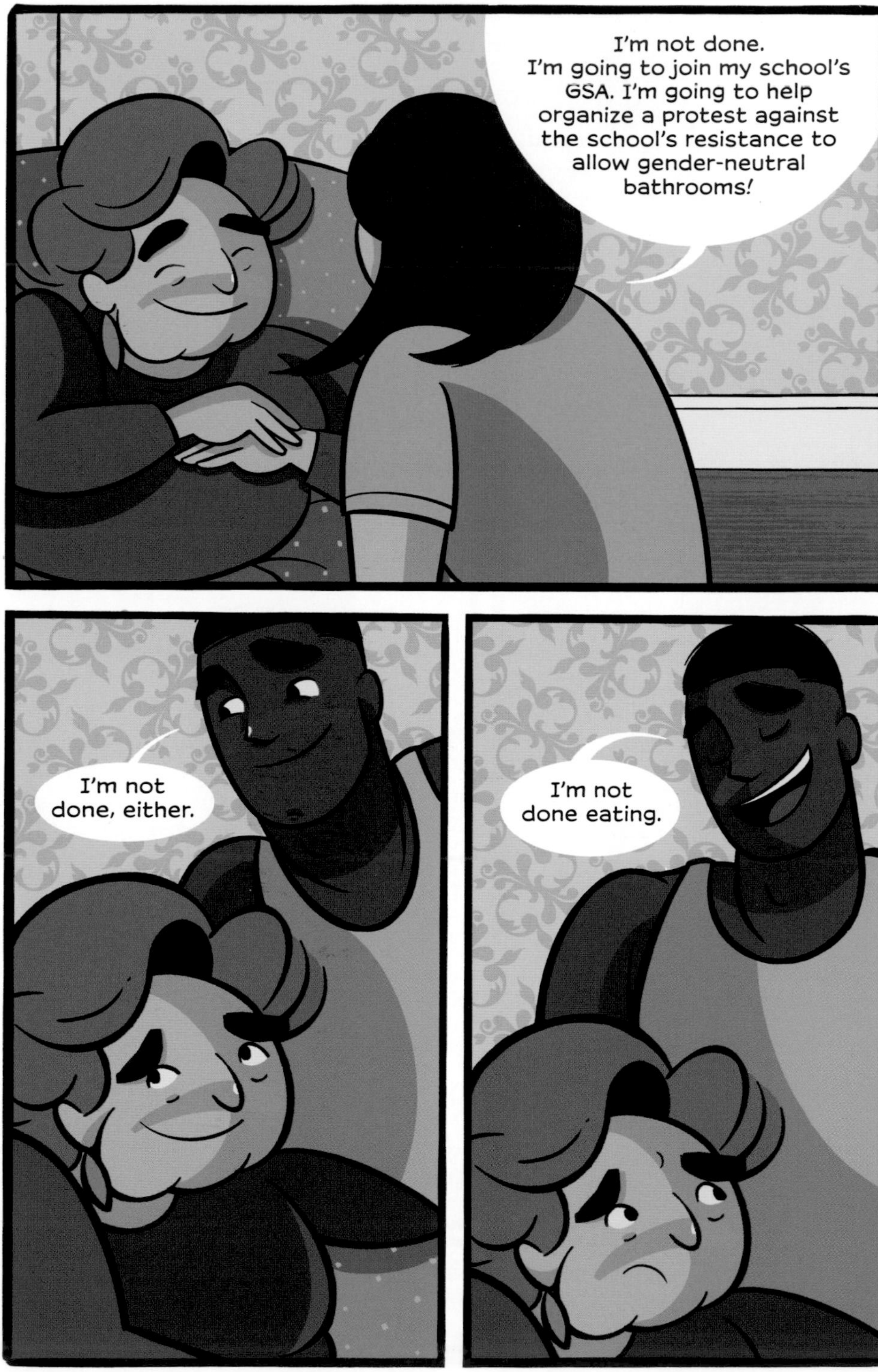
I'm not done. I'm going to join my school's GSA. I'm going to help organize a protest against the school's resistance to allow gender-neutral bathrooms!
I'm not done, either.
I'm not done eating.

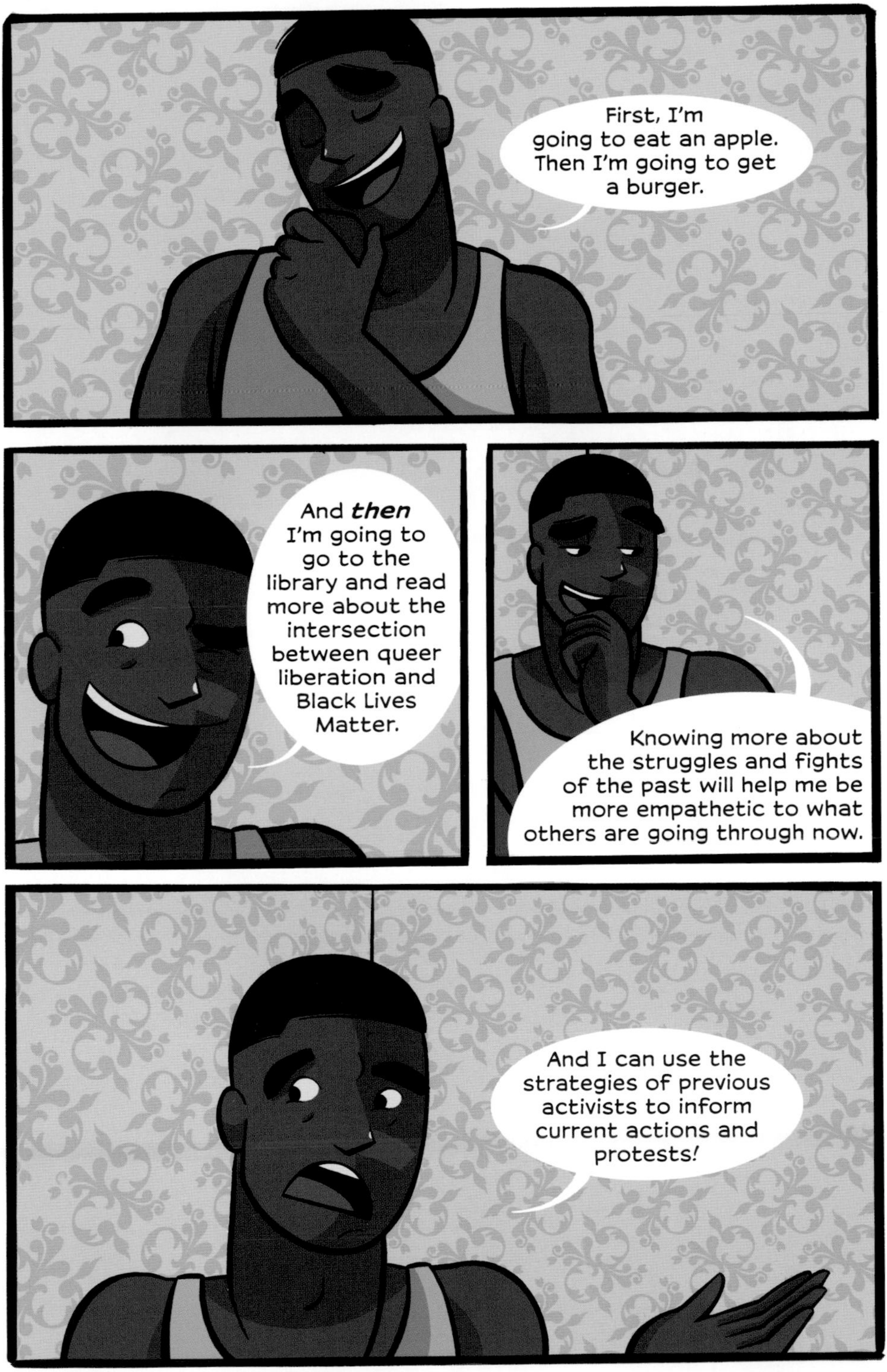
First, I'm going to eat an apple. Then I'm going to get a burger.
And *then* I'm going to go to the library and read more about the intersection between queer liberation and Black Lives Matter.
Knowing more about the struggles and fights of the past will help me be more empathetic to what others are going through now.
And I can use the strategies of previous activists to inform current actions and protests!

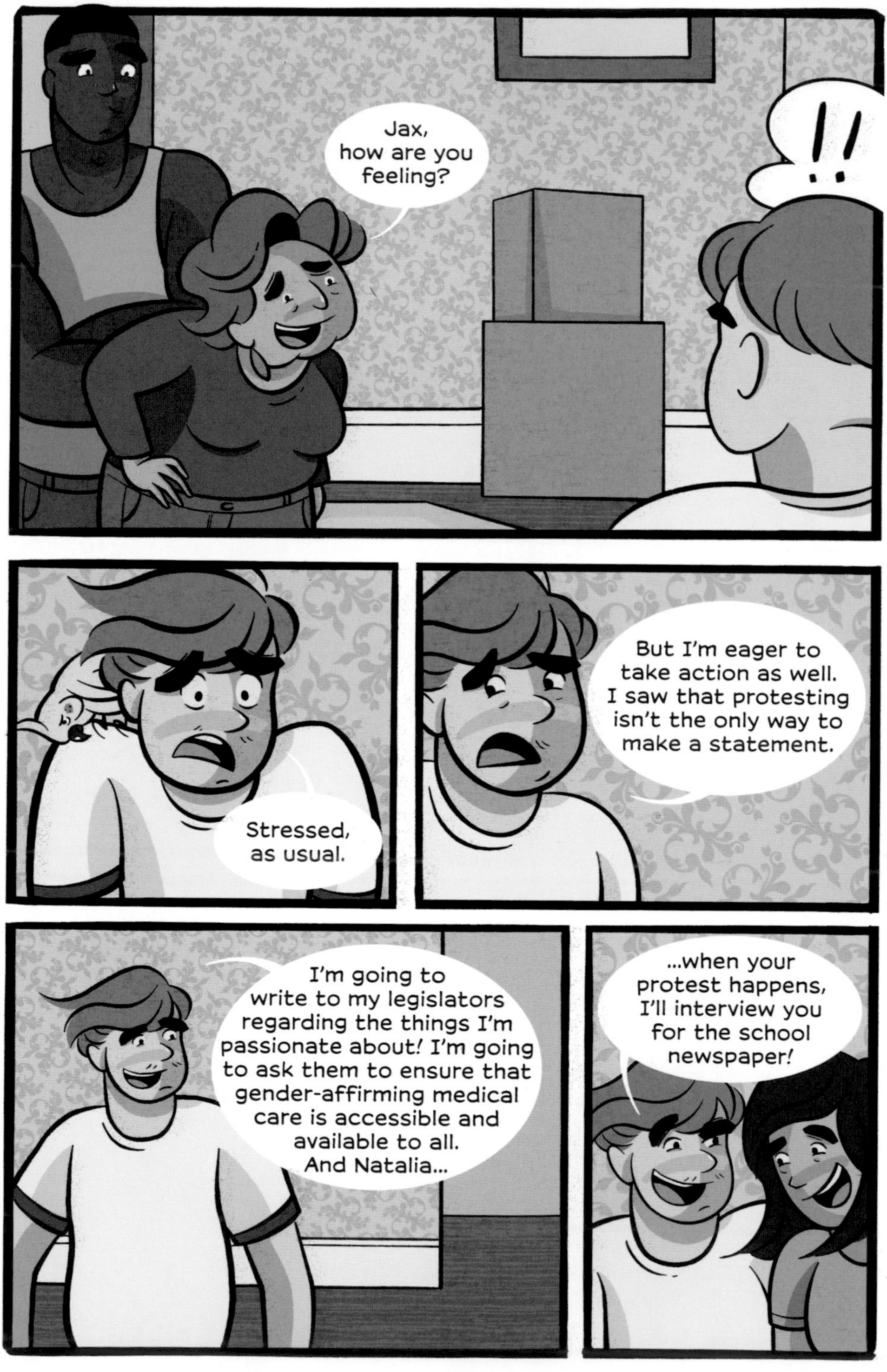
Jax,
how are you
feeling?
!!
Stressed,
as usual.
But I'm eager to
take action as well.
I saw that protesting
isn't the only way to
make a statement.
I'm going to
write to my legislators
regarding the things I'm
passionate about! I'm going
to ask them to ensure that
gender-affirming medical
care is accessible and
available to all.
And Natalia...
...when your
protest happens,
I'll interview you
for the school
newspaper!

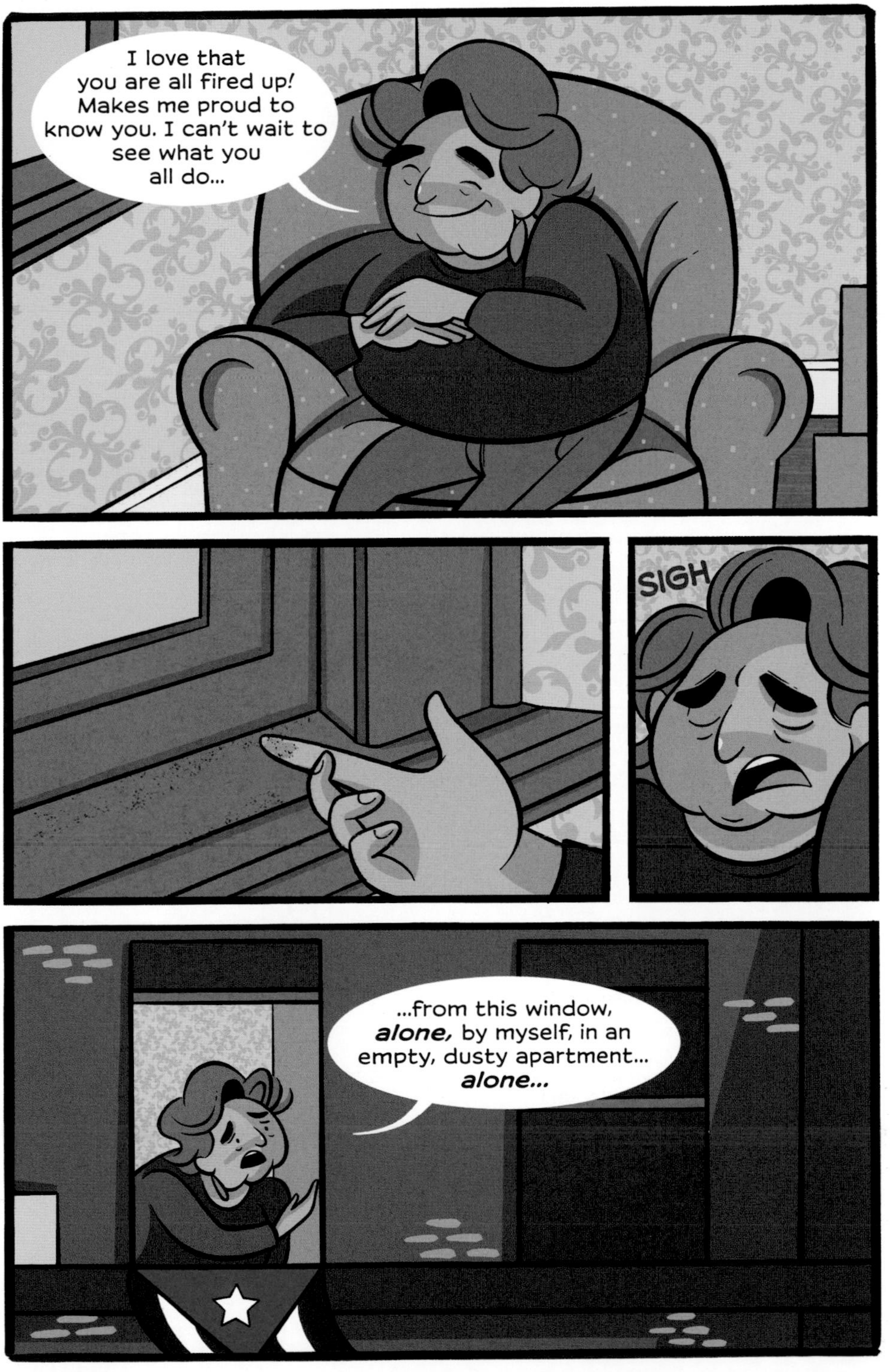
I love that you are all fired up! Makes me proud to know you. I can't wait to see what you all do...
SIGH
...from this window, ***alone,*** by myself, in an empty, dusty apartment... ***alone...***

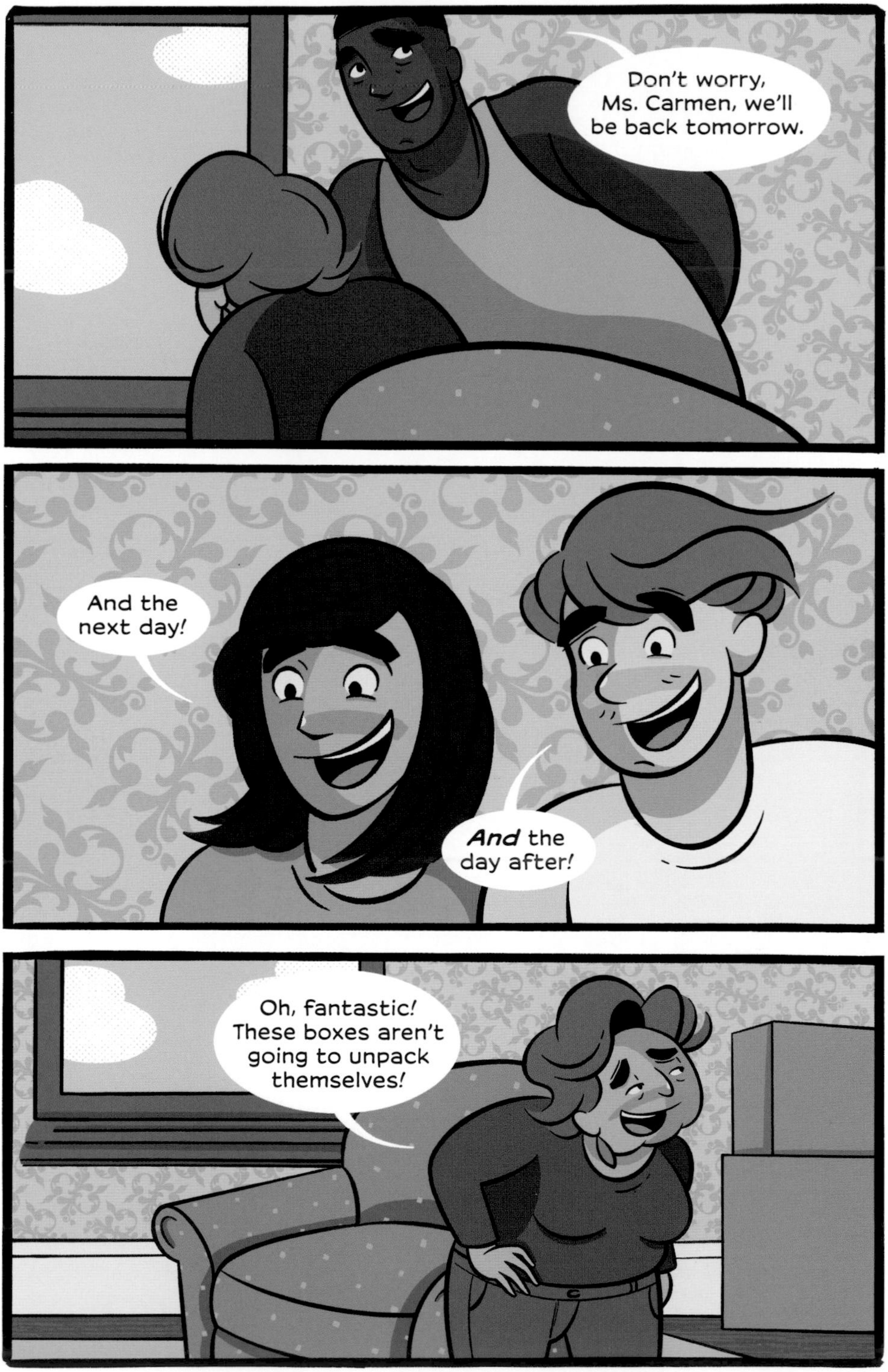
Don't worry, Ms. Carmen, we'll be back tomorrow.
And the next day!
And the day after!
Oh, fantastic! These boxes aren't going to unpack themselves!

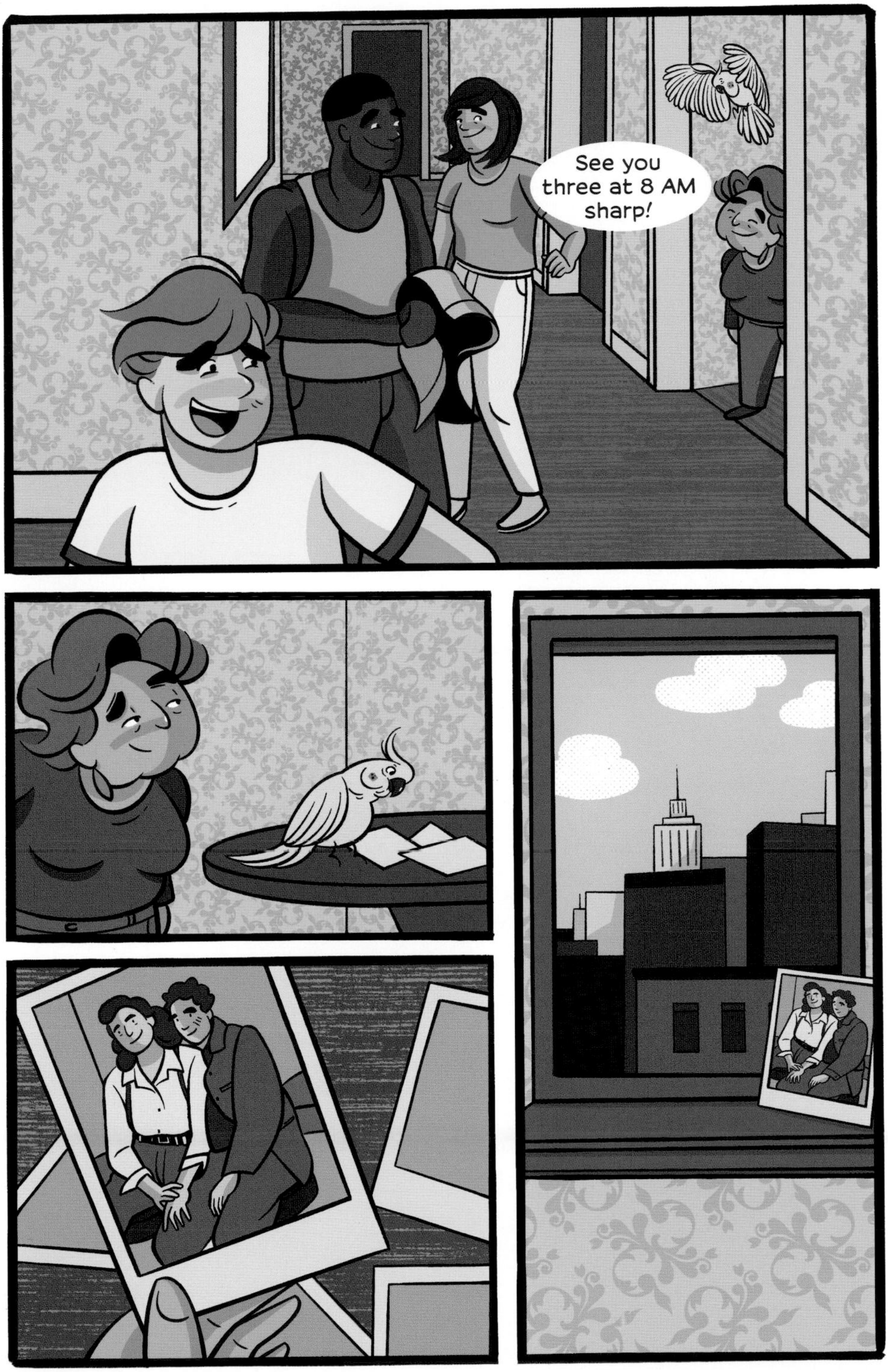
See you three at 8 AM sharp!

Author's Note

This graphic novel is not 100 percent true. Much of what we know about the Stonewall riots comes from oral history, meaning one account might not match another person's description of that night and sometimes people's narratives contradict each other. This is a common issue with history—whoever tells the story or documents the story alters the record. There's some playfulness in this particular version—Marsha P. Johnson and Sylvia Rivera did not talk to three kids from the future in Stonewall on that fateful night. My hope is that my account of the Stonewall riots—the essence, heart, and courage—remains the same as those of the people who were experiencing the riots in 1969.

—Archie Bongiovanni

Other LGBTQ Resources for Youth

The Trevor Project: a national organization providing crisis intervention and suicide prevention services to lesbian, gay, bisexual, transgender, queer, and questioning youth. *thetrevorproject.org*

GLSEN: GLSEN works to ensure that LGBTQ students are able to learn and grow in a school environment free from bullying and harassment. *glsen.org*

GSA NETWORK: trans and queer youth uniting to fight for racial and gender justice. *gsanetwork.org*

The Safe Zone Project: an online resource for LGBTQ awareness and ally training workshops. *thesafezoneproject.com*

A Letter To Young LGBTQI Activists
(Written by an Activist)

Dear Young LGBTQI Activists,

The truly difficult thing about being an advocate for equality is that the time, tears, and effort you pour into this important work are an imposition. Even as you refuse to exist as those who hate you say you must, the ability to live in society as freely as cisgender heterosexual people do will be withheld from you. Even if we achieved equality tomorrow, our history will be defined by our reactions to hate, and in this way, another's toxicity will, at least in part, define who we become: survivors.

As Audre Lorde wrote, "Caring for myself is not self-indulgence, it is self-preservation, and that is an act of political warfare." It is the difficult work of an activist to be aware of one's own needs and boundaries, ensuring that the fire of compassion burns just as bright for our own well-being. That isn't to say that activism is about never inconveniencing oneself; rather, the goal of activism is to extend respect to yourself even as you extend it to others. In fact, it is this relationship of respect—one of mutual consideration—that is the basis of community, and community is the only power that can truly stand against oppression.

Respectfully yours,

Cristan Williams

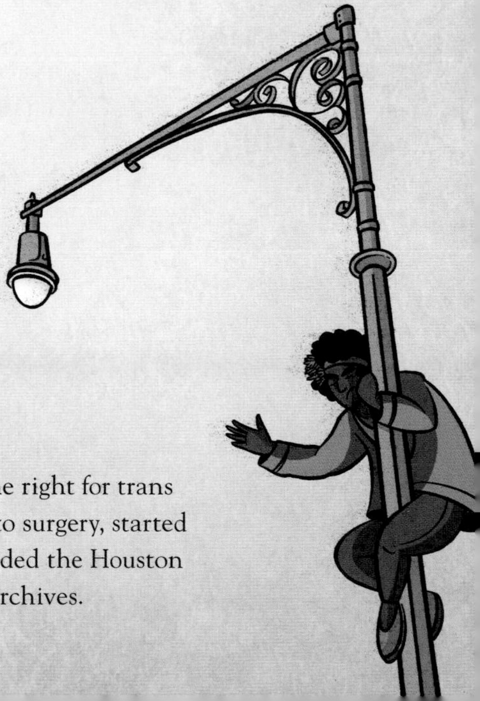

Cristan Williams is a trans historian and pioneer in addressing the practical needs of underserved communities. She started the first trans homeless shelter in Texas and cofounded the first federally funded housing-first homeless program, pioneered affordable health care for trans people in the Houston area, won the right for trans people to change their gender on Texas ID prior to surgery, started numerous trans social service programs, and founded the Houston Transgender Center as well as the Transgender Archives.

Helpful Definitions

Activism: An action, such as a protest or a sit-in, that emphasizes support or opposition to a controversial issue.

Ally: Someone who does not identify as LGBTQ, but whose actions and beliefs are in support of the LGBTQ community.

Asexual: An umbrella term that refers to someone who isn't attracted to anyone; however, this term is broad and can have many different meanings.

Bisexual: People who love or are attracted to people of more than one gender.

Cisgender: When a person's gender identity is the same as what doctors assigned them at birth.

Direct action: A type of demonstration, protest, or other form of civil disobedience meant to create change. Nonviolent direct action includes protests, sit-ins, creating flyers or posters, strikes, and blockades.

Gay: People who love or are attracted to people of the same gender. Frequently used by people who identify as men but has evolved over time to include other identities as well.

Gender identity: A person's internal sense and understanding of who they are/their gender.

GSA: Gender and Sexuality Alliance, an organization that holds meetings at schools where LGBTQ students and allies can gather.

Heterosexual: People who identify as women who only love or are attracted to people who identify as men. Also, people who identify as men who only love or are attracted to people who identify as women.

Intersex: An umbrella term that refers to people who are born with bodies that are naturally different from what is traditionally considered female or male. This is what the "I" stands for in LGBTQIA.

Lesbian: People who love or are attracted to people of the same gender. Frequently used by people who identify as women but has evolved over time to include other identities as well.

LGBTQ: LGBTQ is an acronym for lesbian, gay, bisexual, transgender, and queer or questioning. These terms are used to describe a person's sexual orientation or gender identity.

Nonbinary or gender nonconforming: People who do not feel like the word girl or boy fits. They may feel like both or neither. They sometimes use pronouns such as they/them/theirs.

Queer: People use this word as a way to identify and celebrate people of all gender identities and sexual orientations. When used in a mean way, this is a hurtful word. It has been reclaimed and is now often used in a positive, powerful way.

Questioning: Someone who is questioning their sexual orientation or gender identity.

Sexual orientation: Whom a person loves or is attracted to.

Transgender: When a person's gender identity is different from what doctors assigned them at birth.